Divine Simplicity

Divine Simplicity

A Biblical and Trinitarian Account

JORDAN P. BARRETT

FORTRESS PRESS
MINNEAPOLIS

DIVINE SIMPLICITY
A Biblical and Trinitarian Account

Cover design: Alisha Lofgren

Print ISBN: 978-1-5064-2482-8
eBook ISBN: 978-1-5064-1483-5

The paper used in this publication meets the minimum requirements of American National Standard for Information Sciences — Permanence of Paper for Printed Library Materials, ANSI Z329.48-1984.

Manufactured in the U.S.A.

Contents

Acknowledgments

Theology is never done outside of a community, and therefore I have many to thank. The initial idea for this dissertation stems from a brief conversation with Stephen R. Holmes over email. His works and further questions about divine simplicity fueled my interest and, unexpectedly, eventually led to my continued studies at Wheaton College. My doctoral supervisor, Kevin Vanhoozer, has been an incredibly wise and able guide. His example of how to do and live out theology has always been insightful, refreshing, and challenging. I could not have asked for a better supervisor. I am also grateful to my second reader, Dan Treier. His ability to balance honesty and encouragement is rare and admirable, and his feedback made this a much better dissertation. Fred Sanders was a wise and careful external reader, and I am indebted to his questions, challenges, and wise insights. Special thanks are also due to Kevin Hector, who read various drafts of my section on Karl Barth, and to Scott Swain, who helped me navigate the careful use and definitions of divine names, attributes, and perfections.

I am especially grateful for the consistent support of my family. The many prayers and encouraging conversations with my parents and siblings played a significant role in my ability to persevere and finish. I have also been blessed with incredible in-laws who have been equally supportive and provided relief with the occasional football game, board game, and gardening.

Special thanks go to my cohort for their time, insights, and encouragement. The PhD community at Wheaton College is a gift, especially Michael Kibbe, Ashish Varma, Jeremy Treat, Stephen Pardue, and James Gordon. Uche Anizor played a special role from this project's conception to its finish. His friendship and interest in this project helped me persist during the most difficult of times. I am also indebted to the help from Greg Morrison and the staff at Buswell Library. Their support and skills have been outstanding and helped save me time on many occasions. In addition, none of this would have been possible without the gracious financial assistance of the Buyse family. Thank you so much for your selfless gift.

Michael Gibson, Jeff Reimer, and Alicia Ehlers were incredible editors and I am thankful for their patience, grace, and expertise. This is a better book because of their excellent work at Fortress Press.

Most of all, thanks must be given to my patient wife, Erin. She endured the stress and difficulties of this project as much as I did and has done so with grace, kindness, and love. She walked with me the entire way, constantly pointing me to Jesus, and encouraging me at every turn. My gratefulness extends beyond these words.

Jordan Barrett
August 2017

Abbreviations

CCT	Challenges in Contemporary Theology
CD	Karl Barth. *Church Dogmatics*. Edited by Geoffrey Bromiley and Thomas F. Torrance. Translated by G. W. Bromiley, J. C. Campbell, Ian Wilson, and J. Strathearn McNab. 4 vols in 14 parts. Edinburgh: T&T Clark, 1956–1975.
CHRC	*Church History and Religious Culture*
CIT	Current Issues in Theology
ConCT	Contours of Christian Theology
CSCD	Cambridge Studies in Christian Doctrine
CSEMBH	Cambridge Studies in Early Modern British History
CSPR	Cornell Studies in the Philosophy of Religion
CTC	Christian Theology in Context
CTHPT	Cambridge Texts in the History of Political Thought
DDCT	Distinguished Dissertations in Christian Theology
ECR	*Eastern Churches Review*
EES	The Eerdmans Ekklesia Series
ES	Emerging Scholars
FCT	Formation of Christian Theology
FET	Foundations of Evangelical Theology
FoC	Fathers of the Church
FPh	*Faith and Philosophy*
GMT	Great Medieval Thinkers
HBM	Hebrew Bible Monographs
HBT	*Horizons in Biblical Theology*
HCOT	Historical Commentary on the Old Testament
HJ	*Heythrop Journal*
HTR	*Harvard Theological Review*
IBC	Interpretation: A Bible Commentary for Teaching and Preaching
IJPR	*International Journal for Philosophy of Religion*
IJST	*International Journal of Systematic Theology*

IPQ	*International Philosophical Quarterly*
IST	Issues in Systematic Theology
JAAR	*Journal of the American Academy of Religion*
JAT	*Journal of Analytic Theology*
JECS	*Journal of Early Christian Studies*
JETS	*Journal of the Evangelical Theological Society*
JR	*Journal of Religion*
JRT	*Journal of Reformed Theology*
JTI	*Journal of Theological Interpretation*
JTISup	Supplements to the Journal for Theological Interpretation
MCT	Milestones in Catholic Theology
ModTheo	*Modern Theology*
MPTT	Mediaeval Philosophical Texts in Translation
MS	*Mediaeval Studies*
MSch	*Modern Schoolman*
MST	Mediaeval Sources in Translation
NBf	*New Blackfriars*
NPNF²	*Nicene and Post-Nicene Fathers*, Second Series. Edited by Philip Schaff. 14 vols. 1886–1889. Reprint, Peabody, MA: Hendrickson, 1994.
NSBT	New Studies in Biblical Theology
NS	*New Scholasticism*
NSD	New Studies in Dogmatics
NV	*Nova et Vetera*
NZSTR	*Neue Zeitschrift für systematische Theologie und Religionsphilosophie*
OCT	Outstanding Christian Thinkers
OECS	Oxford Early Christian Studies
OECT	Oxford Early Christian Texts
ORP	Oxford Readings in Philosophy
OSAT	Oxford Studies in Analytic Theology

OSHT	Oxford Studies in Historical Theology
OTL	Old Testament Library
OTM	Oxford Theological Monographs
P&T	*Philosophy and Theology*
PACPA	*Proceedings of the American Catholic Philosophical Association*
PC	*Philosophia Christi*
PP	The Problems of Philosophy
ProEccl	*Pro Ecclesia*
PRRD	*Post-Reformation Reformed Dogmatics*
PTM	Princeton Theological Monographs
PTUNS	Publications of the Thomas Instituut te Utrecht, New Series
RD	*Reformed Dogmatics*
RelS	*Religious Studies*
RR	Reason and Religion
SAJ	*Saint Anselm Journal*
SBET	*Scottish Bulletin of Evangelical Theology*
SHCT	Studies in the History of Christian Thought
SECT	Sources of Early Christian Thought
SEMH	Studies in Early Medieval History
SIET	Strategic Initiatives in Evangelical Theology
SJT	*Scottish Journal of Theology*
SMRT	Studies in Medieval and Reformation Traditions
SP	*Studia Patristica*
SPT	Studies in Philosophical Theology
SRT	Studies in Reformed Theology
SST	Studies in Systematic Theology
STGM	Studien und Texte zur Geistesgeschichte des Mittelalters
SVC	Supplements to Vigiliae Christianae
SVTQ	*St. Vladimir's Theological Quarterly*

SWJT	*Southwestern Journal of Theology*
TJT	*Toronto Journal of Theology*
TMT	Texts in Modern Theology
TRS	Thomistic Ressourcement Series
TS	*Theological Studies*
TT	*Theology Today*
TynBul	*Tyndale Bulletin*
VC	*Vigiliae christianae*
WJO	Works of John Owen
WSA	Works of Saint Augustine
WTJ	*Westminster Theological Journal*
ZNT	*Zeitschrift für Neuere Theologiegeschichte*
ZTK	*Zeitschrift für Theologie und Kirche*

Introduction

This book began as a dissertation at Wheaton College under the supervision of Kevin Vanhoozer. The aim of the project is to present the biblical roots of the doctrine of divine simplicity and to clarify its connection to the doctrine of the Trinity. In short, I argue that the divine name(s) and indivisible operations of the Trinity *ad extra* are the biblical roots of the more developed doctrine of divine simplicity. Similar to the doctrine of the Trinity and its biblical derivation, divine simplicity is a culminating doctrine based on these two roots. This means that the origin of divine simplicity is not Plato, Aristotle, Plotinus, natural theology, substance metaphysics, or perfect being theology. Rather, Scripture is the source of its motivation and content even if its form and terminology, like the Trinity and other doctrines, is borrowed from outside Scripture. Furthermore, I argue that the doctrine of the Trinity offers guidance for navigating the problem of "identical divine attributes" by serving as a formal analogy—what I call the *analogia diversitatis*—that leads to a distinction between the divine attributes that I call an "idiomatic distinction." Briefly stated, the divine attributes are identical to the divine essence, but the divine attributes are not identical to each other. The strength of this argument is that it builds on the biblical roots and closely ties itself to trinitarian insights. Rather than divine simplicity dictating to the Trinity, simplicity takes it cues from the Trinity so that anyone who affirms the doctrine of the Trinity should see how divine simplicity naturally flows from its teachings.

This argument proceeds in six chapters. Chapter 1 surveys the recent critics of divine simplicity and develops a taxonomy to explain why the doctrine is often rejected: for historical, biblical, or theological reasons. I then present recent revisionists and proponents and explain how their accounts have not sufficiently responded to the objections. Chapter 2 analyzes how and why key patristic theologians, East and West, developed a doctrine of divine simplicity. At this stage, the divine names and indivisible operations of the Trinity *ad extra* begin to emerge. Chapter 3 examines central theologians from Pseudo-Dionysius to Thomas Aquinas, and does so with special reference to their use of Scripture. Chapter 4 continues from the Reformation to Karl Barth, arguing that of all places, one would expect divine simplicity to be rejected during the Reformation if it was truly foreign to Scripture. Rather, it was quietly maintained and was incorporated into later confessions. If divine simplicity were a product of natural theology, then one would expect Barth to be a severe critic. Although he finds some problems, he retains its teachings and furthers its connection to Scripture and the doctrine of the Trinity. This chapter also concludes the historical chapters by arguing that divine simplicity developed in order to avoid errors (e.g., gnostics, Eunomius, Socinians) and the misreading of Scripture, specifically 1 Corinthians 1:24 and John 4:24, but more generally the name(s) of God and the understanding of indivisible operations. Chapter 5 turns to Scripture and deepens the connection to divine simplicity by arguing that the name(s) of God (including images, titles, and perfections) and the indivisible operations of the Trinity *ad extra* are its two biblical roots. With these in mind, chapter 6 argues that the doctrine of the Trinity provides divine simplicity with a formal analogy—the *analogia diversitatis*—so that proper distinctions can be drawn between the divine attributes and the divine essence, and the divine attributes themselves. The *analogia diversitatis* also helps solve the problem of "identical attributes," and by identifying Scripture as the primary source of divine simplicity, my argument voids any claims that simplicity is a product of any origin other than Scripture. The remainder of the chapter offers a summary of my overall argument and explores the implications of my account.

1.

Divine Simplicity in Contemporary Theology

Abstract doctrines of God have had their day. It is time for evangelicals to take more seriously their affirmation of the deity of Jesus Christ and begin to think about God on a thoroughly christological basis.
—Bruce McCormack, "The Actuality of God"

Could it be that the classical theology of God is less a metaphysics than a theology, that is, the explication of a mystery that attends faith?
—Edward Farley, *Divine Empathy*

Contemporary theological treatments of the doctrine of God and his perfections often neglect the doctrine of divine simplicity.[1] Discussions of simplicity are more often found in philosophical literature,[2] and the theologians who do address it usually express concerns

---

1. Unless otherwise indicated, all Scripture references are taken from the New Revised Standard Version.

2. I will not address the long-standing debates in analytic philosophy, philosophy of religion, or philosophical theology because these disciplines have nothing to offer my project. Rather, the debates seek different goals (e.g., analytic precision) and therefore ask different questions and use different tools to engage those questions. Significantly, there is rarely any engagement with scripture, especially in terms of a proposed solution or response to recent critics. Furthermore, philosophical accounts are often overly concerned with Thomas's (sometimes Anselm's) account of divine simplicity to the exclusion of other voices. This book, however, will include more than just Thomas and will make scripture a major focal point. Therefore, philosophical works on divine simplicity will be used as needed, but will not be central to the discussion. For a discussion on the distinctions between dogmatics and analytic philosophy as it relates to divine simplicity, see Steven J. Duby, *Divine Simplicity: A Dogmatic Account*, SST (London: Bloomsbury T&T Clark, 2016), 67–79.

instead of its importance. Chapter 2 will detail how the doctrine of divine simplicity has always had critics. However, reactions to the doctrine in the latter half of the twentieth century were of a different kind and greater degree. Although criticisms of divine simplicity are nothing new, modern theology developed a new narrative of the origins and content of divine simplicity that partially led to its dismissal. While this project does not allow space for a comprehensive treatment of this historical shift, it will be beneficial to survey the recent critics of this long-standing doctrine in order to understand where shifts began to take place and why. The survey will also help clarify the background and recent context for the recent criticisms of divine simplicity.

The aim of this chapter is primarily descriptive, analytical, and historical: I will first present the major critics of the doctrine of divine simplicity with the aim of understanding how the doctrine was received and how its reception may have contributed to its rejection. Second, I will outline the views and arguments of those who find problems with the traditional account of divine simplicity but seek to modify it to various degrees. Third, I will present the proponents of a more traditional account of divine simplicity and will describe how they have responded to the recent critics and revisionists. Last, I will conclude that many criticisms remain insufficiently answered despite the latest efforts to defend and rearticulate a doctrine of divine simplicity. What I will show, and crucially for this project, is that contemporary responses insufficiently attend to the relationship between the doctrine of divine simplicity and scripture. Not only does scripture play a key role in its development throughout the theological tradition, but the doctrine can also be shown to have key biblical roots that shape its content and point to it as a revealed teaching with great significance for Christian theology.

THE PROBLEM OF DIVINE SIMPLICITY: A BRIEF TAXONOMY

The Christian church has consistently confessed that the triune God of the gospel is simple and therefore beyond composition. The various divine perfections do not represent parts of God that, when combined, make up God's nature. However, in 1983, Ronald Nash observed that divine simplicity now has a "public relations problem."[3] What was once part of the theological tradition from Irenaeus to Edwards can now be said to have "nothing at all to do with the God of the Christian Faith."[4]

How did divine simplicity become a problem when for so long it was understood as a necessary doctrine? What this chapter demonstrates is that some theologians arrive at their rejection of divine simplicity because of its reception among other theologians, mainly Augustine and Aquinas. Others find problems within the tradition in general (for example, Greek philosophy), which they believe to be incompatibility with a doctrine of the Trinity, or in the doctrines purported lack of scriptural support. One might summarize these as historical, biblical, or theological critiques.[5]

AUGUSTINE AND THE PROBLEM OF DIVINE SIMPLICITY: ROBERT JENSON

Rejections of divine simplicity are often staged as critiques of particular trajectories within the historical tradition. Contemporary theology commonly ascribes to Augustine's theology an overemphasis on the oneness of God and often finds his theology to be dependent upon Neoplatonic metaphysics. Some root the source of his problems within his trinitarian theology, but others see it as the result of his stress on a doctrine of absolute divine simplicity. Robert Jenson is a clear proponent of the latter. In fact, "discarding [Augustine's doctrine of divine simplicity] is one purpose" of his work *The Triune Identity*.[6] What is the problem with Augustine's view? Partly, first,

3. Ronald H. Nash, *The Concept of God: An Exploration of Contemporary Difficulties with the Attributes of God* (Grand Rapids: Zondervan, 1983), 85.

4. Emil Brunner, *The Christian Doctrine of God*, trans. Olive Wyon (London: Lutterworth, 1949), 1:294. It is surprising that Brunner commends Irenaeus and Athanasius's approach to the divine attributes. Their views "reveal scarcely a trace of the speculative bias in comparison with the Biblical foundation" (243). However, as will become clear, both theologians held to a doctrine of divine simplicity.

5. Not every theologian mentioned above will fall into one category. For example, many of the historical critiques involve conceptual-dogmatic concerns. My point, however, is that the rejection (or qualification) comes *primarily* through one of the three categories: historical, biblical, and conceptual-dogmatic.

6. Robert W. Jenson, *The Triune Identity: God according to the Gospel* (1982; repr., Eugene, OR: Wipf & Stock, 2002), 124. Stephen John Wright argues that "Jenson has a complicated relationship with the doctrine of divine simplicity, neither explicitly rejecting nor unequivocally accepting the doctrine" (Stephen John Wright, *Dogmatic Aesthetics: A Theology of Beauty*

from his view of divine timelessness. A timeless view of God results in a doctrine of divine simplicity "that comes very close to the Arian refusal of all differentiation in God."[7] If God is in time, then God has a past, present, and future and can be divided into these aspects. Jenson worries that a timeless and simple view of God creates problems for divine action within human history. The second problem is that Augustine misses the Cappadocian achievement—namely, the understanding that the relations between the three persons are constitutive in God: according to Jenson, Augustine "did not see that Nicaea asserts eventful differentiation in God. The reason he did not is apparent throughout his writings: unquestioning commitment to the axiom of his antecedent Platonic theology, that God is metaphysically 'simple,' that *no* sort of self-differentiation can really be true of [God]."[8] Jenson admits that there is truth to the doctrine of divine simplicity, but it cannot avoid causing problems for the doctrine of the Trinity. For example, "if everything predicable of God is his divine being and nothing *else*, then nothing can be said specifically of a triune identity relative to its deity without collapsing the distinction between that identity and the divine *ousia*." The trouble is that "the three identities not only *equally* possess the one *ousia* but *identically* possess it, so that the differentiating relations between them are irrelevant to their being God."[9] Therefore, Augustine's theology and

---

in Dialogue with Robert W. Jenson [Minneapolis: Fortress Press, 2014], 61). He states that "Jenson employs some form of the doctrine of divine simplicity" and that some "misinterpret Jenson as completely denying simplicity" (ibid., 62) when, in fact, Jenson "makes frequent use of the doctrine" (ibid., 99). Jenson may hold to some sense of divine simplicity—although this is not clear—but what is sufficiently clear is that he is critical of Augustine's view. For two other critics of Augustine's doctrine of divine, see William Hasker, *Metaphysics and the Tri-personal God*, OSAT (Oxford: Oxford University Press, 2013), 40–49, 55–61, and Paul R. Hinlicky, *Divine Simplicity: Christ the Crisis of Metaphysics* (Grand Rapids: Baker Academic, 2016), 97–142.

7. Jenson, *Triune Identity*, 118. Elsewhere, he states that "the *mutual structure* of the identities . . . is flattened into an *identical possession* by the identities of an abstractly simple divine essence" (ibid., 120 [emphasis original]). For a critical engagement with Jenson's doctrine of God, see Scott R. Swain, *The God of the Gospel: Robert Jenson's Trinitarian Theology*, SIET (Downers Grove, IL: IVP Academic, 2013).

8. Robert W. Jenson, *Systematic Theology*, vol. 1, *The Triune God* (New York: Oxford University Press, 1997), 111. Jenson also writes that "Augustine rejected the Cappadocian doctrine for the sake of his simplicity axiom" (*Triune Identity*, 119). Interestingly, David Bentley Hart faults Jenson for not having sufficient distinctions in his trinitarian theology: "God's eternal being, thus, is not to be distinguished from [the] historical achievement [of Jesus's crucifixion and resurrection]" (*The Beauty of the Infinite: The Aesthetics of Christian Truth* [Grand Rapids: Eerdmans, 2004], 161).

9. Jenson, *Triune God*, 112 (emphasis original). Elsewhere, Jenson criticizes Thomas's problematic view of divine beauty due to his view of divine simplicity. See Robert W. Jenson, "*Deus*

Western classical metaphysics in general are in need of serious revision, and the removal of a determinative doctrine of divine simplicity is crucial in order to maintain a proper doctrine of the Trinity.[10]

AQUINAS AND THE PROBLEM OF DIVINE SIMPLICITY: ALVIN PLANTINGA

While Augustine is often identified as the primary influence on Western theology, particularly in regard to divine simplicity, others link the problem with Aquinas and his classical version of the doctrine. Aquinas is also at the heart of the battlegrounds for divine simplicity in philosophical theology. Therefore, it is not surprising that one of the most influential philosophical critiques of divine simplicity stems from Alvin Plantinga's Aquinas Lecture, *Does God Have a Nature?*[11]

Plantinga is clear that divine simplicity is "exceedingly hard to grasp or construe" and that "it is difficult to see why anyone would be inclined to accept it."[12] According to Plantinga, for Aquinas "the fundamental reason is to accommodate God's aseity and sovereignty."[13]

---

est ipsa pulchritudo (God Is Beauty Itself)," in *Theology as Revisionary Metaphysics: Essays on God and Creation*, ed. Stephen John Wright (Eugene, OR: Cascade, 2014), 211. He adds the following: "I will admit that recent heavy critique of Thomas' doctrine of divine simplicity was sometimes overdone, also by me," but Jenson still feels that Augustine's and Thomas's accounts remain problematic (ibid.).

10. Although Jenson does have a separate account of the divine attributes in his *Systematic Theology*, he gives one in 1984 in which he was also critical of Augustine, including "the method of negative analogy" where "the revelation in Christ simply adds special items to the total of the effects in the world from which God's character as its reason [is] intuited." See "The Attributes of God," in *Christian Dogmatics*, ed. Carl E. Braaten and Robert W. Jenson (Philadelphia: Fortress Press, 1984), 1:182. William Hasker also struggles with Augustine's doctrine of divine simplicity in *Metaphysics and the Tri-personal God*, 40–49, 55–61, 244–45.

11. Alvin Plantinga, *Does God Have a Nature?*, AL (Milwaukee: Marquette University Press, 1980). Even though my project does not directly engage the reception of divine simplicity in analytic philosophy, the influence of Plantinga's criticisms extends beyond philosophy and therefore requires mention. For additional critics of Aquinas's doctrine of divine simplicity, see Christopher Hughes, *On a Complex Theory of a Simple God: An Investigation in Aquinas' Philosophical Theology*, CSPR (Ithaca, NY: Cornell University Press, 1989); Mark D. Jordan, "The Names of God and the Being of Names," in *The Existence and Nature of God*, ed. Alfred J. Freddoso (Notre Dame: University of Notre Dame Press, 1983), 161–90; Hinlicky, *Divine Simplicity*, 27–72.

12. Plantinga, *Does God Have a Nature?*, 28. Cf. Paul Maxwell, "The Formulation of Thomistic Simplicity: Mapping Aquinas's Method for Configuring God's Essence," *JETS* 57 (2014): 371–403.

13. Plantinga, *Does God Have a Nature?*, 28.

God has a nature and is identical with it. If his nature and its properties were distinct from him, then he would depend on these parts to be who he is. Why? Because "if [God] *had* an essence (or nature), as opposed to being *identical* with it, then that essence would be his cause."[14] But as Plantinga makes clear earlier, this conclusion would infringe upon God's sovereignty and aseity.

What about the "Platonic menagerie"—those things that exist necessarily and essentially and are therefore independent from God? Their existence also violates God's sovereignty. At this point the attraction toward nominalism is clear: in order to uphold God's sovereignty we must hold that properties do not actually exist. Aquinas does not want to hold to nominalism and so, once again, asserts that God is identical with his properties and his essence. This move gets to the heart of the matter for Plantinga—"the most important and most perplexing denial of divine composition: the claim that there is no complexity of properties in [God] and that he is identical with his nature and each of his properties."[15] If each property is identical with the other properties, then God has but one property. And if God is identical with this one property, then God has just one property: himself. God "isn't a person but a mere abstract object. . . . So taken, the simplicity doctrine seems an utter mistake."[16]

Plantinga admits that it is possible he has not correctly understood Aquinas. "Perhaps when he argues that God is identical with his essence, with his goodness, with goodness itself, and the like, he doesn't mean to identify God with a property or state of affairs at all, but with something quite different." But the problem still remains for Plantinga: "Taken at face value, the Thomistic doctrine of divine simplicity seems entirely unacceptable."[17] At best, it appears that divine simplicity causes more problems than it solves. At worst, divine simplicity seems to reduce God to an impersonal, indistinguishable property who might lack agency and is therefore incapable of creating this world.

14. Ibid., 31–32.
15. Ibid., 46.
16. Ibid., 47.
17. Ibid., 53.

SCRIPTURE AND THE PROBLEM OF DIVINE SIMPLICITY:
JOHN FEINBERG AND BARRY D. SMITH

Although some theologians do not find problems with the doctrine of divine simplicity within the theological tradition, others reject or question it because of its purported absence in scripture. For example, John S. Feinberg presents divine simplicity as the teaching that "God is free from any division into parts; he is free from compositeness" and adds that "God's essence *is* his attributes, and those attributes must be identical with one another and with him."[18] After briefly describing William Mann, Alvin Plantinga, and Anselm's views, Feinberg lists three problematic motivations for the doctrine. First, sympathetic with Plantinga's criticisms, Feinberg sees that "in order to safeguard divine aseity, many theologians have opted for divine simplicity."[19] Since God is identical with his perfections, he does not depend on these perfections to be who he is. Second, there is a strong connection between divine simplicity and atemporal eternity. A being in time would experience temporal succession and therefore create temporal parts to its existence. Third, for God to be supremely good he must be his own goodness rather than by something external. A perfect being would not depend on its attributes to be who it is. In other words, perfect being theology also grounds divine simplicity.

The most significant negative aspect of divine simplicity is that "there is no verse that explicitly teaches that God is simple."[20] Other theologians have argued for it inferentially, such as Louis Berkhof and Herman Bavinck. Texts such as Jeremiah 10:10, 23:6; John 1:4, 5, 9; 14:6; 1 Corinthians 1:30; 1 John 1:5, 4:8; and others appear to equate God's essence with his attributes. However, Feinberg worries that associating the surface grammar in scripture of God's attributes with the metaphysical view that "God is his attributes" is "dubious" and "question begging." For Feinberg, "there needs to be further evidence in the text before we can conclude that the author intends to say either that the attribute named is equal to God's being or that it is only a part of God's being."[21] At this point, there appears to be no biblical support for divine simplicity and "for anyone committed

18. John S. Feinberg, *No One Like Him: The Doctrine of God*, FET (Wheaton, IL: Crossway, 2001), 325.

19. Ibid., 326.

20. Ibid., 327.

21. Ibid., 328.

to a biblically based notion of God, the lack of biblical evidence for divine simplicity should be disconcerting at least, and a good argument against it at most."[22]

Barry Smith presents a somewhat different perspective from Feinberg, arguing that both scripture and tradition teach that God is numerically one and therefore unique. However, some theologians extended these teachings to a different kind of oneness in which God is noncomposite or simple. Smith argues that this teaching "enters Christian theology through the influence of Greek philosophy"[23] and reminds his readers that it was never established as dogma until the Fourth Lateran Council (1215).[24]

Nevertheless, Smith sees that divine simplicity functioned polemically against Gnosticism and Arianism and that it aimed to eliminate all forms of composition in God. Yet, for Smith, this teaching produces "two unusual implications": first, the "property-deity identification" in which there is no distinction between God's essence and his attributes. The result is that God does not really *have* attributes and so it is difficult to understand what a predicate like "love" is referencing. Second, the "property-property identification," which asserts that God's attributes are all identical.[25] In this view, God does not have *many* attributes since they are all identical to one another. Despite finding these two claims unusual, Smith attempts to listen to some of the traditional arguments for divine simplicity from scripture. He considers the argument from the following: (1) God's numerical oneness in Deuteronomy 6:4; (2) God is Spirit in John 4:24; (3) the divine name in Exodus 3:14 and its parallel in Revelation 1:4; and (4) God's identification with nouns such as light (John 1:4; 1 John 1:5) and love (1 John 4:16).[26] He concludes that each argument fails to justify its point. Therefore, "the arguments from Scripture for God's simplicity are weak to the point of being unconvincing."[27] Divine simplicity does not arise from scripture, but from Greek philosophy, and "the Remonstrants were correct that

22. Ibid., 329. Interestingly, Feinberg elsewhere comments that "frequently we must go beyond the biblical testimony about these attributes [i.e., nonmoral attributes] to formulate a definition or to resolve problems surrounding them" (238). Is this not what the doctrine of divine simplicity is attempting to do?

23. Barry D. Smith, *The Oneness and Simplicity of God* (Eugene, OR: Pickwick, 2013), 23.

24. Ibid., 33.

25. Ibid., 48–52.

26. Ibid., 56–60.

27. Ibid., 61.

the simplicity doctrine was not scriptural but what they referred to as 'metaphysical.'"[28] Because this teaching has "no basis," the entire dichotomy between simple or composite should be rejected in favor of the otherness of God and an apophatic approach to our knowledge of him.[29]

A THEOLOGICAL CRITIQUE OF DIVINE SIMPLICITY: BRUCE MCCORMACK

Some of the previously mentioned scholars have already raised concerns about the compatibility of divine simplicity and other orthodox doctrines. For example, Christopher Hughes questions Aquinas's doctrine of divine simplicity in relation to the Trinity and Christology. Robert Jenson also worries that divine simplicity so flattens out all distinctions in God that it makes it difficult, if not impossible, to adequately distinguish the three divine persons. These questions and concerns, however, remain underdeveloped (Jenson) and are more strongly works of philosophy than theology (Hughes). Bruce McCormack, though, offers a much stronger theological critique of divine simplicity. For McCormack, "commitment to the twin ideas of divine impassibility and divine simplicity constitutes the single greatest impediment to the full coherence of the traditional doctrine of the penal substitutionary theory of the atonement."[30]

Simplicity "remained unqualified by the triunity of God (which was carefully interpreted so as to preserve divine simplicity)" and denied that God had a body, soul, or physical passions.[31] It was difficult, therefore, to say that the Son truly suffered in his divinity on the cross. Rather, he suffered in his human nature alone. This "instrumentalization" of the human nature was common in the patristic period until Cyril of Alexandria, whose theory of kenosis "understood the Logos to be receptive to that which came to Him from His human nature."[32] If the Logos is receptive to his human nature, and

---

28. Ibid.

29. Ibid., 120–26. For Smith's account of the otherness of God, see Barry D. Smith, *The Indescribable God: Divine Otherness in Christian Theology* (Eugene, OR: Pickwick, 2012).

30. Bruce L. McCormack, "The Only Mediator: The Person and Work of Christ in Evangelical Perspective," in *Renewing the Evangelical Mission*, ed. Richard Lints (Grand Rapids: Eerdmans, 2013), 254.

31. Ibid., 255.

32. Ibid., 260. McCormack also faults the "instrumentalization" view with ignoring the

if the communication of attributes is therefore no longer figurative but real, then there is no simple Subject in the "person of union." Human attributes are divisible, and Jesus's body is a "part" of him, not all that he is. In other words, the Logos is a complex Subject. But does this complexity imply a change in God? "The only way to preserve immutability while affirming passibility is by making the appropriation that occurs in time, in the incarnate state, to be the result of an eternal 'determination' of the Person of the Logos precisely *for* this appropriation. If the Logos is a composite subject in time, He must already be so in Himself in eternity."[33] In this framework, divine simplicity prevents us from affirming these necessary christological truths.

As a "composite unity" the Logos became human in time, but his humanity was not "new" to him and had been eternally planned. But this logic would require a surrender of divine simplicity and, as McCormack argues, someone like Calvin was not ready to do this and therefore argued for a figural communication of attributes of both natures to the one person. These conclusions concern McCormack, for "clearly, impassibility and simplicity were, once again, controlling their thinking."[34] The key example of this controlling influence is that the infinite value of the penal substitutionary atonement can only be attributed to the human nature. Because any human experiences or attributes can only be figuratively communicated to the Logos, penal substitution "could only mean that God had willed (and perhaps contributed directly to) the torture and death of an innocent human being."[35]

To find the solution one must first begin looking at the problem qualitatively rather than quantitatively. The problem and penalty due to us is separation from God. Therefore, God in Christ freely allows himself to be subjected to our penalty. At this stage, the theme of Christ's descent into hell must enter the dialogue. Jesus becomes the subject "of the 'living death'—a contemplation in pure receptivity of the abysmal horror of a separation from God which the man Jesus can do nothing to bridge."[36] This horror is brought to an end not by the Son's omnipotent acts, but by the Holy Spirit's work in raising

power and role of the Holy Spirit in the works of Jesus. Rather, these are attributed to his divine nature. What is needed is a "pneumatically driven two-natures Christology" (262).

33. Ibid., 262.
34. Ibid., 264.
35. Ibid.
36. Ibid., 266.

him from the dead. Divine simplicity and impassibility prevent theologians from arguing this point, limiting any suffering to the human nature (not the "person of union") and therefore leaving the human nature incapable of making an infinite payment through suffering. In other words, the divine nature and Logos are so separated (or protected) from the human nature that it renders a penal substitution theory pointless. The Logos does not suffer, cannot have human experiences, and is in no need of the Holy Spirit because the Logos is simple and impassible.[37]

According to critics, therefore, divine simplicity is a troublesome doctrine generative of many difficulties and stemming from problems.[38] These problems can be related to particular theologians throughout the tradition and are most often tied to readings of Augustine or Thomas. Other works argue that divine simplicity has insufficient or no grounding in scripture and any attempt to draw this connection is the result of mere prooftexting or the forcing of foreign categories onto scripture. Finally, some problems are theological in that simplicity is said to conflict with the Trinity, incarnation, or even penal substitution. However, not everyone who finds problems with divine simplicity is convinced that it must be completely discarded.

37. Sonderegger is critical of making Christology the ground or measure of the doctrine of God. For examples, see her *Systematic Theology*, vol. 1, *The Doctrine of God* (Minneapolis: Fortress Press, 2015), xvii, 157, 394. For another perspective on the function of Christology, see John Webster, "The Place of Christology in Systematic Theology," in *The Oxford Handbook to Christology*, ed. Francesca Aran Murphy (Oxford: Oxford University Press, 2015), 611–27.

38. See also R. T. Mullins, who finds divine simplicity to be "impossible" according to the present taxonomy, finding problems with simplicity in the tradition, scripture, and the Trinity and incarnation ("Simply Impossible: A Case against Divine Simplicity," *JRT* 7 [2013]: 181–203). It is unclear whether Mullins has dismantled the core of the theological tradition's doctrine of divine simplicity or his own version. For example, he simply asserts that "divine simplicity is part of a package of divine perfections that includes timelessness and immutability. One cannot have divine simplicity without timelessness and immutability" (181). While some theologians throughout the tradition include these three perfections together, it is not clear that this *collection* of perfections is necessary, nor does Mullins offer sufficient evidence that proves this is true of the tradition. See also by Mullins, "An Analytic Response to Stephen R. Holmes, with a Special Treatment of His Doctrine of Divine Simplicity," in *The Holy Trinity Revisited: Essays in Response to Stephen Holmes*, ed. Thomas Noble and Jason Sexton (Milton Keynes, UK: Paternoster, 2015), 82–96; Mullins, *The End of the Timeless God*, OSAT (Oxford: Oxford University Press, 2016).

REVISIONIST ATTEMPTS

Some theologians hear these criticisms and agree that the more traditional doctrine of divine simplicity is problematic. Others work to revise the teaching rather than throw out the doctrine altogether, appropriating and reconfiguring divine simplicity to a lesser or greater degree. While they are critical of the doctrine, they attempt to modify the teaching by finding alternative expressions and functions for the doctrine of divine simplicity.

F. G. IMMINK

F. G. Immink argues that simplicity is "best understood as a logical characterization of God's aseity and otherness," but "otherness" cannot be defined in a Thomistic sense.[39] Immink worries that Aquinas's view stresses God's otherness and transcendence so much that it "ends in a complete identity. Since no distinctions can be made in God, God is identical with each of his properties and each of his properties is identical with each of his properties. I believe this conclusion ought to be rejected."[40] This "identity thesis" is an unnecessary conclusion that takes God's unity too far. For Immink, "God has more than one perfection, and although God's perfections are *united* in a special way, they are not one and the same thing."[41] Unity along the lines of divine simplicity, therefore, is more about harmony than identity.[42] Even this qualified doctrine of divine simplicity, however, is not found in scripture. Its role in theology is "to secure God's aseity and otherness, and this aseity and otherness is certainly taught by Scripture."[43] Immink does not clarify *why* divine aseity and otherness need securing, especially if they are clearly found in scripture.

39. F. G. Immink, *Divine Simplicity* (Utrecht: J. H. Kok, 1987), 35. Immink also argues for divine simplicity in the following: "The One and Only: The Simplicity of God," in *Understanding the Attributes of God*, ed. Gijsbert van den Brink and Marcel Sarot, Contributions to Philosophical Theology 1 (Frankfurt: Peter Lang, 1999), 99–118.

40. Immink, *Divine Simplicity*, 173. He also states that "[the identity thesis] is a consequence of Aquinas' overaccentuation of God's otherness" (176) and that "this identity is either a remnant of Platonic philosophy or follows from a mistaken idea of God's transcendence" (177).

41. Ibid., 176.

42. For a critique of this "harmony account," see James E. Dolezal, *God without Parts: Divine Simplicity and the Metaphysics of God's Absoluteness* (Eugene, OR: Pickwick, 2011), 136–39.

43. Immink, *Divine Simplicity*, 35. Immink actually faults Barth and Miskotte for believing that divine simplicity is a revealed doctrine (26).

Nevertheless, an account of divine simplicity that avoids Aquinas's identity thesis and argues for a special unity of God's perfections remains beneficial.[44]

COLIN GUNTON

Colin Gunton follows Jenson's criticisms in many ways but is stronger in his criticism of Augustine.[45] For Gunton, "the God of most Western philosophy is single, simple, and unchanging. And that is the problem."[46] Although it is not the only problem—Gunton also faults contemporary theology with the failure to give sufficient weight to the Trinity, Holy Spirit, and humanity of Christ—he sees it as the influential position in Western theology since Augustine. When it comes to divine simplicity, "it will not do," as Augustine argued, to speak of one attribute as identical to all the others. Gunton's criticisms may be similar to Jenson's, but Gunton still finds a role for divine simplicity: "The point of the doctrine of divine simplicity is rather that the attributes must be defined from and through one another as a function of the trinitarian perichoresis."[47] So, Gunton has room for a softer rendering of divine simplicity as long as it is not Augustine's version. We must be careful with statements such as "God is without body, passion or parts," since these speak of "God and creation in terms of opposing attributes: material things have parts; God, by a process of negation, is supposed to be simple."[48] These opposing attributes come from the Neoplatonic theology that was so influential for Augustine. Turning in a different direction, Gunton wants to define divine simplicity positively and therefore lays greater stress on the divine persons: "The Trinity is indeed not constituted of parts—which can be separated—but of persons, who are distinguishable but not separable, and therefore

44. For a longer survey and assessment of Immink, see Dolf te Velde, *The Doctrine of God in Reformed Orthodoxy, Karl Barth, and the Utrecht School: A Study in Method and Content*, SRT (Leiden: Brill, 2013), 571–81.

45. See the well-known essay, Colin Gunton, "Augustine, the Trinity and the Theological Crisis of the West," *SJT* 43 (1990): 33–58.

46. Colin E. Gunton, *The One, the Three and the Many: God, Creation and the Culture of Modernity* (Cambridge: Cambridge University Press, 1993), 24.

47. Colin E. Gunton, *Act and Being: Towards a Theology of the Divine Attributes* (Grand Rapids: Eerdmans, 2003), 123. For a broader assessment of Gunton's view of the divine attributes, see Uche Anizor, *Trinity and Humanity: An Introduction to the Theology of Colin Gunton* (Milton Keynes, UK: Paternoster, 2016), 25–53.

48. Ibid., 122.

constitute a 'simple' God."[49] Similar to Jenson, Gunton sees Augustine's doctrine of divine simplicity as a strict identity of attributes that destroys all differentiation in God, thus removing sufficient distinction between the divine persons and causing problems for the Trinity.[50] Gunton prefers, instead, the trinitarian theology of Irenaeus and the Cappadocians.

PAUL R. HINLICKY

Hinlicky recognizes various errors in modern Protestant systematic theology, but "challenging the Platonic dogma of simplicity in the name of the crucified God is not one of them."[51] Rather than being simple in a Platonic sense, God is *complex*, although Hinlicky is not entirely clear what he means by "complexity." At the very least, he notes that divine complexity is "in complement, not contradiction, of 'simplicity.'"[52] What is left of divine simplicity? First, divine simplicity says nothing *positive* about God's being since it is "not an ontological insight" into God's nature.[53] Instead, Hinlicky modifies simplicity so that it is a rule for our speech about God, directing our faith toward God, who is unique and incomparable.[54] God is to be thought of as a "perfect harmony" whose life is complex. He arrives at this particular form of the doctrine "relatively, from the revelation of God as eschatological creator, not by attempts of the creature at self- and world-transcendence."[55]

49. Ibid.
50. "Augustine's chief weakness is that he asked the wrong question . . . about how to reconcile the absolute simplicity of God with the apparent plurality of persons, rather [seeking] a concept of divine unity on the basis of the economy" (Colin Gunton, *A Christian Dogmatic Theology*, vol. 1, *The Triune God: A Doctrine of the Trinity as Though Jesus Makes a Difference* [2003], unpublished manuscript, chap. 5), cited and quoted in Robert W. Jenson, "A Decision Tree of Colin Gunton's Thinking," in *The Theology of Colin Gunton*, ed. Lincoln Harvey (London: T&T Clark, 2010), 10. Jenson also notes that "the incompatibility of this doctrine with the Scriptural portrayal of God never ceased to agitate Gunton" (ibid.).
51. Paul R. Hinlicky, *Divine Complexity: The Rise of Creedal Christianity* (Minneapolis: Fortress Press, 2010), 241n11. Hinlicky is clear that divine simplicity can be traced through the apophatic tradition and directly to Platonism (245n69). See also his *Beloved Community: Critical Dogmatics after Christendom* (Grand Rapids: Eerdmans, 2015), 15–18.
52. Hinlicky, *Divine Complexity*, xi.
53. Ibid., 176.
54. Ibid., xi. For this "ruled" reading, see also 22, 156, and 176–77.
55. Ibid., 176. I am sympathetic to Hinlicky's concerns with a directly Platonic doctrine of divine simplicity; however, his work does not show evidence that the Platonic version he presents and rejects is synonymous with, or even mostly similar to, the positions within the theological tradition. Furthermore, in his treatment of the Trinity, Hinlicky speaks of "the gospel's

In his more recent work, Hinlicky argues against Aquinas's "strong simplicity" based on perfect being theology and natural theology and seeks a "weak simplicity" in relation to a "social model of the Trinity" and a univocal understanding of theological language.[56] "Consistent perichoresis" functions better than "protological" or strong simplicity in terms of expressing divine unity. Augustine and Aquinas had their problems—strong apophaticism, natural theology, analogy of being, starting with the divine essence or one God—which "muddled" their thinking, leaving the need for revisions to divine simplicity.[57] Hinlicky's "weak simplicity" provides an eschatological, univocal, christological, hermeneutical, and positive statement of simplicity that differs significantly from accounts found throughout the tradition, but which claims to revise, rather than reject, divine simplicity.

JOHN FRAME

John Frame is critical of the theological tradition (that is, Aquinas), but for different reasons than either Gunton or Hinlicky. Frame worries that for Aquinas "unity must always be prior to multiplicity" and that any plurality "is in our minds" and therefore "only apparent. In reality, God is a being without any multiplicity at all, a simple being for whom any language suggesting complexity, distinctions, or multiplicity, is entirely unsuited."[58] This is the "Plotinian neo-Platonic view" and Aquinas's "argument for a total absence of multiplicity in God is quite inadequate."[59] Frame worries that this view causes unnecessary problems for the Trinity, and scripture demands that we account for the diversity of attributes and characterizations of God. Frame would rather do away with the term "simplicity" and replace it

---

encounter with Platonism" that resulted in the adoption of terms and concepts such as *hypostasis* and *ousia*. This adoption is acceptable to him because "to adopt this terminology for purposes of conceptual clarity in ontological description does not entail adoption of any specific metaphysical baggage, as is often confusedly maintained" (211). Hinlicky never addresses why this adoption is acceptable for the doctrine of the Trinity, but not for divine simplicity. Perhaps he believes the formulation of the Trinity was more successful than divine simplicity in terms of leaving behind the "metaphysical baggage."

56. Paul Hinlicky, *Divine Simplicity: Christ the Crisis of Metaphysics* (Grand Rapids: Baker Academic, 2016), xv–xix. For an assessment of Hinlicky's book, see my forthcoming review in the *International Journal of Systematic Theology*.

57. Hinlicky, *Divine Simplicity*, 27–71, 97–142.

58. John Frame, *The Doctrine of God*, A Theology of Lordship (Phillipsburg, NJ: P&R, 2002), 227.

59. John Frame, *Systematic Theology* (Phillipsburg, NJ: P&R, 2013), 430.

with "necessary existence," a term much more in line with scripture.[60] The pattern of thinking given in scripture demonstrates that God's attributes are not synonymous, but "describe different aspects of [his essence]" and even "refer to genuine complexities in his essence," yet one in which we still see "the unity within this complexity."[61] Therefore, for Frame, "there is a legitimate biblical motive in the doctrine of simplicity," although he goes no further in explaining how this looks.[62]

EBERHARD JÜNGEL

The most significant revision of divine simplicity comes from the German Lutheran theologian Eberhard Jüngel. He wants to uphold the tradition's emphasis on the unity of God's essence and existence, but he has serious reservations about the tradition's formulation of this unity. The early church was not critical enough of its adoption of terms and concepts from Greek philosophy and fell prey to the "dictatorship of metaphysics," failing to think of God's being as the Crucified One.[63] The traditional concept of God was taken captive to an account of the absolute nature of God and therefore a doctrine of absolute simplicity. Regarding God's essence and existence, "the existence of God follows with logical necessity from his essence. Accordingly, God was thought of as an 'essential being' . . . , which as such was a 'necessary being.'"[64] Attempts at the teaching that there is no "real distinction" between God's essence and existence were disrupted since human theological thought could not avoid making a distinction (*distinctio rationis*), even if it was for methodical reasons.[65] For Jüngel, the problem is that essence determines existence and,

---

60. Frame, *The Doctrine of God*, 227, 228. See also Frame, *Systematic Theology*, 430.

61. Frame, *Systematic Theology*, 432. Elsewhere, Frame states that "simplicity embraces distinctness, rather than canceling it out" (Frame, *The Doctrine of God*, 705).

62. Frame, *Systematic Theology*, 433. Depending on what Frame implies from his univocal view of language, it is difficult to understand how univocity would fit with any account of divine simplicity. See Frame, *The Doctrine of God*, 208.

63. Eberhard Jüngel, *God as the Mystery of the World: On the Foundation of the Theology of the Crucified One in the Dispute between Theism and Atheism*, trans. Darrell L. Guder (Grand Rapids: Eerdmans, 1983), 39. See also 48–49.

64. Ibid., 106.

65. DeHart notes that "Jüngel's picture of exactly how [the harmful compulsion to make a 'rational distinction' between essence and existence] is supposed to have occurred is obscure and quite impressionistic." See Paul J. DeHart, *Beyond the Necessary God: Trinitarian Faith and Philosophy in the Thought of Eberhard Jüngel* (Oxford: Oxford University Press, 1999), 162.

crucially, the divine essence was predetermined in abstraction from the incarnation.[66]

Even though Jüngel finds serious problems in the tradition's account of divine simplicity, he still believes the doctrine to be significant as long as it is reconstructed and removed from its uncritical relation to traditional metaphysics. God's essence can no longer dictate the terms of his existence. This "inversion" keeps Jüngel within the tradition but critically moves beyond it by rethinking God's unity. "God's mode of existence is itself God's identity or essence. God's existence is not the actualization of an essence which could be abstracted from it and made the object of independent reflection."[67]

Divine simplicity must also take account of God's many and diverse perfections. In this sense, reconfiguring divine simplicity also speaks to "the simplicity of the divine self-relation, . . . i.e., *simplicity is to be thought of relationally as the living concentration of the inexhaustibly diverse characteristics of God, comparable to the character of a fire that burns in countless many flames.*"[68] Jüngel calls this the "analogy of advent," an event that "is only possible because God has introduced himself linguistically."[69] This view "understands the attributes of God to be an inexhaustible multiplicity of divine characteristics" that "conceives the differentiated multiplicity of God's attributes to be distinguished from one another in the sense of a *distinctio realis*, and thus to be an expression of the *concrete simplicity* of God."[70] The "old theology and metaphysics" created an opposition between simplicity as undifferentiated and a differentiated way of multiplicity that must be overcome "for the sake of the concrete speakability of the essence of God which is simple precisely in the inexhaustibly differentiated character of its characteristics."[71]

---

66. In a later essay, Jüngel notes that the traditional account of divine simplicity was supposed to maintain the Creator-creature distinction and defend against polytheism. Yet the drawback is that it pushed this distinction so far that it threatened to make God's essence inexpressible since our language naturally differentiates (or divides) a thing that is spoken about. See Eberhard Jüngel, "Theses on the Relation of the Existence, Essence and Attributes of God," trans. Philip G. Ziegler, *TJT* 17 (2001): 107–24.

67. DeHart, *Beyond the Necessary God*, 160.

68. Jüngel, "Theses," 56, 1.3.1.2 (emphasis original).

69. Ibid., 66, 4.4.3. For more on Jüngel's "analogy of advent," see Joseph Palakeel, *The Use of Analogy in Theological Discourse: An Investigation in Ecumenical Perspective* (Rome: Gregorian University Press, 1995), 163–224.

70. Jüngel, "Theses," 66, 4.4.4.3.

71. Ibid., 66, 4.4.5.

It would be tempting to see Jüngel as a traditional critic (for example, Aquinas's articulation of God's essence and existence, or the metaphysical tradition in general) or as a theological critic (that is, a traditional doctrine of divine simplicity cannot and does not account for the incarnation and death of Christ). However, Jüngel's criticisms of the theological tradition are expressions of his frustration with their inability to be sufficiently critical of the metaphysics of their time. Turning toward a more critical metaphysics, Jüngel restructures divine simplicity such that God's existence *is* his essence—where we "perceive existence as that which is essential"[72]—in the sense that the Christian faith "can speak of no other God than the 'incarnate God' and the 'human God.'"[73]

Immink, Gunton, Hinlicky, Frame, and Jüngel find some form of the doctrine of divine simplicity to be suitable, but in need of reform. Frame desires a revision based more strongly on scripture, whereas Immink, Gunton, Hinlicky, and Jüngel are concerned more directly with theological and historical problems. For the latter three, a common theme emerges: the so-called Hellenization Thesis.[74] The adoption of Greek philosophy by some in the early church, even if necessary and unavoidable, altered the gospel and Christian concept of God. However, despite this supposed problem, Gunton, Hinlicky, and Jüngel attempt to reframe and reshape divine simplicity rather than reject it in whole.

RECENT DEFENSES OF DIVINE SIMPLICITY

Despite the shift against divine simplicity (or toward a revision of the doctrine), a minority is starting to rise against the critical readings of

72. Jüngel, *God as the Mystery of the World*, 153.

73. Ibid., 37. Regarding Jüngel and the divine attributes, see Colin E. Gunton, "The Being and Attributes of God: Eberhard Jüngel's Dispute with the Classical Philosophical Tradition," in *The Possibilities of Theology: Studies in the Theology of Eberhard Jüngel*, ed. John Webster (London: T&T Clark, 1994), 7–22; Christopher R. J. Holmes, "The Glory of God in the Theology of Eberhard Jüngel," *IJST* 8 (2006): 343–55; Christopher R. J. Holmes, "Eberhard Jüngel and Wolf Krötke: Recent Contributions toward a Trinitarian Doctrine of God's Attributes," *TJT* 22 (2006): 159–80.

74. On this issue, see W. V. Rowe, "Adolf von Harnack and the Concept of Hellenization," in *Hellenization Revisited: Shaping a Christian Response within the Greco-Roman World*, ed. Wendy E. Helleman (Lanham, MD: University Press of America, 1994), 69–99. See also Matthew Levering, "God and Greek Philosophy in Contemporary Biblical Scholarship," *JTI* 4 (2010): 169–86; C. Kavin Rowe, "God, Greek Philosophy, and the Bible: A Response to Matthew Levering," *JTI* 4 (2010): 69–80.

the tradition regarding the doctrine. For example, Stephen Holmes points out that "a dogmatic tradition stretching from at least as early as Basil in the fourth century to at least as late as Francis Turretin in the seventeenth century and from as far east as John in Damascus to as far west as Jonathan Edwards in Stockbridge, Massachusetts, never had any of these problems."[75] Have the critics and revisionists truly revealed the weaknesses and problems of divine simplicity that went unnoticed for so many centuries? This question is not meant to halt discussion but to fuel it. Nevertheless, it should cause theologians to stop and reevaluate the call for rejection and revision. At this point, we will turn to see how proponents of divine simplicity have defended and argued for the doctrine.

CARL F. H. HENRY

Henry's fifth volume of *God, Revelation and Authority* was published in 1982 and includes a section on "God's Divine Simplicity and Attributes." Henry notes that the attributes "define" or "constitute" the essence of God.[76] Ultimately, divine simplicity teaches that

> God is not compounded of parts; he is not a collection of perfections, but rather a living center of activity pervasively characterized by all his distinctive perfections. The divine attributes are neither additions to the divine essence nor qualities pieced together to make a compound. . . . God's variety of attributes does not conflict with God's simplicity because his simplicity is what comprises the fullness of divine life.[77]

Divine simplicity also means that one attribute cannot be elevated over another since "each attribute is involved in every other attribute." The result is that "each attribute is rightly definable and defined only in relation to every other attribute."[78] For example, God's love, holiness, or infinity is not more basic than any other attribute, all of which, Henry asserts, is confirmed by Scripture.

---

75. Stephen R. Holmes, "'Something Much Too Plain to Say': Towards a Defence of the Doctrine of Divine Simplicity," in *Listening to the Past: The Place of Tradition in Theology* (Grand Rapids: Baker Academic, 2002), 53.

76. Carl F. H. Henry, *God, Revelation and Authority: God Who Stands and Stays*, 2nd ed. (Wheaton, IL: Crossway, 1999), 5:127, 130.

77. Ibid., 5:131.

78. Ibid., 5:135–36.

When it comes to the relation of divine simplicity and Scripture, Henry states that "Scripture represents God's attributes as a living unity" and cites Louis Berkhof and Bavinck as support.[79] Henry's account is a clear evangelical restatement of the doctrine, but he does not clarify the doctrine's relationship to Scripture nor how it bears on the Trinity.

MILLARD ERICKSON

In the late 1990s Millard Erickson noted that "many, if indeed not most, recent systematic theologies do not even discuss [divine simplicity]." In contrast, Erickson argues that divine simplicity expresses an "important truth" for the Christian doctrine of God: "the unity of his nature, the harmony of his attributes, and the fact that his actions involve the whole of what he is."[80] These "values" are important to maintain despite Erickson's desire to avoid the "full traditional meaning " of the doctrine. Erickson fears that this form of divine simplicity leads to the problems raised by Plantinga (see above). In order to uphold these values, Erickson proposes that "what we need is a new metaphysic of persons. . . . A better way of thinking may be to conceive of reality as fundamentally personal rather than impersonal."[81] He never offers a perspective on how this "metaphysics of persons" would affect divine simplicity. His concern is that the "classical" version of divine simplicity borders on an impersonal view of God's nature. In contrast to Henry, Erickson is sympathetic but more apprehensive toward divine simplicity.

RON HIGHFIELD

Ron Highfield owes much to the doctrine of divine simplicity. He admits that his "book stands or falls with the doctrine of divine simplicity" since his work argues that "our knowledge of God will be deepened when we contemplate the different attributes as mutually

79. Ibid., 5:138.

80. Millard J. Erickson, *God the Father Almighty: A Contemporary Exploration of the Divine Attributes* (Grand Rapids: Baker, 1998), 232. See also his brief discussion of the "certain basic values" of the doctrine (229–31).

81. Ibid., 231. He is also comfortable calling God both "rich" and, similar to John Frame, "complex".

enriching each other."[82] Following from the uniqueness of God, divine simplicity was held throughout the great tradition. "Negatively, the doctrine of simplicity denies that God's wholeness, fullness, and perfection is a composite of separable entities or properties. Positively, it affirms that God's wholeness is his free action of self-determination, which is transparent and fully present to him." This means that God is "indivisible but rich and full in his indivisibility."[83] Like others, Highfield worries that a compound God implies dependence on something outside Himself for being and existence. He confesses that "the Bible does not explicitly discuss divine simplicity," but asserts that "divine uniqueness cannot be sustained without affirming divine simplicity."[84] Because God's uniqueness is a biblical doctrine, divine simplicity is *indirectly* linked to Scripture. A Christian doctrine of divine simplicity affirms distinctions that point to the perfect harmony of God's being without creating composition. These distinctions do not violate the doctrine of the Trinity and expresses how "God can be rich without being composite."[85]

JAMES DOLEZAL

James Dolezal offers a more in-depth argument for divine simplicity than any of the previous theologians. His thesis is that if God is absolute (that is, self-existent and independent), then he is also simple. In this sense, divine simplicity is a necessary corollary of God's absolute existence and forms its ontological framework. To deny divine simplicity leads to the view that God depends on something outside himself for his existence and therefore "cannot be the ultimate sufficient explanation for himself or anything else."[86] And, "if God is not the ontological sufficient reason for himself and all other things then he is not God."[87]

Dolezal's aim is to restore divine simplicity "to its traditional role as a controlling and vital concern in the orthodox Christian doctrine of God."[88] He demonstrates that those who deny divine simplicity

82. Ron Highfield, *Great Is the Lord: Theology for the Praise of God* (Grand Rapids: Eerdmans, 2008), 261.
83. Ibid., 264.
84. Ibid., 265.
85. Ibid., 274.
86. Dolezal, God without Parts, 30.
87. Ibid., 213.
88. Ibid., 216.

exhibit a clear theme: a strong commitment to ontological univo-cism. "Each critic speaks as if God and creatures were 'beings' in the exact same sense, reducing the Creator-creature distinction to a difference of degrees. . . . Given this outlook it is no wonder that the doctrine of divine simplicity appears incoherent to many modern philosophers and theologians."[89] This leads him to critique "property accounts" of divine simplicity and argue for the "truth-maker" account with regard to the identity of God's attributes with his essence.[90] In many ways, Dolezal's work is a positive extension of Aquinas's account of divine simplicity carried on through the Protes-tant Scholastics and in dialogue with modern analytic philosophy's concerns, problems, and questions.[91]

PETER SANLON

Peter Sanlon understands divine simplicity to be the crucial aspect of a doctrine of God that is personal, triune, and classical. He is clear that "the simplicity of God is the most fundamental doctrinal gram-mar of divinity"[92] even though it "is counter-intuitive and difficult to grasp; but without it our attempts to describe God's attributes become idolatrous."[93] He finds Jeffrey Brower's and others' arguments for "truthmakers" to be the best way forward for describing how God's attributes are identical. God is his own truthmaker such that "what-ever is being described, the same God guarantees the truthfulness of this statement."[94] Coupled with the important ontological distinction between Creator and creature, this teaching provides crucial guid-ance throughout Sanlon's work.

While divine simplicity may be a traditional doctrine and seem-ingly important to one's grammar of divinity, Sanlon also argues that

---

89. Ibid., 29.

90. Ibid., 144–63. To say that God is the "truthmaker" of his attributes is to ascribe their logical necessitation. On truthmakers and divine simplicity, see Jeffrey E. Brower, "Making Sense of Divine Simplicity," FPh 25 (2008): 3–30; Jeffrey E. Brower, "Simplicity and Aseity," in The Oxford Handbook of Philosophical Theology, ed. Thomas P. Flint and Michael C. Rea (Oxford: Oxford University Press, 2009), 105–28; Brian Leftow, "Divine Simplicity," FPh 23 (2006): 365–80.

91. Dolezal also discusses the relationship between divine simplicity and the Trinity in "Trin-ity, Simplicity and the Status of God's Personal Relations," IJST 16 (2014): 79–98.

92. Peter Sanlon, Simply God: Recovering the Classical Trinity (Nottingham, UK: Inter-Varsity Press, 2014), 58.

93. Ibid., 61.

94. Ibid., 63.

the teaching is biblical. He offers four reasons why this connection is often not made. First, an "uninformed rejection of systematic theology" leads some to see divine simplicity as a foreign concept.[95] There is no passage that uses the word or the concept, so how could it be called biblical? Second, some Christians, especially those who are new to their understanding of the Christian faith, are suspicious of new concepts or terms. Third, an "unduly low view of the importance of church tradition" leads others to neglect divine simplicity as an old teaching with little to offer our modern culture.[96] Finally, the academic "championing of theology as drama or narrative—over against what is unfairly caricatured as impersonal, timeless, doctrinal facts"—leads some scholars to ignore or reject divine simplicity.[97]

Sanlon is unconvinced by the critics, and asserts that divine simplicity "is the term used by generations of Christians and the church to describe the kind of existence God must have if he is indeed all the Bible says he is."[98] Although I agree with this statement, Sanlon regrettably does not offer any arguments or support for this claim. He outlines the implications of simplicity for a biblical teaching like "God is love," but never makes the argument *for* divine simplicity *from* scripture itself.[99] Are there particular passages that teach the simplicity of God? Particular themes?

DAVID BENTLEY HART

David Bentley Hart has argued for a doctrine of divine simplicity in various works,[100] but his clearest articulation is found in *The Experience of God*. There, he argues that "no claim, I think it fair to say, has traditionally been seen as more crucial to a logically coherent concept of God than the denial that God is in any way composed of separable parts, aspects, properties, or functions" and that "any denial of divine simplicity is equivalent to a denial of God's reality."[101] Divine simplicity is the "total absence" of any "limitations" or "conditions," meaning

---

95. Ibid., 65–66.
96. Ibid., 68.
97. Ibid., 69.
98. Ibid., 72.
99. Ibid., 125–27.
100. For example, Hart, *Beauty of the Infinite*, 173–74, 205.
101. David Bentley Hart, *The Experience of God: Being, Consciousness, Bliss* (New Haven: Yale University Press, 2013), 134.

that "there is not even any distinction between [God's] essence and existence."[102]

Hart also identifies two "metaphysical implications" of divine simplicity: God is eternal and impassible (this includes immutability). God is "beyond time," changeless, and cannot be externally affected. The philosophical problems that arise are often due to "a failure properly to think of God's way of being as truly transcendent of ours, rather than as merely another version of our way of being."[103] A doctrine of creation coupled with a theological account of analogy is crucial for making proper sense of divine simplicity. Nevertheless, Hart recognizes that various religious traditions elaborate divine simplicity differently, and this observation leads him to stress "the elementary metaphysical premise . . . that God is not like a physical object, composed of parts and defined by limits, and so is dependent upon nothing and subject to neither *substantial* change nor dissolution."[104]

STEPHEN R. HOLMES

A longtime defender of a theological account of divine simplicity is Stephen Holmes, who argues that the doctrine of divine simplicity is comprehensible and theologically useful,[105] is important for soteriology,[106] and has demonstrated simplicity's importance for the Trinity throughout the tradition.[107] Holmes locates two problems with contemporary responses to divine simplicity: (1) Problems associated with the incarnation and Trinity are "the result of a failure to work with the same doctrine of simplicity as the Christian dogmatic tradition."[108] (2) There is a misunderstanding of ontology. While there

102. Ibid., 136.

103. Ibid., 137.

104. Ibid., 140.

105. Holmes, "Something Much Too Plain to Say," *NZSTR* 43 (2001): 137–54. A slightly revised version was published in Holmes, *Listening to the Past*, cited above. Citations will be from the revised 2002 essay.

106. Stephen R. Holmes, "A Simple Salvation? Soteriology and the Perfections of God," in *God of Salvation: Soteriology in Theological Perspective*, ed. Ivor Davidson and Murray Rae (Aldershot: Ashgate, 2011), 35–46.

107. Stephen R. Holmes, *The Quest for the Trinity: The Doctrine of God in Scripture, History and Modernity* (Downers Grove, IL: IVP Academic, 2012), 97–99, 104–8, 136–37, 156–60, 192–93. See also Stephen R. Holmes, "The Attributes of God," in *The Oxford Handbook of Systematic Theology*, ed. John Webster, Kathryn Tanner, and Iain Torrance (Oxford: Oxford University Press, 2007), 54–71.

108. Holmes, "Something Much Too Plain to Say," 61.

is no traditional ontology, or account of God's being, the tradition is clear that God is incomprehensible. "The problems—all the problems, I think—raised by the doctrine of divine simplicity are results of an improper assumption that we can understand God's essence."[109] These two closely related problems aid Holmes in his positive account of divine simplicity in relation to an ontology of personhood.

To speak of God's nature as simple means that in the incarnation "the personal character displayed by the man Jesus Christ is an accurate revelation of the personal character of God—an important point, but hardly an original or difficult one."[110] Divine simplicity and the Trinity have gone "hand-in-hand for much of Christian history," and Holmes finds this most clearly illustrated in John of Damascus's *An Exposition of the Orthodox Faith*.[111] In terms of usefulness, divine simplicity provides a middle road between the nominalism-realism debates by positing that God's very being is the standard, for example, of righteousness.[112] However, Holmes's strongest point is historical: many theologians throughout the tradition never noticed the problems raised against divine simplicity in the last thirty years. Following this vein, those who reject or seek to modify divine simplicity must face the question of whether they have rejected a form of divine simplicity from the tradition or their own problematic construction of the doctrine.[113]

STEVEN J. DUBY

One recent deliberately dogmatic account of divine simplicity is found in the work of Steven Duby. He argues that divine simplicity includes "a network of theological commitments" that require both

---

109. Ibid., 55.

110. Ibid., 61.

111. Ibid., 61, 62–64.

112. Ibid., 66.

113. Nicholas Wolterstorff argues that the difficulty for modern theologians and philosophers is the clash of ontologies. The medieval "constituent" ontology and contemporary "relation" ontology think very differently about essences and properties. See Nicholas Wolterstorff, "Divine Simplicity," in *Inquiring about God: Selected Essays*, ed. Terence Cuneo (Cambridge: Cambridge University Press, 2010), 91–111. Although there is truth to Wolterstorff's argument, the problems cannot be reduced to mere difference of ontological categories. Rather, as Holmes notes, one of the primary problems is whether divine simplicity has been received according to its traditional understanding. See also Richard A. Muller, *Post-Reformation Reformed Dogmatics*, vol. 3, *The Divine Essence and Attributes*, 2nd ed. (Grand Rapids: Baker Academic, 2003), 297–98.

biblical and dogmatic articulation.[114] In relation to scripture, Duby argues that scripture's teachings on God's singularity, aseity, immutability, infinity, and *creatio ex nihilo* imply, or entail, a doctrine of divine simplicity.[115] Although Duby distinguishes dogmatics from exegesis, he also points out that "in another sense [dogmatics] just is exegesis carried out in a certain elaborative manner."[116] His approach also incorporates the metaphysics of Thomas Aquinas and other Thomistic Reformed orthodox theologians. Metaphysics and philosophy have a ministerial role and are always governed by scripture.

At the core of Duby's project is what he calls "a cartography of divine simplicity," a list of ten statements that summarize the doctrine's key tenets.[117] (1) "God is pure act and is therefore not composed of act and potency." (2) "God is entirely spiritual and is therefore not composed of corporeal parts." (3) "God is his own form (*deitas*) and is therefore not composed of matter and form." (4) "God is his own divinity subsisting and is therefore not composed of nature and *suppositum* or individual." (5) "God is really identical with each of the persons of the Trinity and is not composed by them." (6) "God, who is his own essence, is identical with his own existence also." (7) "God transcends classification and demarcation and is therefore not composed of genus and species." (8) "God is identical with each of his own attributes." (9) "God is wholly himself and not susceptive of any composition at all." (10) "Finally, while God is fully himself and incomposite in himself, he is also not joined to other things as though he might become part of a composite."[118] Briefly stated, God does

---

114. Duby, *Divine Simplicity*, 2. See also Steven J. Duby, "Divine Simplicity, Divine Freedom, and the Contingency of Creation: Dogmatic Responses to Some Analytic Questions," *JRT* 6 (2012): 115–42.

115. On the exegetical and dogmatic connections between these teachings and scripture, see *Divine Simplicity*, 91–177. Similarly, Turretin argues that divine simplicity can be proved from God's independence, unity, perfection, and activity (*Institutes of Elenctic Theology*, ed. James T. Dennison Jr., trans. George Musgrave Giger [Phillipsburg, NJ: P&R, 1992], 3.7.4 [1:191]). The first four biblical teachings that Duby argues imply divine simplicity are also similar to Dolezal's "theological rationale for divine absoluteness." He argues in a somewhat different direction, stating that divine aseity, unity, infinity, immutability, and eternity require divine simplicity. "Without simplicity these dogmatic claims would not be sufficient to distinguish God absolutely from his creation. Indeed, absolute simplicity is the theological rationale underlying each of these claims" (*God without Parts*, 67).

116. Ibid., 56.

117. Ibid., 80.

118. Ibid., 81–86.

not have "'proper' parts" or "'improper' parts."[119] Each statement is demonstrated through careful exegesis and theological consideration.

These statements are significant because a portion of them is located in each of the five biblical teachings that imply a doctrine of divine simplicity. For example, the biblical teaching of divine singularity presents "the universality of God's sovereignty, the distinction between the God of Israel and other gods and the absolute and direct descriptions of God as the only God."[120] God's singularity entails, first, "the identity of nature and *suppositum* in God"; second, that God "transcends the categories of genus and species"; third, "that God is really identical with each of his own perfections"; and fourth, "that all that is in God is really identical with God himself."[121] Put differently, God's singularity includes statements four, seven, eight, and nine from the cartography of divine simplicity. Another example, aseity, includes statements one, four, six, eight, and nine. For Duby, the ten statements summarize the key elements found in the biblical teachings of God's singularity, aseity, immutability, infinity, and the doctrine of *creatio ex nihilo*.

My project finds continuity with Duby's in that it seeks to broaden and clarify the connection of the doctrine of divine simplicity to scripture. His work guides the conversation back to neglected sources that engage scripture, dogmatics, and metaphysics. He makes a strong argument for divine simplicity as an implied and strongly entailed biblical teaching. However, as the remainder of my work will demonstrate, I locate the roots of divine simplicity in the name(s) of God and the individual operations of the Trinity *ad extra*. These two biblical teachings are prominently at work through the early, medieval, and Reformation periods. While these teachings are not included in Duby's work, I find them to be complementary and aimed toward the goal of clarifying simplicity's origins in scripture.

THE NEED FOR FURTHER STUDY

I have argued that one of the best ways to understand the contemporary critiques of divine simplicity is to categorize them according to the traditional, biblical, and theological criticisms. Each critique

119. Ibid., 87.
120. Ibid., 100.
121. Ibid., 102, 103, 106, 107.

does not fit perfectly in these categories, but they still provide a helpful basis for understanding the fundamental problems with divine simplicity. Overall, divine simplicity appears to present biblical, doctrinal, and conceptual problems for Christian theology and is at best a speculative and difficult doctrine to understand. Revisionists agree with some of the criticisms, but disagree that divine simplicity should be discarded. Apart from Jüngel, those who attempt to modify the doctrine have merely offered suggestions for ways forward, but have not developed their insights into extended or comprehensive accounts.

One of the most confusing aspects of the contemporary articulation and reception of divine simplicity is the divergent explanations of its demise. Holmes is partially correct that the problems stem from the belief that the divine essence can be sufficiently understood and that, to a large extent, the version of divine simplicity being rejected cannot be found throughout the tradition.[122] Nicholas Wolterstorff adds another helpful piece to the puzzle by locating some of the problems in the realm of differing ontologies. What about scripture? Was divine simplicity ever understood to be a biblical teaching? If so, which passages, which themes, and why?

DEFINING TERMS

The analysis of the contemporary reception of divine simplicity raises a number of questions about the definition and use of particular terms like *being, substance, attribute,* or *names.*[123] These terms are common throughout the tradition depending on each context, but they must be carefully used and defined since they are largely absent from scripture. These terms and concepts were not pointless developments or improvements on scripture, but, as Calvin points out, "the novelty of words of this sort (if it must be called) becomes especially useful when the truth is to be asserted against false accusers."[124]

I will use the terms *nature, being, essence,* and *substance* to refer to

---

122. As I will show in the following chapters, the development of the doctrine of divine simplicity is not monolithic. There is no single "traditional" view of divine simplicity. However, this does not mean that the various perspectives do not have strong similarities or continuity.

123. I am thankful for Scott Swain's input on this section.

124. John Calvin, *Institutes of the Christian Religion,* ed. John T. McNeill, trans. Ford Lewis Battles, LCC 20–21 (Philadelphia: Westminster, 1960), 1.8.4 (1:124).

what God is.[125] Therefore, these terms refer to what the three divine persons have in common. This does not mean that God's essence is a fourth "thing" in relation to the three divine persons, but refers to the perfections that characterize God as God. Rather, the terms identify and point to the fact that the triune God is *one* in being, nature, essence, or substance.

Aside from some of the historical sections, I will largely avoid the term *property*. My concern with *property* language is that many contemporary analytic theologians and philosophers refer to properties as something God possesses.[126] Instead, I will use the language of divine attributes, perfections, and names. Attributes refer to "any term that adequately completes the sentence 'God is. . . .'"[127] On the one hand, divine attributes are qualities of God's being; on the other hand, they are not something God possesses, but rather descriptions of what God is. I will also sometimes use the term *perfection* and understand it to be nearly synonymous with *attributes*. For Barth, perfections "[point] at once to the thing itself instead of merely to its formal aspect, and because instead of something general it expresses at once that which is clearly distinctive."[128] Like attributes, perfections are descriptions God's being and refer to what God is. Unlike the term *attributes*, the language of perfections is more particular (that is, they are *God's* perfections and they are supremely perfect), whereas attribute language is broader and requires more clarification since both God and creatures are said to have attributes.

I understand the term *divine name(s)* to refer not only to God's proper names but also to attributes of all kinds (absolute, relative, metaphorical). In this sense, *divine names* is the best of all terms, first, because of its more inclusive nature. Second, it is more directly connected to the grammar of scripture. Finally, the divine names

125. Depending on the translation, the language of "divine nature" (θειότης, Rom 1:20), "nature" (φύσει, Gal 4:8), "deity" (θεότητος, Col 2:9), or "nature" (φύσεως, 2 Pet 1:4) is found in Scripture. Of course, the meaning of these terms is not identical to the philosophical definitions often attached to them, but they do provide a biblical basis for the use of such language as long as they are used and defined carefully.

126. For two examples, see Plantinga, *Does God Have a Nature?*; Thomas V. Morris, "On God and Mann: A View of Divine Simplicity," in *Anselmian Explorations: Essays in Philosophical Theology* (Notre Dame: University of Notre Dame Press, 1987), 98–123.

127. Stephen R. Holmes, "Divine Attributes," in *Mapping Modern Theology: A Thematic and Historical Introduction*, ed. Bruce L. McCormack and Kelly M. Kapic (Grand Rapids: Baker Academic, 2012), 48.

128. *CD* II/1, 322. To be clear, the term "perfection" is not original in Barth's theology. See Muller, *Divine Essence and Attributes*, 199–200.

were significant throughout church history to bridge the language of scripture to the language of divine attributes.[129] These points will become clearer in the following chapters.

The use of metaphysical language throughout this work is not a capitulation to what is sometimes called "substance metaphysics," if such a view even exists.[130] Nevertheless, this project will demonstrate how "metaphysical analysis sustains the believer's ability to express, both within scripture and in Christian theologies that interpret scripture as a channel of divine Revelation, the Holy Trinity's radical and mysterious presence."[131] The use of metaphysics or ontology—which I see as functionally equivalent—is made serviceable to theology and must be governed by scripture. Rather than repudiating the role of metaphysics, this project analyzes and uses metaphysics in a ministerial rather than magisterial sense.[132]

Last, it is important to present the definition of divine simplicity, for which I argue throughout the present project. Divine simplicity is a concept that elaborates what is implicit in scripture's depiction of God—namely, that the divine attributes and the divine essence are identical, whereas the divine attributes are distinct from one another.[133] The divine essence is not a composite of attributes but is rather identical to the divine attributes taken as a whole, even though the divine attributes themselves are not identical with one another. Divine simplicity yields a number of apophatic implications. The simple nature of God admits of no composition or parts. Traditionally, to be composed, or to be made of parts, implies dependence on

129. See Muller, *Divine Essence and Attributes*, 246–70. Hart sees a greater difference between a study of divine names and divine attributes: "There is a vast difference between the theological enunciation of the 'divine names' and the philosophical enumeration of the 'attributes of deity,' which is nothing less than the difference between two ontologies: between a metaphysics of participation, according to which all things are embraced in the supereminent source of all their transcendental perfections, and a 'univocal' ontology that understands being as nothing but the bare category of existence, under which all substances (God no less than creatures) are severally placed" (*Beauty of the Infinite*, 301).

130. D. Stephen Long argues that "substance metaphysics" arose after 1725 based on supposed errors throughout the theological tradition. See *The Perfectly Simple Triune God: Aquinas and His Legacy* (Minneapolis: Fortress Press, 2016), 307–62.

131. Matthew Levering, *Scripture and Metaphysics: Aquinas and the Renewal of Trinitarian Theology*, CCT (Oxford: Blackwell, 2004), 5.

132. See also Duby's reasoning for the use of metaphysical language and philosophy in *Divine Simplicity*, 58–67.

133. For example, God's love is not identical to God's holiness, yet God's love and holiness are nothing other than the divine essence in its entirety. My definition of divine simplicity as a "theological concept" is different from Duby's understanding of divine simplicity as a perfection (e.g., *Divine Simplicity*, 2–3).

the parts for existence, the possibility of change, a lack of freedom, corruptibility, and measurability.[134]

OVERVIEW OF THE ARGUMENT

This study is an exercise in systematic theology, making use of historical theology and biblical studies. One of my primary aims is to listen closely to the tradition in order to best understand and present its readings of scripture and the perspectives on divine simplicity in each particular context. With careful attention, this enables me to compare understandings of simplicity to scripture and make use of the insights as I present my own account. My fundamental claim is that divine simplicity is a uniquely Christian doctrine rooted in scripture that developed in order to combat opposition and in response to false readings of scripture. To locate the origins of divine simplicity in Greek philosophy, natural theology, perfect being theology, or "classical theism" is the result of misunderstandings. Rather, it is a revealed doctrine that is best understood when governed by scripture and when it follows the theological discernment of trinitarian distinctions.

Chapters 2, 3, and 4 will survey key figures throughout the theological tradition—from Irenaeus to Karl Barth—in order to see how, if at all, their doctrine of divine simplicity was constructed, received, and informed by scripture. A patristic, Thomistic, Barthian, or other label does not frame my account of divine simplicity. To be sure, my perspective is shaped and influenced by many works, but my overall aim is not to articulate a doctrine according to a particular theologian or time period. Chapter 5 argues that divine simplicity originates from two biblical sources—the divine name(s) and the indivisible operations of the Trinity *ad extra*—and that they are the true Christian basis of the doctrine. The chapter on scripture follows the chapters on historical theology not because scripture is of little importance, but for two reasons: first, because there is great wisdom to be found by listening to interpreters who have gone before us; second, so that scripture may be used to test the claims made throughout the tradition with specific attention to whether divine simplicity can be called biblical in any sense. Chapter 6 presents distortions and errors that

---

134. For a summary of the various forms of composition that divine simplicity denies, see Duby, *Divine Simplicity*, 81–88; Dolezal, *God without Parts*, 31–66.

must be avoided when formulating a doctrine of divine simplicity. It is here that the doctrine of the Trinity provides a key formal analogy: as the triune God is one nature in three distinct persons, so the simplicity of God affirms one nature in multiple and distinct perfections. I call this distinction between the divine attributes an idiomatic distinction, which states that the divine attributes are identical to the divine essence, but are not identical to one another. Based on this distinction, what contemporary critics are rejecting is much closer, if not identical, to a Eunomian version of divine simplicity than the biblical and trinitarian version I present in the following chapters.

2.

Early Christian Approaches to Divine Simplicity

The doctrine of divine simplicity has a long history involving complex accounts that interweave philosophy, scripture, and theology. Without a doubt, there is no single doctrine of divine simplicity that remained perfectly unaltered throughout the Christian tradition. Perhaps this is because, as Christopher Stead argues, throughout the early church various senses of divine simplicity were used to speak about God without ever clarifying which sense was in use. In other words, "we must not think that simplicity is itself a simple notion."[1] However, the simplistic versions of divine simplicity represented in much contemporary theology—primarily from critics—might lead others to see it as a clear and easy target. What is missing in these accounts is attention to the crucial fact that "the doctrine of God emerged out of contexts within which hotly contested common texts and images sustained a number of traditions of thought."[2] Not every version of divine simplicity was the result of a magisterial metaphysics, speculation, or perfect being theology. Similar to the Trinity, Christology, and other debated teachings, the core belief that God is without parts

1. Christopher Stead, "Divine Simplicity as a Problem for Orthodoxy," in *The Making of Orthodoxy: Essays in Honour of Henry Chadwick*, ed. Rowan Williams (Cambridge: Cambridge University Press, 1989), 256–57.

2. Lewis Ayres and Andrew Radde-Gallwitz, "Doctrine of God," in *The Oxford Handbook of Early Christian Studies*, ed. Susan Ashbrook Harvey and David Hunter (Oxford: Oxford University Press, 2008), 866.

developed as a result of disputing texts of scripture and as a response to false teachings.

Even in light of this, there are still disagreements as to whether the development of divine simplicity was a positive or negative progression. On the one hand, Stead finds "radical defects in the neat antithesis of simple and compound." He is also concerned that the early church fathers, "inheriting a richer though far more complex tradition, struck out new lines of thought which were never (I think) connected in a logically coherent whole, but which, if pursued, should have exhibited the notion of wholly undifferentiated divine simplicity as an unwanted survival."[3] For example, with the Cappadocians, Stead finds "a peculiar weakness" in the relation of Trinity and simplicity. The three "distinguishing peculiarities" contradict the "simple undivided divine substance," and the "multiplicity of descriptions" (*epinoia*) corresponds to the energies while leaving the simple substance unaltered.[4] On the other hand, Lewis Ayres and Andrew Radde-Gallwitz point out that older scholarship, including Stead's views on divine simplicity, saw the relation of scripture and philosophy's doctrines of God as blending contrary views. That is, there is little if anything in common between the God of the philosophers and the God of Abraham, Isaac, and Jacob. Furthermore, recent patristic scholarship now draws a key distinction between doctrine and method which demonstrates that "one can use another school's doctrines to explicate the texts and traditions to which one is more fundamentally committed."[5] In this way, divine simplicity functions as a shorthand concept used to elaborate scripture's language and teaching about God and "was not discussed by patristic authors as a 'purely philosophical' concept easily separable from exegetical and doctrinal concerns. Rather, it entered into basic debates about who God is in light of revelation."[6] When seen differently, it becomes clearer that divine simplicity should be viewed "as part of the set

---

3. Stead, "Divine Simplicity," 261, 265.

4. Ibid., 267.

5. Ayres and Radde-Gallwitz, "Doctrine of God," 872. Elsewhere, Ayres adds that while Stead is right to desire greater clarity on the meaning of the various sources used to support divine simplicity, he finds that "Stead has simply missed the function of this terminology in pro-Nicene authors" (Ayres, *Nicaea and Its Legacy: An Approach to Fourth-Century Trinitarian Theology* [Oxford: Oxford University Press, 2006], 287n41). This particular issue will be discussed below. Regarding Stead, see also Andrew Radde-Gallwitz, *Basil of Caesarea, Gregory of Nyssa, and the Transformation of Divine Simplicity*, OECS (Oxford: Oxford University Press, 2009), 9–14.

6. Radde-Gallwitz, *Transformation of Divine Simplicity*, 7.

of concepts that Christians used to deal with problems and tensions involved in reading scripture as a coherent whole."[7] While divine simplicity was clearly a borrowed concept, this does not lead to the conclusion that it is contrary to scripture. If the mere borrowing of a concept made a doctrine suspect, then the creeds would be just as suspect due to their borrowed terms and concepts.[8]

Currently, no comprehensive historical account of divine simplicity exists. Recent surveys of the history of divine simplicity tell the story primarily from the angle of philosophy.[9] Consequently, Augustine, Anselm, and Aquinas receive most of the attention—the supposed champions of classical theism—and are typically read as philosophers rather than theologians. Most narratives also tend to leave out crucial voices (for example, the Cappadocians) or ignore the historical and theological significance of various opponents that contributed to the rise and development of divine simplicity in the first place. While the origins of the concept of a simple being have clear ties to pre-Christian philosophy,[10] it is crucial to see that the deployment of this doctrine *by Christian theologians* throughout history is motivated by theological and biblical concerns. After beginning with Irenaeus, I will present the views of Basil of Caesarea and Gregory of Nyssa, Augustine, John of Damascus, and Aquinas. In the next chapter I will look at the Reformation and post-Reformation, including Jonathan Edwards, Friedrich Schleiermacher, Herman Bavinck, and Karl Barth. The aim of this chapter is not to provide an exhaustive

7. Ayres and Radde-Gallwitz, "Doctrine of God," 875.

8. I agree with David Bentley Hart that "it seems undeniable to me that the early development of the Christian understanding of God implicitly involved a metaphysical revision of certain prevailing understandings of being." See his "The Hidden and the Manifest: Metaphysics after Nicaea," in *Orthodox Readings of Augustine*, ed. Aristotle Papanikolaou and George E. Demacopoulos (Crestwood, NY: St. Vladimir's Seminary Press, 2008), 191. Divine simplicity surely involves metaphysics, but it is a theological and ministerial metaphysics that underwent serious revisions in its adoption from various philosophies.

9. For example, Stump finds its origin in Parmenides via Plotinus and traces it through Augustine, Anselm, and Aquinas (Eleonore Stump, "Simplicity," in *The Blackwell Companion to Philosophy of Religion* [Oxford: Blackwell, 1997], 253–55). James E. Dolezal is a recent exception. He briefly describes divine simplicity from the patristic to the twentieth century in his *God without Parts: Divine Simplicity and the Metaphysics of God's Absoluteness* (Eugene, OR: Pickwick, 2011), 3–10. For brief historical accounts, see Gavin Ortlund, "Divine Simplicity in Historical Perspective: Resourcing a Contemporary Discussion," *IJST* 16 (2014): 436–53; Steven J. Duby, *Divine Simplicity: A Dogmatic Account*, SST (London: Bloomsbury T&T Clark, 2015), 7–53.

10. See Katherin A. Rogers, "The Traditional Doctrine of Divine Simplicity," *RelS* 32 (1996): 167–70. Stead argues that the Christian view of divine simplicity derives from Xenophanes (c. 570–475 BCE), although he admits the possibility of other intermediate sources and differing doctrinal motivations (*Divine Substance* [Oxford: Clarendon, 1977], 188).

survey of divine simplicity, but to attend to the key theological and biblical themes in the most representative works and thinkers. In particular, I will give attention to the use of scripture in relation to divine simplicity, the way divine simplicity affected readings of scripture, and when appropriate, the polemical nature of divine simplicity in the face of false teachings and other pressures.

IRENAEUS OF LYONS

Irenaeus's statements on divine simplicity are likely the earliest Christian witness to this teaching.[11] His understanding and use of divine simplicity is not fully developed, but the seeds of the doctrine are present and his use of divine simplicity in response to false teaching indicates its importance for the church fathers from an early time. It is also significant that Irenaeus makes use of divine simplicity in light of the important role scripture plays in response to gnostic teachings and other theological formulations. While he does not directly connect or quote scripture to support his doctrine of divine simplicity, his aim is to be faithful to scripture and apostolic teaching and this does not lead him to reject divine simplicity but to use it as a Christian response to false teaching.

Against Heresies marks one of Irenaeus's responses to the gnostic teachings of his time. It is plausible that the central theme of this work is "the thesis that God is one, and is himself the maker of everything that is."[12] Gnostic teaching violates this notion because of its doctrine of divine emanation. Irenaeus notes that various gnostics believed that "in the invisible and ineffable heights above there exists a certain perfect, pre-existent Aeon [Αιών]" who is also "eternal and unbegotten."[13] This Aeon generated many other Aeons by which other

11. Stead argues that Irenaeus is the first in Christian literature to suggest that "the divine attributes are identical with each other and their possessor" (*Divine Substance*, 187). Depending on the dating of texts, Athenagoras may be the earliest. See his *Plea for the Christians* 8, 12 (*ANF* 2:133–34).

12. Richard A. Norris, "The Transcendence and Freedom of God: Irenaeus, the Greek Tradition and Gnosticism," in *Early Christian Literature and the Classical Intellectual Tradition: In Honorem Robert M. Grant*, ed. William R. Schoedel and Robert L. Wilken, Théologie Historique (Paris: Beauchesne, 1979), 88.

13. Irenaeus, "Against Heresies," in *Ante-Nicene Fathers*, ed. Alexander Roberts and James Donaldson, trans. Ernest Cushing Richardson and Bernard Pick (Peabody, MA: Hendrickson, 1994), 1.1.1. Hereafter *AH*. For more on the structure and content of *AH*, see John Behr, *Irenaeus of Lyons: Identifying Christianity* (Oxford: Oxford University Press, 2013), 73–203. See also Richard A. Norris, "Who Is the Demiurge? Irenaeus' Picture of God in *Adversus haereses* 2,"

"Aeons were sent forth just as rays are from the sun."[14] Part of Irenaeus's response is that "if they had known the Scriptures . . . they would have known, beyond doubt, that God is not as men are; and that His thoughts are not like the thoughts of men." Rather, God

> is a simple, uncompounded Being, without diverse members, and altogether like, and equal to himself, since He is wholly understanding, and wholly spirit, and wholly thought, and wholly intelligence, and wholly reason, and wholly hearing, and wholly seeing, and wholly light, and the whole source of all that is good.[15]

God does not generate a multiplicity of Aeons from himself as though these "parts" of his being could be separated from him. Diversity, at least in the gnostic sense, does not exist in God. Nevertheless, to describe God as light is to express something true about God's *entire* being, without summing up all that he is or all that can be said about him. "God is all mind, all reason, all active spirit, all light, and always exists one and the same, as it is both beneficial for us to think of God, and as we learn regarding Him from the Scriptures, such feelings and divisions [of operation] cannot fittingly be ascribed to Him" (*AH* 2.28.4).

Although divine simplicity is a borrowed concept—similar to *homoousios*—Irenaeus did not adopt it without significant revision. The philosophical emphasis on a transcendent deity devoid of any involvement with creation and one that transcends all forms of distinction is missing from his account, even in its undeveloped form. As Douglas Farrow puts it, "In a departure demanded by the scriptures, [Irenaeus] built instead on the freedom of God to involve himself with his creatures. For 'the Father of all' is already in his transcendent simplicity the triune God, who with his two hands—Word and Wisdom, the Son and the Spirit—is well able to embrace the world, and has in fact done so."[16] In Irenaeus we find a crucial response to gnostic teaching that divided God. Divine simplicity means that God

---

in *God in Early Christian Thought: Essays in Memory of Lloyd G. Patterson*, ed. Andrew B. T. McGowan, Brian E. Daley, and Timothy J. Gaden (Leiden: Brill, 2009), 9–38.

14. Irenaeus, *AH* 2.17.7.

15. Irenaeus, *AH* 2.13.3. See also 2.13.8. Norris finds the origins of this wording in Xenophanes ("Irenaeus, the Greek Tradition and Gnosticism," 96). The Latin for "simple" is *simplex* and "wholly" is from *totus*. See St. Irenaeus of Lyons, *Five Books Against Heresies, Volume II*, ed. W. Wigan Harvey (Cambridge: Cambridge University Press, 1857).

16. Douglas Farrow, *Ascension and Ecclesia: On the Significance of the Doctrine of the Ascension for Ecclesiology and Christian Cosmology* (Edinburgh: T&T Clark, 1999), 48.

is completely all that he is, without division, and truly (not literally) *is* these names because scripture names him as such. However, these names are true in a sense different from creatures, who are composite beings. Other early church fathers held to similar understandings of divine simplicity such as Clement of Alexandria, Origen, and Athanasius.[17] However, the next significant development stems from the Cappadocians' understanding of divine simplicity in response to Eunomius.

DIVINE SIMPLICITY IN THE EAST

Similar to Irenaeus and his response to gnostic teachings, Basil's and Gregory's views developed in relation to their polemical dialogues with Eunomius of Cyzicus (d. ca. 394).[18] Eunomius was a secretary to Aetius and was made bishop of Cyzicus in 360. While his thought follows the theology of Aetius in many ways, he was a central figure in the development of "heterousian" theology in the fourth century and his thought progressed beyond Aetius's in many ways.[19] Although his theology and the context of his debate with Basil and Gregory is complicated, my concern here is for the way he understood the doctrine of divine simplicity and the work it did in his theology. Eunomius did not reject divine simplicity, but agreed with his opponents that it plays an important role in the doctrine of God. The problem is that it was so important for him that he ended up *misusing* the doctrine of divine simplicity in ways that actually worked against the doctrine of the Trinity and caused difficulty when it came

17. For more on Clement of Alexandria, Origen, and Athanasius, see chaps. 2 and 3 in Radde-Gallwitz, *Transformation of Divine Simplicity*. He notes that there are subtle differences between the three. For example, Clement's view of divine simplicity means that "God falls under no category." For Origen, divine simplicity "means that God is being itself, with no admixture of relative or accidental being" (ibid., 64).

18. Three of Eunomius's works survive in part and in whole. The first is the *Apology* (ca. 360), which Basil attacks in *Adversus Eunomium* (ca. 364) and survives due to Basil's quotations. Second, *Apology for an Apology* (ca. late 370s) only survives in portions from quotations given by Gregory of Nyssa and is a response to Basil's *Adversus Eunomium*. Last, *Confession of Faith* was preserved by Gregory of Nyssa and written for the council summoned by Theodosius in 383. The following quotations for these works will be drawn from the critical texts and translations found in Richard P. Vaggione, *Eunomius: The Extant Works*, OECT (Oxford: Oxford University Press, 1987). See also Richard P. Vaggione, *Eunomius of Cyzicus and the Nicene Revolution*, OECS (Oxford: Oxford University Press, 2001).

19. The term comes from Ayres, *Nicaea and Its Legacy*, 145. However, Richard P. C. Hanson also uses it in *The Search for the Christian Doctrine of God: The Arian Controversy, 318–381* (1988; repr., Grand Rapids: Baker Academic, 2006), 625, 633.

to making sense of scripture's presentation of the names of God. Therefore, it is crucial to locate and clarify the role of divine simplicity in Eunomius's thought in order to see why Basil and Gregory of Nyssa responded with great seriousness.

EUNOMIUS OF CYZICUS

For the purposes of this project, it is important to highlight two key teachings of Eunomius: the essence of God as unbegotten and the essence of God as simple. These beliefs work together in the *Apologia* and contribute to Eunomius's overall theology in significant ways. Eunomius is clear that "God is one," and "he was brought into being neither by his own action nor by that of any other."[20] Nothing existed before him since he is before all things. What follows from these statements is that God is thus named "the Unbegotten, or rather, that he is unbegotten essence."[21] Crucial to Eunomius's point is that

> when we say "Unbegotten," then, we do not imagine that we ought to honour God only in name, in conformity with human invention; rather, in conformity with reality, we ought to repay him the debt which above all others is most due God: the acknowledgement that he is what he is.[22]

Radde-Gallwitz explains that the debt is both "'religious' and 'epistemological': as the former, acknowledging God as God really exists is something we owe as worshippers; as the latter, such an acknowledgment . . . tell[s] us what the object known really is, not merely what we perceive it to be or how it relates to us."[23] On the one hand, Eunomius wants to avoid what later theologians would call nominalism. The names of God actually conform to reality and to his very essence and, as saints, we must worship God as he truly is. On the other hand, one might be tempted to anachronistically call this a univocal view of language, as Stephen Hildebrand does, or, as Radde-Gallwitz asserts, a form of "hyper-realism."[24]

20. Eunomius, *Apologia* 7 (Vaggione, 41).

21. Eunomius, *Apologia* 7 (Vaggione, 41).

22. Eunomius, *Apologia* 8 (Vaggione, 42–43).

23. Radde-Gallwitz, *Transformation of Divine Simplicity*, 97. For more on Eunomius's concern about "human invention" (or conceptualization), see ibid., 98–104.

24. Stephen M. Hildebrand, *The Trinitarian Theology of Basil of Caesarea: A Synthesis of Greek Thought and Biblical Truth* (Washington, DC: Catholic University of America Press, 2007), 41; Radde-Gallwitz, *Transformation of Divine Simplicity*, 112.

If language and names directly correspond to reality, and to God, then the name unbegotten refers to all that God is rather than a part or one aspect. However, Eunomius takes this idea further: if unbegotten "is not applied to a part of him only (for his is without parts), and does not exist within him as something separate (for he is simple and uncompounded), and is not something different alongside him (for he is one and only he is unbegotten), then 'the Unbegotten' must be unbegotten *essence*."[25] To be God is to be unbegotten. This is his name. To be simple and unbegotten also means that God "could never undergo a generation which involved the sharing of his own distinctive nature with the offspring of that generation."[26] The implications of this thinking are paramount: the "only-begotten" Son cannot equally be God since to be God is to be unbegotten.[27]

Eunomius's doctrine of divine simplicity is also closely tied to his epistemology and theory of divine names.[28] In contrast to Basil, Gregory, and others assert that "by distinguishing the names they show the difference in essence as well."[29] Names are "tools" in that they "[put] us *in actual contact* with the essence."[30] As it pertains to God, "we take it that his substance is the very same as that which is signified by his name, granted that the designation applies properly to the essence."[31] In this way, God's essence can be known, and because the Father (unbegotten) and Son (begotten) have different names, they end up having different essences as well. What follows is that all other names spoken of God must be seen in light of the name unbegotten, otherwise these names would divide God into parts (or essences) and violate the doctrine of divine simplicity that Eunomius is trying to maintain. "If, then, every word used to signify the essence of the Father is equivalent in force of meaning to 'the Unbegotten' because

25. Eunomius, *Apologia* 8 (Vaggione, 43).

26. Eunomius, *Apologia* 9 (Vaggione, 43).

27. Elsewhere Eunomius argues that one must believe the Son "to be neither *homoousios* nor *homoiousios* [with the Father], since the one implies a generation and division of the essence and the other an equality" (*Apologia* 26 [Vaggion, 71]). Eunomius's problem with "equality" stems from his belief that if both the Father and Son were equally God, then both would have to be unbegotten. But since the Son is called only-begotten and because names ontologically correspond to essences, the Son cannot be unbegotten and is therefore not equal to the Father.

28. For a deeper reflection on this topic in relation to Basil, see Mark DelCogliano, *Basil of Caesarea's Anti-Eunomian Theory of Names: Christian Theology and Late-Antique Philosophy in the Fourth Century Trinitarian Controversy*, SVC 103 (Leiden: Brill, 2010).

29. Eunomius, *Apologia* 12 (Vaggione, 49).

30. Vaggione, *Eunomius*, 254 (emphasis original).

31. Eunomius, *Apologia* 12 (Vaggione, 49).

the Father is without parts and uncomposed, by the same token that same word used of the Only-begotten is equivalent to 'offspring.'"[32] All other names are subordinated to the one name, unbegotten, and this conclusion contributes further to Eunomius's attack against the doctrine of the Trinity.[33]

I conclude this section with two main points. First, Eunomius operates with a radical doctrine of divine simplicity that is overly determinative for much of his theology. This view of simplicity translates into the view that "unity can only be monism."[34] Put differently, there are no distinctions in God. Coupled with his theory of divine name(s), his doctrine of divine simplicity makes Nicene trinitarianism impossible and creates serious problems when it comes to interpreting the many divine names throughout scripture. Second, the content and function of Eunomius's doctrine of divine simplicity rules out an orthodox doctrine of the Trinity. The Father, or the unbegotten one, cannot have multiple names (for example, Father, Son, and Holy Spirit), and this also makes any doctrine of eternal generation or spiration impossible since both teachings would divide God's nature and so violate divine simplicity.

BASIL OF CAESAREA'S RESPONSE

Basil was the first to respond to Eunomius's teachings, in his *Adversus Eunomium.*[35] While Gregory of Nyssa would later develop his ideas

---

32. Eunomius, *Apologia* 19 (Vaggione, 59).

33. For more on the broader discussion of Eunomius and trinitarian theology, see John Behr, *The Nicene Faith: Part Two: One of the Holy Trinity*, FCT (Crestwood, NY: St. Vladimir's Seminary Press, 2004), 2:267–82; Hanson, *The Search for the Christian Doctrine of God*, 617–36; Khaled Anatolios, *Retrieving Nicaea: The Development and Meaning of Trinitarian Doctrine* (Grand Rapids: Baker Academic, 2011), 69–79; Stephen R. Holmes, *The Quest for the Trinity: The Doctrine of God in Scripture, History and Modernity* (Downers Grove, IL: IVP Academic, 2012), 97–110. See also two essays by Michel Barnes: "The Background and Use of Eunomius' Causal Language," in *Arianism after Arius: Essays on the Development of the Fourth Century Trinitarian Conflicts*, ed. Michel R. Barnes and Daniel H. Williams (Edinburgh: T&T Clark, 1993), 217–36; Barnes, "Eunomius of Cyzicus and Gregory of Nyssa: Two Traditions of Transcendent Causality," *VC* 52 (1998): 59–87.

34. Anatolios, *Retrieving Nicaea*, 166.

35. See Basil of Caesarea, *Against Eunomius*, trans. Mark DelCogliano and Andrew Radde-Gallwitz, FoC 122 (Washington, DC: Catholic University of America Press, 2011). Additional citations of this work will be abbreviated as *AE* with parenthetical citations of the page numbers from this text. For another helpful guide to Basil's *AE*, see Milton V. Anastos, "Basil's Κατὰ Εὐνομίου: A Critical Analysis," in *Basil of Caesarea, Christian, Humanist, Ascetic: A Sixteen-Hundredth Anniversary Symposium*, ed. Paul Fedwick (Toronto: PIMS, 1981), 1:67–136.

more fully, Basil set the necessary groundwork for a response to Eunomius. It should also be noted that divine simplicity was not the primary issue—it was the Trinity and with it Christology and pneumatology—but Basil and Gregory certainly saw that Eunomius's faulty doctrine of divine simplicity undermined Nicene theology and the teachings of scripture, driving them to respond by means of exegetical, theological, and philosophical arguments.

Basil "develops his doctrine of God by reflecting upon and interpreting Scripture" since "good theology consists in explicating what Scripture reveals about God and standing in silent adoration before the mystery of what it does not reveal."[36] This does not mean that his use of scripture is devoid of metaphysical assumptions. As Hildebrand observes, Basil's theology is a "synthesis of Greek and Christian thought" that "is informed by Greek metaphysics as well as by the Bible."[37] However, it is crucial to note that Basil "is not in the business, thereby, of constructing a philosophical system of metaphysics or ontology."[38] The synthesis is one, as we will see, that finds its starting and end point with scripture while incorporating concepts and language borrowed from his time to help clarify, carry on, and construct theology in response to false teachings.

Basil agrees that unbegotten may be said of God: "I too would say that the substance of God is unbegotten, but I would not say that unbegottenness is the substance."[39] He qualifies his agreement because the substance, or essence, is incomprehensible and cannot be known as Eunomius claims to know it. This is also because "our notion of unbegottenness does not fall under the examination of 'what it is,' but rather . . . under the examination of 'what it is like.'"[40] Instead of giving us knowledge of God's essence, which is impossible for Basil due to divine incomprehensibility, the name unbegotten "is a conceptualization derived from the scriptural designation of God as 'life.'"[41] I will briefly attend to his and Gregory's notion of conceptualization below, but for now it is important to see that for Basil, our knowledge of God is fragmentary and incomplete, telling us something true about God's life without exhaustively describing it.

36. Mark DelCogliano and Andrew Radde-Gallwitz, introduction to *Against Eunomius*, FoC 122 (Washington, DC: Catholic University of America Press, 2011), 55.
37. Hildebrand, *The Trinitarian Theology of Basil of Caesarea*, 30, 41.
38. Ibid., 46.
39. *AE* 1.11 (107).
40. *AE* 1.15 (114).
41. DelCogliano and Radde-Gallwitz, introduction, 62. See *AE* 1.15 (114).

If the name unbegotten truly but incompletely identifies God, what does it mean? Basil is clear that it means that the essence of God "does not have the origin of its being from another source"[42] and that this is "the name we give him because his life is without a beginning, when we consider the name through conceptualization."[43] This "conceptualization" (*epinoia*) is an important aspect of Basil's argument. Mark DelCogliano and Radde-Gallwitz describe it as a "subsequent reflection on an initial concept" that indicates "both the *act* of reflection and the *concepts* devised from it."[44] So, unbegotten is a subsequent reflection on the initial concept of God's life. Crucially, it "allows real knowledge of objects, especially simple objects, without comprehension of their essence."[45] Eunomius rejected conceptualization, believing that it was mere human conception that did not accord with reality, leaving open the possibility for conceiving of something or some quality that did not actually exist. For Basil (and Gregory of Nyssa), it was a process of reflection that does not fully reach the essence of God, but allows a person to understand his qualities or activities (*energeia*).[46]

The use of *epinoia* is something Basil "learned from the divine word,"[47] and when applied to the name unbegotten, it only communicates what God is *not* (that is, God never had a beginning). In other words, it helps remove inappropriate concepts or qualities of God. This apophatic function still leaves room for Basil to use positive terms for God, and these are demonstrated through God's

---

42. *AE* 1.16 (115).

43. *AE* 1.7 (100). Elsewhere, Basil states that "unbegotten" "is classified with what is not present in God." That is, there is no dependence on any cause or principle in God. See *AE* 1.10 (105–6).

44. DelCogliano and Radde-Gallwitz, introduction, 48 (emphasis mine). For more on conceptualization in Basil, see Radde-Gallwitz, *Transformation of Divine Simplicity*, 143–54.

45. DelCogliano and Radde-Gallwitz, introduction, 62.

46. For more on God's energies in the Cappadocians and later Eastern theology, see Torstein Tollefson, "Essence and Activity (Energeia) in St. Gregory's Anti-Eunomian Polemic," in *Gregory of Nyssa: Contra Eunomium II*, ed. Lenka Karfíková, Scot Douglass, and Johannes Zachhuber, SVC 82 (Leiden: Brill, 2007), 433–44; Giulio Maspero, "Energy," in *The Brill Dictionary of Gregory of Nyssa*, ed. Lucas F. Mateo-Seco and Giulio Maspero, trans. Seth Cherney, SVC 99 (Leiden: Brill, 2010), 258–62; Alexis Torrance, "Precedents for Palamas' Essence-Energies Theology in the Cappadocian Fathers," *VC* 63 (2009): 47–70; Kallistos Ware, "God Hidden and Revealed: The Apophatic Way and the Essence-Energies Distinction," *Eastern Churches Review* 7 (1975): 125–36; David Bradshaw, "The Concept of Divine Energies," *P&T* 18 (2006): 93–120; C. Athanasopoulos and C. Schneider, eds., *Divine Essence and Divine Energies: Ecumenical Reflections on the Presence of God in Eastern Orthodoxy* (Cambridge: James Clarke, 2013).

47. *AE* 1.7 (99).

"distinguishing marks." On the one hand, there are "common names" that are said of the Father and Son that carry the same sense (for example, light). On the other hand, certain "distinguishing marks" such as the Son's being "begotten" and the Father's being "unbegotten" show us what is unique to each person without causing division between the two. "The distinctive features, which are like certain characters and forms observed in the substance, differentiate what is common by means of the distinguishing characters and do not sunder the substance's sameness in nature." Furthermore, they "show otherness in the identity of the substance," and "they certainly do not rupture the unity of substance."[48] For Basil, both common and distinguishing names are said of God and speak truly of him, carrying three key implications: (1) these names do not define the divine essence, therefore preserving divine incomprehensibility; (2) many names may be said of God's simple essence without dividing the essence or losing the meaning of the name; and (3) no single name can define or describe God's essence on its own.[49]

Basil's trinitarian theology asserts that the Son is equal with and generated by the Father in contrast to Eunomius's claim that the Son is a separate essence willed by the Father. This equality means that "just as the Father is entirely free from composition, so too is the Son altogether simple and without composition."[50] If equal in simplicity, the same qualities may be predicated of the Son as are said of the Father. At this point, Basil relates scripture and divine simplicity by attending to 1 Corinthians 1:24, a passage that was a source of debate throughout the early stages of the tradition. "It is clear that all the Father's power is contained in him [i.e., the Son]. Hence, whatsoever he should see the Father doing, these same the Son does likewise [John 5:19]."[51] Elsewhere, Basil states that to say "that Christ *the power of God* [1 Cor 1:24] is deficient in power characterizes those who are altogether infantile and have not heard the voice of the Lord, who said: *I and the Father are one* [John 10:30]." He adds that "the Lord takes this *one* as equality in power"[52] and that the Son is "the power of

---

48. *AE* 2.28 (174–75). See also Basil's discussion of absolute and relative names in *AE* 2.9 (142). Absolute names designate the essence whereas relative names posit relationship.

49. For more on Basil's theology of divine names, see DelCogliano, *Basil of Caesarea's Anti-Eunomian Theory of Names*, 135–260.

50. *AE* 1.23 (124). See also 1.7 (99).

51. *AE* 1.23 (124).

52. *AE* 1.25 (126).

God that has appeared from power itself."[53] Here, there is an equality of essence that carries with it an equality of simplicity, divine activity, and unity of divine works. Contrary to Eunomius's claim that divine simplicity must imply the inequality of the Father and the Son, Basil demonstrates their equality in being, qualities, and action (or power) without rupturing the simple essence.

While the focus of my attention has been on Basil's use and understanding of divine simplicity, his arguments may be summarized, following Hildebrand, in the following points: (1) "The divine *ousia* may be described, but not defined." (2) "The divine nature is simple and uncomposed, and by virtue of this, *ousia* and power (*dynamis*) coincide in God." (3) "The *ousia* of God is wholly light, wholly life, and wholly goodness [see *AE* 2.29 (176)]. It remains, however, ultimately unknowable, while admitting description by many and varied predicates, none of which holds preeminence over the others." (4) "God [as] Father, Son, and Holy Spirit does not violate divine simplicity. Rather, the divine plurality must be explained—insofar as possible—within the rules for thinking and speaking about the one God."[54] Divine simplicity is a form of divine unity and indivisibility that welcomes many names as true descriptions without subsuming the divine essence under any one of them as Eunomius does with unbegotten. Last, God is both one and many, in persons and names, without violating or forfeiting his simple essence.

GREGORY OF NYSSA'S RESPONSE

Shortly after Basil died, Eunomius finished his response to Basil's *Against Eunomius*: *Apologia apologiae*. Gregory wrote two books responding to Eunomius before the Council of Constantinople in 381.[55] I will focus on the first text, particularly the first two books, and

---

53. *AE* 2.27 (172).

54. Hildebrand, *The Trinitarian Theology of Basil of Caesarea*, 56.

55. I will use the following two translations: *A Refutation of the First Book of the Two Published by Eunomius after the Decease of Holy Basil*, in *El "Contra Eunomium I" en la Producción Literaria de Gregorio de Nisa*, ed. Lucas F Mateo-Seco and Juan L. Bastero, trans. Stuart G. Hall (Pamplona: Ediciones Universidad de Navarra, SA, 1988), 35–135; *The Second Book against Eunomius*, in *Gregory of Nyssa: Contra Eunomium II*, ed. Lenka Karfíková, Scot Douglass, and Johannes Zachhuber, trans. Stuart George Hall, SVC 82 (Leiden: Brill, 2007), 59–201. I will refer to them as *CE* 1 and *CE* 2. Additional responses to Eunomius in translation may be found in NPNF2, vol. 5, although readers should be aware that this particular translation does not have the works in proper order (e.g., *Contra Eunomium* II is listed as the *Refutatio*).

will present Gregory's view of divine simplicity along with some of his particular emphases that are not found in Basil.

After Basil's death in 378, Gregory of Nyssa saw himself as the defender of his brother's teachings.[56] Gregory summarizes their view and helps illustrate the continuity of thought between the brothers:

> Our position therefore—I am adopting my master's teaching—is that we have a faint and slight apprehension of the divine Nature through reasoning, but we still gather knowledge enough for our slight capacity through the words which are reverently used of it. We claim that the meaning of all these names is not uniform, but some denote things that appertain to God, others those that are absent. So we call him just and indestructible, by "just" indicating that justice appertains to him, and by "indestructible," that destruction does not.[57]

Gregory maintains the themes of divine incomprehensibility, that no single name can define the nature of God, that our knowledge of God through many names must be understood by way of conceptualization, and that these names either tell us what God is not or name a feature of his works. Unbegotten, therefore, is one name among many that represents what God is *not* since, in contrast to Eunomius, we cannot know what God's essence or nature is in that way that Eunomius desires.

Contra Eunomium 1 and 2 respond to a problem developed more fully in Eunomius's *Apology for an Apology*. In book 1, Gregory quotes Eunomius's teaching on the Father and Son: "Each of these beings . . . both is and is perceived to be absolutely simple and altogether one in its own rank."[58] This ontological hierarchy of simplicity troubles Gregory since the result of this logic is that the Father is "absolutely simple" whereas the Son and Spirit are less simple to varying degrees. The Father is not superior since "the Only begotten and that of the Holy Spirit are indefectibly perfect in goodness and power and all such things."[59] The equality of essence means not only that there is no ontological hierarchy but also that Father, Son, and Holy

---

56. I will refer to Gregory of Nyssa as "Gregory" throughout the rest of this chapter. This is not to be confused with Gregory of Nazianzus. He also responded to Eunomius, but in a more popular fashion and also did not carry on Basil's theology in ways as significant as Gregory of Nyssa.

57. CE 2.130–31. Radde-Gallwitz argues for continuity between Basil and Gregory (*Transformation of Divine Simplicity*, 175–82).

58. CE 1.225.

59. CE 1.167.

Spirit are equal in all qualities. This leads Gregory to move beyond the arguments of Basil by deploying the idea of divine infinity. All three *hypostases* are "unlimited in goodness, and unlimited is the same as infinite. But to apply the concepts of greater and less to the infinite and unlimited is utterly absurd."[60] This also means that "there can be no lack of wisdom or power or any other good thing in one to whom goodness is not something acquired, but who is by nature constituted essentially such."[61] Each *hypostasis* is equally simple and infinite, lacking nothing and incapable of being ranked or defined in "more or less" categories.[62]

To be simple means that in God "there is no diversity in the simple life, no addition, no subtraction, no variation of quantity or quality generating change."[63] This is not merely true of the Father, and so, in contrast, Gregory formulates a doctrine of divine simplicity that denies any ontological rank by affirming that all three *hypostases* are equal in essence and qualities. "Being thought of as in utter perfection and incomprehensible transcendence, it [the uncreated nature] possesses unconfused and clear differentiation through the characteristics to be found in each of the *hypostases*, being invariable in the common possession of uncreatedness, and singular in the special characteristics of each."[64] In the simple Trinity, there is differentiation amid the equality and unity of the qualities that are commonly possessed among the divine persons.

Recall that Eunomius argued that the plurality of names given in scripture are all determined and defined by the one name, unbegotten. The Father's goodness is unbegotten goodness, but the Son is begotten goodness. Even when identical names are used (for

60. *CE* 1.169. For more on divine infinity in Gregory, see Mark Weedman, "The Polemical Context of Gregory of Nyssa's Doctrine of Divine Infinity," *JECS* 18 (2010): 81–104; Albert-Kees Geljon, "Divine Infinity in Gregory of Nyssa and Philo of Alexandria," *VC* 59 (2005): 152–77.

61. *CE* 1.234. Later, Gregory adds that not only is the quality not acquired, but it is also not received via participation since it has these qualities by nature in itself. See *CE* 1.276–77.

62. On properties and rank, see Michel R. Barnes, *The Power of God: Δύναμις in Gregory of Nyssa's Trinitarian Theology* (Washington, DC: Catholic University of America Press, 2001), 272–74.

63. *CE* 2.489.

64. *CE* 1.277. Elsewhere he writes that "the simplicity of the life in Father and Son is understood as one, and since, as has been said, the principle of simplicity admits no variation, it necessarily follows that the title which fits one belongs to the other. If therefore the simplicity of the Father's life is signified by the appellation 'unbegottenness,' that word will not be unsuitably applied to the Son as well" (*CE* 2.490).

example, light), they are still different qualities. Gregory responds by developing his doctrine of divine simplicity in conjunction with his theory of divine names in ways similar to Basil. Each name has its own distinct meaning: Unbegotten means that God is without cause whereas simplicity means that he is not compound.[65] Therefore, the consequence of divine simplicity is not the flattening of divine names but the attending to their meaning and equality found through the scriptures. As Khaled Anatolios puts it, "The fundamental principle is that divine simplicity cannot be apprehended simply. The effect of this principle is to throw us back on the whole range of scriptural language and narrative, indeed, on the whole creation, as a complex manifestation of the Creator."[66] Instead of reducing God's many names (or being) to unbegotten by way of a monadic homogeneity, readers of scripture must focus on the fullness of God's self-presentation, which includes distinct meanings of each name without dividing his nature.[67]

God is called good because he is good eternally and intrinsically rather than by participation in a form of goodness outside himself. "If good things come to be by participation in what is better, then clearly before their participation they were not such." If this were the case, "the divine nature will be understood as not so much a provider of good things as itself in need of a benefactor. How can one provide another with what it does not itself possess?"[68] Even though God "possesses" or is goodness himself, such names, titles, and even divine works are "guides" and all "have something in common with the analogous kind of names which indicate the individuality of a particular man."[69] We describe a person by their "recognizable characteristics," but it must also be remembered that none of them "describe the inward nature of the one described, but some of the characteristics known about him."[70] This example leads Gregory to the conclusion

65. To ignore the multitude of names moves Gregory to ask the following: If Eunomius is correct, why do "the scriptures waste time referring to the divine Nature by many names" (*CE* 2.473)?

66. Anatolios, *Retrieving Nicaea*, 166.

67. There is not sufficient space to discuss the additional and important aspects of the "goods" and the "*propria*" in Gregory's account. For a more detailed description of these issues, see Radde-Gallwitz, *Transformation of Divine Simplicity*, 175–224. See also his important discussion of the divine *propria* as essential attributes that are still not identical with the divine essence (ibid., xx–xxi, 17, 108, 162–69, 184, 200–207, 225).

68. *CE* 1.277 (77).

69. *CE* 2.104 (82). For "guide" language, see *CE* 2.102 (82).

70. *CE* 2.104 (82).

that "similarly, all the words found in holy scripture to indicate God's glory describe some feature of God, each providing its particular emphasis. . . . His being itself, however, scripture leaves uninvestigated, as beyond the reach of mind and inexpressible in word."[71]

Gregory argues that many names are used for God since "no one title has been discovered to embrace the divine Nature" and "we hunt amid the pluriform variety of terms applying to him for sparks to light up our understanding of the object of our quest."[72] Gregory follows Basil by understanding the names conceptually. This means that the names "do not signify the Nature; but none would dare claim that the application of the titles is improper or meaningless."[73] These are not empty names, but neither are they all-encompassing. In scripture we see that "the Divinity is given names with various connotations in accordance with the variety of his activities, named in such a way as we may understand. . . . We ourselves call this 'conceptual thought' [epinoia], but if someone wants to call it something else, we shall not object."[74]

INSEPARABLE OPERATIONS

Although *Contra Eunomium* contains aspects of Gregory's doctrine of the unity of divine action, it becomes clearer if attention is given to one of his often-cited texts, *That There Are Not Three Gods*.[75] This is another polemical text where Gregory responds to the charge that his theology implies three Gods.[76] Gregory's understanding and use of divine simplicity does not change, even in this new context. For example, he writes that "the nature is one; it is united to itself, undivided, a precisely undivided unit, not increased through addition, not decreased through subtraction, but being one and remaining one, even if it would appear in a multitude, undivided, continuous,

---

71. *CE* 2.105 (83).
72. *CE* 2.145 (90).
73. *CE* 2.303 (127).
74. *CE* 2.304 (127).
75. References are taken from the following translation: Gregory of Nyssa, *Concerning We Should Not Think of Saying That There Are Not Three Gods to Ablabius*, in *The Trinitarian Controversy*, trans. William G. Rusch, SECT (Philadelphia: Fortress Press, 1980).
76. For more background and detailed analysis on this text, see Lewis Ayres, "Not Three People: The Fundamental Themes of Gregory of Nyssa's Trinitarian Theology as Seen in *To Ablabius: On Not Three Gods*," *ModTheo* 18 (2002): 445–74; Giulio Maspero, *Trinity and Man: Gregory of Nyssa's "Ad Ablabium,"* SVC 86 (Leiden: Brill, 2007).

perfect, and not divided by those who individually share it."[77] Furthermore, he still maintains that "every name, whether it has been invented from human usage or handed down from scripture, is an interpretation of the things thought about divine nature and does not encompass the significance of the nature itself."[78] The simple nature of God is named "according to things thought" (that is, conceptualization) without claiming to fully define or describe the divine nature.

Even after affirming these claims, the problem is that it still leaves Gregory open to the charge of three Gods. For example, in the pursuit of one goal, three creatures would still act individually and their activity can be distinguished. Gregory answers that "every activity which pervades from God to creation and is named according to our manifold designs starts off from the Father, proceeds through the Son, and is completed by the Holy Spirit. On account of this, the name of activity is not divided into the multitude of those who are active."[79] Divine action is trinitarian—ordered, unified, without division, yet admitting distinctions. Gregory offers an example: Father, Son, and Holy Spirit giving life to creatures. "But though we presuppose that there are three persons and names, we do not reason that three lives have been given to us—individually one from each of them." Rather, "it is the same life, activated by the Holy Spirit, prepared by the Son, and produced by the Father's will."[80] There is a "unity of activity"[81] such that the activity "is one and not three."[82] This is not a matter of "possessing distinct actions towards a common goal, but as together constituting *just one distinct action* (because they are one power)."[83] The point is that three distinct actions would result in three Gods, but God's action is not like three people's actions. Furthermore, his indivisible work—or inseparable operations—is the work of one power rather than three powers. This one power is not indistinguishable;

77. Gregory of Nyssa, *Not Three Gods*, 151.
78. Ibid., 152.
79. Ibid., 155.
80. Ibid.
81. Ibid., 156.
82. Ibid., 157. Ayres sees a deeper background including "power" language. Thus, "if the activities are the same, then the power which gave rise to them is the same and the ineffable divine nature in which that power is inherent must also be one" ("Not Three People," 459). For more on the "one power, one nature" theology in Gregory of Nyssa, see Barnes, *The Power of God*, 260–307, and his early essay, "One Nature, One Power: Consensus Doctrine in Pro-Nicene Polemic," *SP* 29 (1997): 205–23.
83. Ayres, "Not Three People," 462.

however, distinctions in God's one power are still far from entailing divisions or divisibility.

SUMMARY

Basil and Gregory represent two important Eastern perspectives on divine simplicity. Basil's perspective develops in response to false teaching and with careful attention to scripture. Gregory follows Basil in certain respects, but furthers his view of divine simplicity as he extends his defense of the teaching and ties it closer to scripture through the divine names and inseparable operations. The irony is that Eunomius is a much more natural target for the modern objections to divine simplicity. As I noted in the previous chapter, some modern critics argue that divine simplicity does not allow for differentiation and distinctions, therefore causing serious problems for the Trinity. It is crucial to see that this criticism is true only if one holds to a Eunomian form of divine simplicity.[84] Eunomius's doctrine of divine simplicity removes all distinction and differentiation and results in a unitary and abstract view of God. That is, because everything can be summed up in the name unbegotten, God is abstracted from the revelation of himself in scripture and creation and reduced to one name capable of being known by the human mind and fully expressed by human language. While his motivation to truly know God in himself is admirable, he diminishes God rather than recognizing his infinite, plentiful nature, which requires many names to even begin to describe it.

Basil and Gregory provided crucial responses that had long-standing consequences for trinitarian theology and Christology. After encountering Eunomius's radical doctrine of divine simplicity, it would have made sense if they seriously altered or even rejected the doctrine. However, they formulated their doctrine of divine simplicity in close proximity to scripture by arguing that each divine name refers to God and carries meaning without causing division, whether between the persons or qualities. Divine simplicity is often assumed as a biblical teaching that, in turn, bears on the way they read scripture: (1) There is no single name, or "primary attribute," that may sum up the divine essence. (2) The divine essence

---

84. This form is similar to the view that most contemporary critics reject and is not an account of simplicity derived from careful attention to scripture.

lacks nothing, cannot lose or gain anything it does not already have, and has no rank. In other words, it is indivisibly equal and without contradiction or conflict. (3) Although indivisible, the divine essence includes differentiation and distinctions, which can be seen in the distinctions of the three divine persons in one action.[85] The three divine *hypostases* are distinguished without dividing the essence or their work, and the divine names carry distinct meanings without implying that these names correspond to "parts" or separate essences. As noted above, these three summary points guide Basil and Gregory as they read scripture whether it be the various titles of Jesus, the names for each individual person, or the names said of all three persons in common.

DIVINE SIMPLICITY IN THE WEST: AUGUSTINE

Whereas Basil and Gregory battled Eunomius in the East, the doctrine of divine simplicity took similar, though different turns through Augustine's theology in the West. It has become natural in much contemporary theology to categorize Augustine as a theologian substantially persuaded by Neoplatonism, as one who began with and emphasized the unity of God to the point of near modalism, and the one who passed on a highly metaphysical view of the nature of God that left an unfortunate influence on Western theology. Recent scholarship, however, has challenged many of these long-accepted readings and began to put forth a "counter-narrative."[86] While some

85. Krivochéine adds that Gregory makes distinctions between the divine nature and the *hypostases*, the divine natures and the "energies," and the divine nature and its names. See Basile Krivochéine, "Simplicity of the Divine Nature and the Distinctions in God, according to St. Gregory of Nyssa," *SVTQ* 21 (1977): 76–104.

86. It is difficult to point to one particular scholar or work, but the initial turn appears to have begun with Rowan Williams's essay "*Sapientia* and the Trinity: Reflections on *De Trinitate*," in *Collectanea Augustiniana: mélanges T.J. van Bavel*, ed. B. Bruning, M. Lamberigts, and J. van Houtem, BETL 92A (Leuven: Leuven University Press, 1990), 1:317–32. From there, Lewis Ayres and Michel René Barnes have also been influential. For Barnes, see esp. "Augustine in Contemporary Trinitarian Theology," *TS* 56 (1995): 237–50; Barnes, "Rereading Augustine's Theology of the Trinity," in *The Trinity: An Interdisciplinary Symposium on the Trinity*, ed. Stephen T. Davis, Daniel Kendall, and Gerald O'Collins (Oxford: Oxford University Press, 1999), 145–76. For Ayres, see *Nicaea and Its Legacy*, 289–91, 364–83; Ayres, *Augustine and the Trinity* (Cambridge: Cambridge University Press, 2010). See also Luigi Gioia, *The Theological Epistemology of Augustine's "De Trinitate,"* OTM (Oxford: Oxford University Press, 2008); Chad Tyler Gerber, *The Spirit of Augustine's Early Theology: Contextualizing Augustine's Pneumatology*, ASPTLA (Burlington, VT: Ashgate, 2012). See also the interactions between La Croix and Wainwright: Richard R. La Croix, "Augustine on the Simplicity of God," in *What Is God? The*

of the difficulties with Augustine appear to stem from the De Régnon paradigm,[87] the most significant problem, at least when it comes to divine simplicity, is that Augustine's teachings are often read out of context. Therefore, it is of great importance to consider Augustine's doctrine of divine simplicity in its context in order to better understand the pressures, concerns, and circumstances that framed his theology of divine simplicity. This does not mean, as William Hasker worries, that we are to "remain within the conceptualities of the ancient writers, making our permanent intellectual home in the ancient world."[88] But it does mean that a fair hearing of Augustine's doctrine of divine simplicity begins with his texts and the context in which he wrote them. Therefore, my goal is to synthesize the best scholarship on Augustine's doctrine of divine simplicity for systematic theologians who may not be as familiar with his theology or the recent scholarship on it.

As I demonstrated in the last chapter, some contemporary theologians struggle with divine simplicity in relation to their struggle with Augustine's theology.[89] While space limitations and the focus of this

Selected Essays of Richard R. La Croix (Buffalo, NY: Prometheus, 1993), 96–108; W. Wainwright, "Augustine on God's Simplicity: A Reply to Richard La Croix," *NS* 53 (1979): 118–23; Richard R. La Croix, "Wainwright, Augustine, and God's Simplicity: A Final Word," in *What Is God*, 130–33.

87. Théodore de Régnon, *Études de théologie positive sur la sainté Trinité*, 4 vols. (Paris: Victor Retaux, 1892–1898). See also Michel René Barnes, "De Régnon Reconsidered," *AugStud* 26 (1995): 51–79; Kristin Hennessy, "An Answer to de Régnon's Accusers: Why We Should Not Speak of 'His' Paradigm," *HTR* 100 (2007): 179–97; D. Glenn Butner Jr., "For and against de Régnon: Trinitarianism East and West," *IJST* 17 (2015): 399–412.

88. William Hasker, *Metaphysics and the Tri-personal God*, OSAT (Oxford: Oxford University Press, 2013), 67.

89. Even if the struggle is not with his theology in particular, it may be related to the acceptance of recent modern narratives about his theology that Barnes, Ayres, and others seek to refute. While I only mentioned Robert Jenson in the last chapter, examples of other critics include John D. Zizioulas, *Being as Communion: Studies in Personhood and the Church* (Crestwood, NY: St. Vladimir's Seminary Press, 1985), 88–89; Zizioulas, *Communion and Otherness: Further Studies in Personhood and the Church*, ed. Paul McPartlan (London: T&T Clark, 2006), 33–34, 124; Colin Gunton, "Augustine, the Trinity and the Theological Crisis of the West," *SJT* 43 (1990): 33–58; David Bradshaw, *Aristotle East and West: Metaphysics and the Division of Christendom* (Cambridge: Cambridge University Press, 2007), 222–29; Hasker, *Metaphysics and the Tri-personal God*, 40–49, 55–61, 244–45. For a response to Zizioulas, see Will Cohen, "Augustine and John Zizioulas," in *T&T Clark Companion to Augustine and Modern Theology*, ed. C. C. Pecknold and Tarmo Toom (London: Bloomsbury T&T Clark, 2013), 223–39. For a response to Gunton, see Bradley G. Green, *Colin Gunton and the Failure of Augustine: The Theology of Colin Gunton in Light of Augustine*, DDCT (Eugene, OR: Pickwick, 2011). Travis Ables also offers a helpful survey of Gunton, Jenson, and Moltmann on Augustine in *Incarnational Realism: Trinity and the Spirit in Augustine and Barth*, SST (London: Bloomsbury T&T Clark, 2013), 17–36.

project do not allow me to deal with every objection, in this section I will look at one of Augustine's main discussions of divine simplicity in *De Trinitate* in order to see how he relates his doctrine of divine simplicity to scripture or if, as critics have argued, his doctrine of divine simplicity is speculative, highly metaphysical, and causes problems for the Trinity due to its modalistic tendencies.[90] I will focus on books 5–7 as they illuminate the content and context for his doctrine of divine simplicity. Then, I will briefly incorporate the importance of Augustine's account of "inseparable operations" for his doctrine of divine simplicity. I will then conclude with a summary of Augustine's doctrine of divine simplicity and offer a brief comparison of his view to Basil and Gregory of Nyssa.

DE TRINITATE 5–7

Augustine's work is sometimes interpreted as an abstract or speculative treatise, seeking to outline the inner workings of the being of God according to Neoplatonic concepts and terms. It may be that the interpretation of his "psychological analogies" in books 8–15 contributes to this narrative, or perhaps problems stem from a shallow reading of those chapters. Either way, it is central to see that this text constantly engages scripture with the purpose of knowing and worshiping the Trinity. In addition, this is a *polemical* work. It is not merely an exercise of the mind for the sake of thinking; rather, it is an intentional work designed to respond to false teaching as well as lead toward right belief and worship of God. At the beginning on book 5, Augustine comments that "in those [books] that follow we shall see with the Lord's help what sort of subtle crafty arguments the heretics bring forward and how they can be demolished."[91] It is at this point

90. Some readers may expect extended attention to Augustine's use of Exod 3:14. Augustine's doctrine of divine simplicity does not entirely depend on his reading of this passage and is more broadly presented in *De Trinitate*. For Augustine's reading of this passage, see Emilie Zum Brunn, *St Augustine: Being and Nothingness in the Dialogs and Confessions*, trans. Ruth Namad (New York: Paragon, 1988), 119; R. Michael Allen, "Exodus 3 after the Hellenization Thesis," *JTI* 3 (2009): 179–96; Andrea Saner, *"Too Much to Grasp": Exodus 3:13–15 and the Reality of God*, JTISup (Winona Lake, IN: Eisenbrauns, 2015), 59–105.

91. Augustine, *The Trinity*, ed. John Rotelle, trans. Edmund Hill, WSA (Hyde Park, NY: New City Press, 1991), 4.32 (177). Further parenthetical citations of page numbers are from this text. For a survey of recent scholarship on books 5–7, see Maarten Wisse, *Trinitarian Theology beyond Participation: Augustine's "De Trinitate" and Contemporary Theology*, SST (London: T&T Clark, 2011), 76–83.

that Augustine incorporates divine simplicity to respond to heretical teachings and problematic language and thought about God.

The "Arians," as Augustine puts it,[92] argued that accidents could not be attributed to God since whatever is said of God is said substance-wise. Father and Son, therefore, refer to two different substances and cannot be said to be one God or the same being.[93] Augustine meets his opponents on the same ontological ground of substance and accidents, agreeing that no accidents can be attributed to God. An accident would predicate change, loss, increase, or decrease of God's being, and none of these things may be attributed to God. That said, not *every* thing said of God is said substance-wise since this would require a person to say that the three divine persons are unequal. Augustine's aim, therefore, "is to deprive them of the possibility of using these logical and ontological distinctions for the purpose of denying the full divinity of the Son."[94] In other words, in book 5 Augustine seeks to reconcile how the Father and Son can have the same substance if what is said about them is said substance-wise.

Augustine attempts a middle way by arguing that some things said of God are said *relationally* (e.g., the Father in reference to the Son). These are said neither of the substance nor as an accident of God's being. Father and Son are said "with reference to something else" and what is signified "belongs to them eternally and unchangeably."[95] Only the Father is called Father, and what this signifies could never be transferred or shared with his Son, nor can the Father be called Son, and so forth. These relational names do not change God—he is eternally the unbegotten Father, the begotten Son, and Holy Spirit—nor are they predicated of the substance such that they create two substances.

How does this relate to divine simplicity? Augustine's "chief point" is to clarify that "whatever is said with reference to self about each of [the three divine persons] is to be taken as adding up in all three

---

92. They are most likely Palladius and Maximinus. See Michel R. Barnes, "The Arians of Book V, and the Genre of *De Trinitate*," *JTS* 44 (1993): 190.

93. Recall that Eunomius argued that each name points to a separate essence. In one sense, therefore, Augustine is battling a similar set of ideas that Basil and Gregory faced in the East. While there are similarities, there are also some key differences between the two. For expositions of these differences, see Michel René Barnes, "*De Trinitate* VI and VII: Augustine and the Limits of Nicene Orthodoxy," *AugStud* 38 (2007): 191–94.

94. Gioia, *The Theological Epistemology of Augustine's "De Trinitate,"* 149.

95. Augustine, *The Trinity* 5.6 (192).

to a singular and not a plural."[96] Similar to the fact that "the Father is God, the Son is God, and the Holy Spirit is God" does not result in three gods, Augustine argues that when we say "the Father is great, the Son is great, the Holy Spirit too is great; yet there are not three great ones but one great one."[97] To end up with three great ones is to admit a division created by the name "great." This conclusion follows from four key points: (1) Relational names—Father, Son, and Holy Spirit—signify each person in themselves (the Father is the Father and not the Son), whereas (2) names like God, great, wise, and good are predicated of all three persons and refer to the substance. They do not partake of or participate in greatness since God "is great with a great-ness by which he is himself this same greatness."[98] (3) Each divine per-son is named great, good, eternal, and so forth equally (if each divine person differed in their qualities then they would not be one sub-stance), yet they are also named Father, Son, Holy Spirit as distinct persons. (4) Neither of these ways of naming destroys or reduces the three distinct persons and elevates the divine substance, nor do the names separate the three persons by dividing the substance into three substances. Because God is simple, there is unity and inseparability amid distinctions and differentiation.

After defending the equality of the three divine persons and stating how God may be named according to substance and relation, Augus-tine moves on in books 6 and 7 to an extended exegesis of 1 Corinthi-ans 1:24—"Christ the power of God and the wisdom of God." These two books are "his most extended engagement with a scriptural text in all of [De Trinitate]" and are therefore significant for our pur-poses.[99] With a long history of anti-Nicene interpretations of this passage, Augustine's concern is that this verse could be taken to mean that "equality seems to be lacking here, since the Father is not himself . . . power and wisdom, but the begetter of power and wisdom."[100] Rather than being powerful and wise in himself, it appears that the Father is only powerful and wise because of the Son, whether by virtue of begetting this power and wisdom or by way of participation.

96. Augustine, *The Trinity* 5.9 (195).
97. Augustine, *The Trinity* 5.9 (195).
98. Augustine, *The Trinity* 5.11 (196).
99. Barnes, "Augustine and the Limits of Nicene Orthodoxy," 190.
100. Augustine, *The Trinity* 6.1 (205). For a brief presentation of the history of anti-Nicene interpretation of this passage, see Barnes, "Augustine and the Limits of Nicene Orthodoxy," 193–94.

This possible conclusion faces problems, however, since "for God it is the same thing to be as to be powerful or just or wise or anything else that can be said about his simple multiplicity or multiple simplicity to signify his substance."[101] In what way is God both simple and multiple? Augustine offers a helpful metaphor by analyzing the body and soul to first show how God is *not* multiple. The body consists of parts, some greater, smaller, and "the whole will be greater than even the greatest part."[102] While the soul appears simple compared to the body, it fails since its qualities are separate from one another and can be greater, lesser, and therefore experience change. In short, "nothing simple is changeable; everything created is changeable."[103]

God, however, is simple and does not change like creatures. This may be true, but God is also "called in multiple ways great, good, wise, blessed, true" and this seems to introduce some form of multiplicity. Yet "his greatness is identical with his wisdom, . . . and his goodness is identical with his wisdom and greatness."[104] As Roland Teske observes, there is a crucial distinction here between speech about God, thought about God, and the being of God.[105] In our speech we apply a multiplicity of predicates and, because the predicates have different meanings, we may think of God in many senses. So while our speech and thoughts are multiple, Augustine reminds us that they express a single reality—the one simple being of God. This does not mean that there is a major disconnect between our speech, thought, and God's being. Aiming to uphold a Creator-creature distinction, it avoids what is later termed a univocal view of language and seeks to maintain that the multiple predicates are true of God without leading to a separation or division of his being into distinct parts.

Augustine sees that the multiple predicates still do not sufficiently solve the problem and begins book 7 with a further examination of

101. Augustine, *The Trinity* 6.6 (209).

102. Augustine, *The Trinity* 6.8 (210).

103. Augustine, *The Trinity* 6.8 (211).

104. Augustine, *The Trinity* 6.8 (211). "Identical" is Hill's translation of *eadem*, which is a form of *idem*. It can also be translated as "sameness." Augustine uses the same term elsewhere, in 6.2 (206) and 15.7 (400). Augustine's language has confused and frustrated many recent theologians and philosophers and has led others to reject divine simplicity. How can identical qualities permit any kind of distinction? I will comment further on this below.

105. Roland J. Teske, "Properties of God and the Predicaments in *De Trinitate* V," in *To Know God and the Soul: Essays on the Thought of Saint Augustine* (Washington, DC: Catholic University of America Press, 2008), 93–111.

1 Corinthians 1:24. It is worth quoting at length the options he finds available:

> Our desire to express the inexpressible seems to have forced us into the position where [i] we either have to say that Christ is not the power of God and the wisdom of God, and thus shamelessly and irreligiously contradict the apostle; or [ii] we admit that Christ is indeed the power of God and the wisdom of God, but that his Father is not the Father of his own power and wisdom, which would be no less irreligious, because in this case he will not be Christ's Father either, seeing that the power of God and the wisdom of God are Christ; or [iii] that the Father is not powerful with his power or wise with his wisdom, and who would have the nerve to say that?; or [iv] that to be for the Father and to be wise must be understood as two different things, so that he is not wise simply by being, and is thus in the same case as the soul which is sometimes unwise sometimes wise, being a changeable nature, and not supremely and perfectly simple; or [v] that the Father is not anything with reference to himself, and that not only his being Father but also his simply being is said with reference to the Son. How then can the Son be of the same being as the Father, seeing that his Father is not even being with reference to himself, but even his "is" or his "to be" is only a reference to the Son?[106]

Augustine begins his answer with an appeal to divine simplicity. If the Father becomes wise because he begets wisdom—and if "to be" is not the same as "to be wise"—then the Son is not his offspring but is actually a quality of his Father. This conclusion is "unthinkable" since "with God to be is the same as to be wise. If then in this case to be is the same as to be wise, it follows that the Father is not wise with the wisdom he has begotten; otherwise he did not beget it, but it begot him."[107] Refusing this option, Augustine argues that the Son "is called the wisdom of the Father in the same way as he is called the light of the Father, that is, that as we talk of light from light, and both are one light, so we must understand wisdom from wisdom, and both one wisdom."[108] At this point we encounter Augustine's crucial move in his doctrine of divine simplicity.

106. Augustine, *The Trinity* 7.2 (218–19).
107. Augustine, *The Trinity* 7.2 (220). Ayres summarizes this passage: "Wisdom, he begins, is wise in itself. Those who become wise share in Wisdom, but it in no way changes as they do so. Thus the Father cannot be wise by the Wisdom he begot, and he is Wisdom itself, the cause of his own being and of his being wise. In the Father Wisdom is the same as essence" (Ayres, *Augustine and the Trinity*, 225).
108. Augustine, *The Trinity* 7.3 (220–21). Ayres comments that "it is the same basic statement

Because wisdom is said of God substance-wise, the Father is said to be wise in himself. The Father begets the Son who is, as Nicaea taught, "light from light" and therefore "wisdom from wisdom." The Father and Son are together one substance, one wisdom, and one power, equal in essence and therefore equal in all qualities. The Father is the source of this wisdom, just as he gave life to the Son (John 5:26), and therefore is the source of the Son's simplicity.[109] Contrary to the "Arians," the Father begets the Son without dividing the substance into two substances. This way of thinking is driven by "an awareness of the weakness of Nicene exegesis of 1 Cor. 1:24 and the vulnerability of that exegesis to anti-Nicene claims on the Pauline passage."[110] In this way, divine simplicity and eternal generation work closely together and affirm the unity, equality, and indivisibility of the divine persons while also declaring their distinctness from one another.[111]

After following the thrust of Augustine's use of divine simplicity in *De Trinitate* 5–7, we may sum up his understanding of divine simplicity in the following four points: (1) For God it is the same thing "to be" as it is "to be wise" since wisdom (and other predicates) is said of God's substance. (2) As predicates of his being, God's qualities do not increase and cannot be lost or change in any way. (3) God does not acquire or participate in wisdom in order to be wise. He does not *have* wisdom but *is* wisdom himself, and this is named *equally* of all three divine persons. (4) Because there is no division or separation between God's being and his qualities, or between the qualities themselves, they are said to be "identical"—God's wisdom is identical to his power, his power to his eternity, and so forth.

This last point has been a source of great confusion and contention, but I believe we can cut through some of the problems by attending to the heart of Augustine's account. First, he clearly states that God is named in multiple ways and that these are true statements of his substance. In God there is a simple multiplicity and a multiple simplicity. If the predications were absolutely identical to one another then they

---

of divine simplicity that grounds Augustine's discussion, and once again the pivotal question concerns the nature of the Son's generation as 'God from God'" (*Augustine and the Trinity*, 222).

109. This view of the Father as source is somewhat clearer in the *City of God*: "For that which is begotten of the simple Good is Itself simple, and is the same as that of which it is begotten." Translated by R. W. Dyson. CTHPT. Cambridge: Cambridge University Press, 1998. (11.10).

110. Barnes, "Augustine and the Limits of Nicene Orthodoxy," 202.

111. While I am using the example of the Father/Son relationship, the Holy Spirit should be understood to be an equal part of this discussion.

would surely lose all meaning and God would be capable of being reduced to one name or quality (like Eunomius). Second, because each name is predicated of God's simple substance, each name implies its inseparable relation to every other name. That is, God is never wise without also being loving, powerful, good, gracious, and so forth. He is never powerful without being wise, just, righteousness, and so forth because his being and qualities are indivisible and inseparable. The core of the identity between the qualities themselves and between the qualities and God's being is one of *equality* in the sense that they are all equally identical with the substance of God and require one another to fully articulate the content of each quality. In other words, God's wisdom describes all that God is, but it cannot be understood on its own apart from God's goodness, love, righteousness, and other qualities. Understood this way, saying that the qualities are identical to God's substance and to one another is not a matter of reducing God or collapsing his attributes into each other, but of recognizing the plentitude of his being.

INSEPARABLE OPERATIONS

Another significant although misunderstood element of Augustine's theology by contemporary critics is his doctrine of the inseparable operations of God *ad extra*. For some, this teaching only seems to further the belief that his account of divine simplicity (or any other account) is so strong that it contributes to his modalistic tendencies. As Robert Jenson remarks, this doctrine "has to mean that there is no difference at all between the agencies of Father, Son, and Spirit. Either, [Augustine] thinks, Father, Son, and Spirit must simply do the *same* thing, or simply *different* things; the possibility of a *mutually* single act cannot occur to him."[112] Jenson also worries that in *De Trinitate* 1.8 Augustine appears to say that "the speaker is indifferently specifiable as the Father or the Son or the Spirit or the whole Trinity."[113] Yet this concern is difficult to sustain and illustrates the lack of a careful reading of Augustine's texts. In order to get a clearer picture,

112. Robert W. Jenson, *Systematic Theology*, vol. 1, *The Triune God* (New York: Oxford University Press, 1997), 111. See George Hunsinger's brief response to Jenson's account of Augustine on divine simplicity and unity of divine action in "Robert Jenson's Systematic Theology: A Review Essay," *SJT* 55 (2002): 161–200, esp. 189–91.

113. Jenson, *The Triune God*, 111. Jenson is not trying to do away with this teaching, but sees a necessary corrective: "The identities' agencies *ad extra* do not achieve an undivided work

I will provide a brief examination of *Sermon 52*.[114] This text will help illuminate his use of scripture to support his view of the inseparable works of the Trinity. From there, I will clarify the relationship between inseparable operations and divine simplicity. But before getting into *Sermon 52* it is important to understand the context for this Nicene axiom.

Similar to the discussion of Gregory and inseparable operations, it is important to pay attention to the theological and exegetical context. The background for this teaching begins with the early interpretations of John 5:19, which "first appears in theological discussion as an anti-Monarchian text: that the Son depends on the Father and looks to him implies the existence of two irreducible realities."[115] Yet two different readings emerged: one that understood the Son to copy what the Father was doing—implying his dependence on the Father—and another that argued that the Son clearly had the power to do what the Father does. Later, Eunomius turned the text against both homoousians and homoiousians, arguing that the Son's act of creation at the Father's command clearly implies two distinct beings. Didymus, for example, responded to the concerns about the "cannot" language of the Son in John 5:19 by noting that "he 'cannot' do anything other because he cannot be separated from the Father."[116] The Son's "seeing" is significant as many Greek Nicenes "treat the Son's seeing as an intrinsic part of what it means for him to possess the divine nature" and "because of his unique mode of generation," which allows him to possess all that the Father possesses.[117] Other passages of scripture entered the debate, and other issues developed, but these debates over John 5:19 form the context that Augustine entered into. In many ways, it was part of the long-standing issue of ontological subordination or separation from the Father that gave rise to the need to articulate the unity of divine works.

Sermon 52 illustrates Augustine's understanding of Jesus's baptism

---

because they are indistinguishable but because they are perfectly mutual" (ibid., 113). However, this corrective is only necessary if Jenson's assessment of Augustine is accurate.

114. Augustine, *Sermon 52*, in *Sermons 51–94 (III/3)*, trans. Edmund Hill, WSA (Hyde Park, NY: New City Press, 1991), 50–65. Henceforth, I will cite this source with a parenthetical page number such as 52.2 (51). While this theme is present throughout *De Trinitate*, it is more assumed than fully explored. See *The Trinity* 1.7–8 (69–70), 1.17–21 (77–81), 1.25 (84), 2.3 (99), 2.8–9 (102–3), 4.30 (175).

115. Ayres, *Augustine and the Trinity*, 234. This paragraph relies on Ayres's work (234–40).

116. Ibid., 236.

117. Ibid., 237.

in Matthew 3. During this event the Father speaks, the Son is baptized, and the Spirit descends like a dove. This clear distinction between the three divine persons appeared to lead to the view that they are separable and therefore different beings. Augustine imagines someone saying to him, "Demonstrate that the three are inseparable," and he is reminded that he must do so according to his Catholic faith, "which is not a bundle of opinions and prejudices but a summary of biblical testimonies."[118]

If the persons act inseparably, then does the Father ever act without the Son? Augustine answers negatively.[119] But does this mean that the Father was also born of a virgin, suffered, was raised, and ascended? Again, he answers negatively.[120] While these were clearly the activities and experience of the Son, it was still the work of both Father and Son together, and Augustine works to demonstrate that this is the teaching of scripture. The Son's birth was brought about by the sending of the Father (Gal 4:4–5) but was also the work of the Son when he emptied himself (Phil 2:6–7). The Son suffered because his Father "gave him up for us all" (Rom 8:32), but the Son also gave himself up (Gal 2:20). Similarly, the resurrection was the work of both Father and Son (Phil 2:9; John 10:18).[121] For Augustine, "The persons [are] quite distinct, and their working inseparable."[122] Contrary to Jenson's worries, Augustine clearly differentiates the actions of the Father and Son, neither collapsing them into one action without differentiation nor separating them into two actions without any unity.[123]

This doctrine was not simply a small piece of Augustine's theology. Rather, "he took this principle as his point of departure for considering the divine unity throughout his career," and, understood in relation to divine simplicity, it "formed a key plank in his defense and presentation of this doctrine."[124] While anti-Nicene theologians saw a division of works in scripture that implied a division of nature, Augustine and other pro-Nicene theologians "argued that as the

118. Augustine, *Sermon 52*, 52.2 (51).

119. Augustine, *Sermon 52*, 52.4 (52).

120. Augustine, *Sermon 52*, 52.6 (53).

121. Augustine, *Sermon 52*, 52.9–13 (54–56).

122. Augustine, *Sermon 52*, 52.14 (56). While Augustine's example only speaks of the Father and Son, it should be clear that the Holy Spirit is to be included in this inseparability as well.

123. See Eunomius, *Apologiae* §20 (Vaggione, 60), referenced in Ayres, *Augustine and the Trinity*, 235.

124. Lewis Ayres, "'Remember That You Are Catholic' (serm. 52.2): Augustine on the Unity of the Triune God," *JECS* 8 (2000): 80.

activity of the three is seen to be one, so must their nature be one,"[125] working from God's activity *ad extra* and developing their beliefs about God *ad intra*. The thrust of the doctrine is that when God acts it is the entirety of God that is acting, not part of him as though he could be divided. Travis Ables helpfully expresses this point.

> The act of God in Jesus Christ is the act of God entire: the whole divine life is in Jesus Christ, not just one member of the Trinity acting on his own. The purpose of this axiom is not to flatten the trinitarian differentiations outside of the immanent Trinity, because it relies upon the simplicity of the divine life, and thus the singularity of the divine act.[126]

God's works are inseparable, but this is not the same as saying that they are indistinguishable. However, it does mean that when one divine person acts, it entails the others since one divine person does not act alone. The unity of action and simplicity of being does not mean that their action is that of a monad who only appears to be three persons.

The doctrine of inseparable operations is more rich and complex than this brief survey allows, but the goal has been to see how Augustine formulates the teaching, how he sees it related to scripture, and how it is related to divine simplicity. Both inseparable operations and divine simplicity are mutually reinforcing, and it is through the undivided works of the triune God that Augustine understands the divine nature to be simple. It is from the simplicity of God that Augustine sees their works as inseparable.

DIVINE SIMPLICITY EAST AND WEST

What conclusions can be drawn in terms of an Eastern and Western conception of divine simplicity? Radde-Gallwitz argues that there are such significant differences that we must speak of a "transformation" of simplicity in the East. He finds that some theologians understand divine simplicity to mean that "every term one attributes to God names God's essence of substance, and that, metaphysically, God's

---

125. Lewis Ayres, "The Fundamental Grammar of Augustine's Trinitarian Theology," in *Augustine and His Critics: Essays in Honour of Gerald Bonner*, ed. Robert Dodaro and George Lawless (New York: Routledge, 2000), 56.

126. Ables, *Incarnational Realism*, 182.

essence and God's properties are in fact identical."[127] He labels this view the "identity thesis" and points out that Basil and Gregory found this teaching in Eunomius's theology. This is an acceptable interpretation, but Radde-Gallwitz's more controversial claim stems from his statement that "in a vastly more sophisticated version, [this] would be the interpretation of divine simplicity given by such theological authorities as Augustine and Aquinas"[128] and "is an interpretation that Basil and Gregory go to great lengths to oppose."[129] In contrast, they transformed the doctrine of divine simplicity by avoiding the extremes of total apophaticism (God has no properties) and the identity thesis (God's properties are identical to his essence).

I am sympathetic to Radde-Gallwitz's assessment, but I remain unconvinced. Because I have not yet interacted with Aquinas's doctrine of divine simplicity, I will limit my comments to Augustine. I find four problems in Radde-Gallwitz's account: first, he does not offer a minimal account of Augustine's doctrine of divine simplicity. Readers must take it as a given that Augustine's view results in the identity thesis, as Radde-Gallwitz describes it, and must also trust that Augustine's view is similar or even identical to Eunomius's account. This mere assertion is vital to Radde-Gallwitz's argument for a transformation and therefore should have been substantially argued and supported rather than merely declared. Otherwise, it appears as a straw-man argument.[130]

Second, his position also assumes that Augustine's assertion of identity implies knowledge of God's essence that is contrary to the doctrine of divine incomprehensibility found in Basil and Gregory. For example, "if one holds that knowing something (as opposed to merely having true beliefs about it) requires one to know its essence, and one wishes to claim knowledge of God, then it is likely that one will be inclined to claim that the attributes one predicates of God name God's essence."[131] However, a cursory reading of *De Trinitate*

---

127. Radde-Gallwitz, *Transformation of Divine Simplicity*, 5.

128. Ibid.

129. Ibid., 6.

130. Contra David Bradshaw, David Bentley Hart argues against "the fanciful idea that there has always been some great difference between eastern and western patristic traditions regarding the nature of divine simplicity." Additionally, he argues that Augustine's view that "the divine essence and divine attributes are identical . . . is a point on which all of the significant eastern fathers certainly agreed" and that "the denial of such an identity would reduce any idea of divine transcendence to absurdity" ("Metaphysics after Nicaea," 213n40). Hart concludes that "Augustine's view does not differ significantly from Gregory of Nyssa's" (ibid.).

131. Radde-Gallwitz, *Transformation of Divine Simplicity*, 3.

reveals a variety of statements to the contrary. For example, "From now on I will be attempting to say things that cannot altogether be said as they are thought by a man. . . . When we think about God the trinity we are aware that our thoughts are quite inadequate to their object, and incapable of grasping him as he is."[132] Or, "it is difficult to contemplate and have full knowledge of God's substance."[133] Or, "God can be thought about more truly than he can be talked about, and he is more truly than he can be thought about."[134] Augustine is exceedingly unlike Eunomius (that is, not just a more "sophisticated" account) in that he never claims complete, comprehensive, or unlimited knowledge of God. Augustine is like Basil and Gregory in that he claims that we have real and true knowledge of God that is nevertheless limited and incomplete.

Third, at best Radde-Gallwitz is unclear and, at worst, contradictory in his discussion regarding knowledge of God's essence. He does not clearly explain whether the properties used to describe God actually exist. If they do not exist, and only exist in relation to human speech or intellect, then can we really claim true knowledge of God even in the weakest sense? If the properties do exist but are not identical, then how does this avoid leading to a composite view of God in all his nonidentical properties? It is also possible that Radde-Gallwitz contradicts himself when it comes to his discussion of *propria*. But perhaps he does not recognize the contrast or irresolvable tension when he notes that "Basil and Gregory do predicate a number of terms of the divine substance"; however, "they are not *identical* with God's nature, but neither are they merely relative, extrinsic properties. Rather, they are propria of the divine nature."[135] *Propria* are "properties co-extensive with and intrinsic to the divine essence, but not individually definitive of that essence."[136] Put differently, they are "unique identifying properties that are inseparably linked to the divine nature, but distinct in some sense from it,"[137] giving real

132. Augustine, *The Trinity* 5.1 (189).

133. Augustine, *The Trinity* 1.3 (66).

134. Augustine, *The Trinity* 7.7 (225). For additional texts, see nn25–30 in Hart, "Metaphysics after Nicaea," 209.

135. Radde-Gallwitz, *Transformation of Divine Simplicity*, 13–14. Part of the problem is that Radde-Gallwitz sees Gregory making a distinction between substance—predicable and knowable—and essence—unknowable (ibid., 216). This distinction allows Radde-Gallwitz to state that "Gregory believes God is essentially good, not that goodness and the divine nature are identical" (197). It is not clear that Radde-Gallwitz proves this point; rather, he merely asserts it.

136. Ibid., 107.

137. Ibid., 184. See also 225.

knowledge of God without defining God. How do these claims represent a transformation of Augustine's (or Thomas's) account? Surely they are in different contexts and use some different categories, but Basil, Gregory, and Augustine operate with a doctrine of divine incomprehensibility without emptying knowledge of God by way of an extreme apophaticism.[138] As Ayres comments, the force of Augustine's teaching that predicates refer to God's substance follows from the belief that "lacking any accidents, God must be any qualities we predicate of God."[139]

Fourth, and finally, some scholars interpret the Eastern view of divine energies to be really distinct from God's essence. Therefore, all that can be known is God's energies, and his essence remains nameless and unknowable. Augustine, and the West, argues that names applied to God refer to his essence and not just his energies. I agree with David Bentley Hart that, whether or not this is the correct interpretation of the Cappadocians and the West, this logic is troubling. "Logically, if the divine energies are genuine *manifestations* of God, however limited, then whatever names apply to the energies also necessarily applies to the essence, even if only defectively, immeasurably remotely, incomprehensibly, and 'improperly.'" He adds that "none of [the Cappadocians] ever suggests that what is revealed of God therein is true of the energies alone (the Cappadocians were not Nominalists)."[140] Basil and Gregory are not claiming to know nothing about the divine essence, nor is Augustine claiming to apply everything he knows to the divine essence. There is a difference in that Augustine does not use the language of activities or energies, and each one's contexts lead them to formulate their responses in different ways. Nevertheless, there is not as much of a divide as is often assumed.

I am not claiming that early Eastern and Western accounts are identical and without conflict. Even still, there are many overlapping

---

138. For example, Holmes summarizes his argument that "Augustine is the most capable interpreter of Cappadocian Trinitarianism" and that "the doctrine of the Trinity received from the fourth century" includes God's ineffability," or incomprehensibility (*The Quest for the Trinity*, 146).

139. Ayres, *Augustine and the Trinity*, 216. For additional critical interaction with Radde-Gallwitz, see Richard Cross, "Divine Simplicity and the Doctrine of the Trinity: Gregory of Nyssa and Augustine," in *Philosophical Theology and the Christian Tradition: Russian and Western Perspectives*, ed. David Bradshaw (Washington, DC: The Council for Research in Values and Philosophy, 2012), 53–66.

140. Hart, "Metaphysics after Nicaea," 212n38.

and similar ideas, terms, and themes. First, both accounts of divine simplicity develop within a polemical context. The doctrine of divine simplicity does not arise out of nowhere, but stems from a response to false teaching that includes debates not only over ideas but about the interpretation of scripture as well.

Second, both attend to the importance of divine names in scripture. No single name is sufficient to provide knowledge of God, yet the many names used of God in scripture are true of him without referring to parts of God or dividing his being. Therefore, the plurality of names does not violate or endanger divine simplicity. Because scripture itself uses many divine names, they follow the grammar of scripture as they articulate a doctrine of divine simplicity—God's being is so rich and plentiful that it takes many names to begin to speak about his being and works. Last, 1 Corinthians 1:24 and the "one power, one nature" theology also play an important role.[141]

Third, neither Basil, Gregory, nor Augustine claim to derive their doctrine of divine simplicity directly from scripture. It surely has roots in scripture, but the conceptual doctrine, just like the developed doctrine of the Trinity, does not spring directly from scripture. Nevertheless, this does not mean that scripture plays a secondary or subordinate role in their theological formations, nor does it mean that the doctrine of divine simplicity is not biblical. Their "piecemeal engagement [with the philosophies of their times were] deeply shaped by a complex notion of the scriptural text as the primary resource for the Christian imagination, as a text that may be explicated through the use of whatever lies to hand and that may be persuasively adapted."[142] scripture grounded the theological formulation of divine simplicity just as it did the Trinity and Christology in the context of their own debates. Divine simplicity developed in ways similar to Nicene trinitarianism and Chalcedonian Christology, resulting from a broad reading of the whole of scripture that helped respond to false teaching and clarify doctrine. In this sense, "the language of Scripture is taken as the primary and most trustworthy language for Christians developing their account of the world and the importation of philosophical

---

141. For more on 1 Cor 1:24, see William McFadden, "The Exegesis of I Cor. 1:24, 'Christ the Power of God and the Wisdom of God' Until the Arian Controversy" (PhD diss., Pontifical Gregorian University, 1963). Ayres adds that it was a common feature of pro-Nicene theology that "God is one power, glory, majesty, rule, Godhead essence, and nature . . . [and] that God is a unity in these respects is universal" (Ayres, *Nicaea and Its Legacy*, 279), and Basil, Gregory, and Augustine do not deviate from this line of thinking.

142. Ayres, *Nicaea and Its Legacy*, 392.

themes and technical language is conceived not as a necessary *trans-position* of ideas, but as an *elucidation* of the text of Scripture."[143]

After exploring some of the similarities between early Eastern and Western conceptions of divine simplicity, there is good reason not to follow Radde-Gallwitz's argument that a significant "transformation" of the doctrine of divine simplicity took place in the East. There are surely differences between East and West, but they are not so significant that it warrants the language of "transformation." Divine simplicity functioned in each region to help Christians combat opposition and misreadings of scripture, read scripture well, and maintain a consistent understanding of God and his perfections in the context of trinitarian theology. As we will see, divine simplicity finds its climax in the West in Thomas Aquinas. But before turning to him, it will be helpful to briefly see how divine simplicity continues throughout the early Middle Ages.

143. Ibid., 277.

3.

Divine Simplicity in Medieval Theology

Divine simplicity is not merely a contextual doctrine limited to patristic theology, nor is it more properly located in the scholastic theology of the Middle Ages. Having been a significant teaching in both the East and West, it was an important doctrine inherited by theologians as a way of both reading scripture and speaking of God. In this section, I will briefly examine the continued importance of divine simplicity in Pseudo-Dionysius, John of Damascus, Anselm, and Peter Lombard. After this, I will transition to the doctrine's culmination in the theology of Thomas Aquinas. With the exception of Pseudo-Dionysius, there is not an explicit connection between divine simplicity and scripture. However, it remains possible that this connection is implicit within the tradition of the divine names found throughout the scholastic period.

DIVINE SIMPLICITY BEFORE THOMAS AQUINAS

Although Basil, Gregory, and Augustine located divine simplicity with the divine names, this emphasis became even more important in the writings of Pseudo-Dionysius in the fifth or sixth century.[1]

1. Paul Rorem provides a commentary on the text in *Pseudo-Dionysius: A Commentary on the Texts and an Introduction to Their Influence* (New York: Oxford University Press, 1993), 133–81. For more on Dionysius's life and works, see Andrew Louth, *Denys the Areopagite*, OCT (London: Continuum, 2002). See also Sarah Coakley and Charles M. Stang, eds., *Re-thinking Dionysius the Areopagite* (Oxford: Wiley-Blackwell, 2009). Following many others, I will refer to Dionysius as Denys from this point forward.

His works were believed to have been authored by the man converted by Paul in Acts 17, and this identification helped deepen their influence on medieval theology. However, modern scholarship has since pointed out the anachronistic terms and thought seen in Denys's Neoplatonism, although questions about his identity go back to Luther and even as far back as the sixth century. Nevertheless, his work was influential for the medieval period and gives another perspective on the relationship between divine simplicity and scripture.

PSEUDO-DIONYSIUS

The Divine Names upholds many aspects of the doctrine of divine simplicity found in the patristic era, but it also develops the doctrine in distinctive ways. For example, Denys maintains a doctrine of divine names in close relation to scripture. Even though the work "employs grammatical and conceptual strategies that are indisputably Neoplatonic, the treatise itself, as well as the unique approach to divine names it embodies, is profoundly biblical."[2] On the one hand, God is beyond the reach of our minds and language and is therefore nameless. On the other hand, he has revealed himself and is named in scripture. Thus "we must not then dare to speak, or indeed to form any conception, of the hidden super-essential Godhead, except those things that are revealed to us from the Holy Scriptures."[3] The revealed names (or perfections) of God found in scripture tell us something true about God without expressing everything about him. Furthermore, "all the Names proper to God are always applied in Scripture not partially but to the whole, entire, full, complete Godhead, and that they all refer indivisibly, absolutely, unreservedly, and wholly to all the wholeness of the whole and entire Godhead."[4] For example, power does not name a part of God, but all that he is, nor does it name one of the persons as if the Father is powerful and the Son is

---

2. Brendan Thomas Sammon, *The God Who Is Beauty: Beauty as a Divine Name in Thomas Aquinas and Dionysius the Areopagite*, PTM (Eugene, OR: Pickwick, 2013), 96. Sammon argues that Denys's approach to the divine names stems from the book of Exodus (see 97–111).

3. Dionysius the Areopagite, *The Divine Names*, in *The Mystical Theology and The Divine Names*, trans. C. E. Rolt (Mineola, NY: Dover, 2004), 1.1 (51). See also 1.2 (53). All citations will come from this translation followed by chapter and section (1.1), with page number in parenthesis.

4. Dionysius the Areopagite, *The Divine Names* 2.1 (65).

not. Finally, the combination of names does not make up God's being since each name is applied to all that God is.

Some may worry that Denys creates too strong a doctrine of divine simplicity in relation to the divine names and eventually, like Eunomius, ends up with a simple monad rather than an indivisible Trinity. Denys does not remove all plurality, but only the kind that results in composition and implies divisibility or separation in the being of God. Here, Denys draws a distinction between "undifferenced names," which belong to the entire Godhead, and "differentiated names," which belong to the divine persons and are not interchangeable or common to the whole Godhead.[5] As a result, some names entail unity while others admit plurality. In other words, Denys can say that God "is an Indivisible Plurality."[6]

Implicit within Denys's doctrine of divine simplicity and divine names is a strong doctrine of transcendence. This doctrine forms the basis of his view of the namelessness and namability of God. As J. Warren Smith puts it, Denys thinks that "although God, in order to accommodate the finitude of his creatures, reveals himself in and through a veritable panoply of images and concepts, God always retains an essential and transcendent simplicity."[7] In one sense, God is good (cataphatic), yet God is not good (apophatic) since he transcends our concept and meaning of goodness. The other way is supereminent, or the way of excellence. God is "supra-good," and this carries the idea that we do not actually fully understand what this means.

JOHN OF DAMASCUS

John of Damascus is a key representative of the doctrine of divine simplicity in the East. In his *Exposition of the Orthodox Faith*, he argues that God is "one substance, one godhead, one virtue, one will, one operation, one principality, one power, one domination, one kingdom; known in three perfect Persons . . . united without confusion and distinct without separation, which is beyond

5. Dionysius the Areopagite, *The Divine Names* 2.3 (68). This distinction is similar to Basil's, Gregory's, and Augustine's distinction between common and relative names.

6. Dionysius the Areopagite, *The Divine Names* 2.11 (80). This statement is somewhat similar to Augustine's "simple multiplicity and multiple simplicity."

7. J. Warren Smith, "Divine Ecstasy and Divine Simplicity: The Eros Motif in Pseudo-Dionysius's Soteriology," *ProEccl* 21 (2012): 223.

understanding."[8] Similar to Augustine's "not three great ones, but one great one" argument, and similar to the "one power, one nature" theology demonstrated by Michel René Barnes and the inseparable operations found in both East and West, the Damascene preserves a doctrine of divine simplicity in its patristic form.

Even though we know that God is simple, this does not mean that he is understood in his very essence. It should be clear that

> one should not suppose that any one of these things which are affirmed of God is indicative of what He is in essence. Rather, they show either [1] what He is not, or [2] some relation to some one of those things that are contrasted with Him, or [3] something of those things which are consequential to His nature or operation.[9]

This threefold understanding of the divine names supports the position clearly held by Basil, Gregory, and Augustine that names do not strictly refer to the divine essence. Otherwise, such a view would create three different essences, parts, or reduce all names to one name that truly applies to God.

John makes an argument similar to the one found in Denys: God is both unnamable and nameable, but this must be properly understood. He argues that

> in his ineffable goodness He sees fit to be named from things which are on the level of our nature, that we may not be entirely bereft of knowledge of Him but may have at least some dim understanding. Therefore, in so far as He is incomprehensible, He is also unnamable. But, since He is the cause of all things and possesses beforehand in Himself the reasons and causes of all, so He can be named after all things—even after things which are opposites, such as light and darkness, water and fire—so that we may know that He is not these things in essence, but is superessential and unnamable. Thus, since He is the cause of all beings, He is named after all things that are caused.[10]

God transcends our minds and language, yet he also descends to our level in order that we may know him on a very small level.

---

8. John of Damascus, *Exposition of the Orthodox Faith*, in *Writings*, trans. Frederic H. Chase Jr., FoC (Washington, DC: Catholic University Press of America, 1958), 1.8 (177; cf. 186). All citations will come from this translation and will cite the book and chapter (e.g., 1.8) and corresponding page number. See also Joseph Steineger, "John of Damascus on the Simplicity of God," *SP* 68 (2013): 337–54.

9. John of Damascus, *Exposition of the Orthodox Faith* 1.9 (189).

10. John of Damascus, *Exposition of the Orthodox Faith* 1.12 (194).

Furthermore, as the cause and source of all things, we can name him from the things of this world (for example, light), all the while remembering that he ultimately transcends them and cannot be reduced to these names. In this process we encounter "negations and affirmations, but the most satisfactory is the combination of both."[11]

Last, John continues the argument that many names are necessary to God and truly describe him without dividing or separating his being according to each name. The names, "both those given by negation and those given by affirmation, are applied jointly to the whole Godhead. They also apply in the same way, identically, and without exception, to each one of the Persons of the Holy Trinity."[12] Just as each person is fully God and yet there are also three persons, so each (common) name applies to the entire Godhead and yet there are many names.

ANSELM

Anselm carries on the tradition of divine simplicity in his *Monologion* and *Proslogion*, which signal strong influence from Augustine. Far from being the origin of "perfect being theology," these works should be read as contemplative theology in accordance with Augustine's *De Trinitate*.[13] In order to read them as perfect being theology, one has to reverse Anselm's order and read him as "understanding seeking faith." The presupposition of faith means that when Anselm contemplates God in the *Monologion*, he contemplates the revealed God who is Father, Son, and Holy Spirit.[14] In the *Proslogion*, he makes frequent reference to scripture. Any supposed "natural theology" or "reasoning alone" is done in the context of faith and is never made the foundation of what he articulates. Rather, the style and function of Anselm's two works are expressions of the Christian faith that include inherited doctrines like the Trinity and divine simplicity.

For Anselm, "the supreme nature is what it is—good, great,

---

11. John of Damascus, *Exposition of the Orthodox Faith* 1.12 (195).

12. John of Damascus, *Exposition of the Orthodox Faith* 1.12 (195).

13. Anselm expects this much in the prologue. See Anselm of Canterbury, *Monologion*, in *Anselm of Canterbury: The Major Works*, ed. Brian Davies and Gareth Evans, trans. Simon Harrison (Oxford: Oxford University Press, 1998), 6. All citations will come from this translation and will cite the chapter and corresponding page number.

14. For example, see Anselm, *Monologion* 43–63 (55–70).

existing—precisely through itself and nothing else."[15] As a simple being, God is also distinct from his creation since "a man cannot be, but may possess, justice."[16] Since God does not possess what he is, it is best to see that "all of these terms, then, indicate not a quality or quantity, but what the supreme nature is."[17] If each term were to denote a quality or quantity then God could be said to be composed. For Anselm, a composite "requires, for its existence, its components and owes its being what it is to them. It is what it is through them. They, however, are not what they are through it."[18] As Augustine says in the *City of God*, God is what he has and is not who and what he is through anything other than himself.

In the *Proslogion*, a condensed version of the *Monologion*, the simplicity of God refers to the way in which God is one. His oneness is not a matter of parts that, when brought together, form a whole, or a mixture of qualities that make up the divine being. Anselm draws this conclusion because "whatever is made up of parts is not absolutely one, but in a sense many and other than itself, and it can be broken up either actually or by the mind—all of which things are foreign to You."[19] Additionally, because God is simple, "life and wisdom and the other [attributes], then, are not parts of You, but all are one and each one of them is wholly what You are and what all the others are."[20] Even though all of the attributes are one, this does not lead Anselm to deny plurality within the unity of God. He notes that "in the supreme unity there is such an amazing multiplicity, a multiplicity as inexpressible as it is irrepressible. This is what I have found. Such an impenetrable mystery!"[21]

Anselm is clearly not attempting to describe God in a Eunomian

15. Anselm, *Monologion* 16 (29). For additional sources on Anselm and divine simplicity, see Siobhan Nash-Marshall, "Properties, Conflation, and Attribution: The Monologion and Divine Simplicity," *SAJ* 4 (2007): 19–36; Gregory B. Sadler, "A Perfectly Simple God and Our Complicated Lives," *SAJ* 6 (2008): 39–61; Oliver D. Crisp, "Anselm and Edwards on God," in *The Ecumenical Edwards: Jonathan Edwards among the Theologians*, ed. Kyle C. Strobel (Burlington, VT: Ashgate, 2015), 33–50, esp. 33–42.

16. Anselm, *Monologion* 16 (29).

17. Anselm, *Monologion* 16 (29).

18. Anselm, *Monologion* 17 (30).

19. Anselm, *Proslogion*, in Davies and Evans, *The Major Works*, 18 (98). All citations will come from this translation and will cite the chapter and corresponding page number.

20. Anselm, *Proslogion* 18 (98). Elsewhere, Anselm states that "any one of [the titles] is the same thing as all of them . . . [and each] signifies the same thing as the others" (*Monologion* 17 [30]).

21. Anselm, *Monologion* 43 (55–56). Later he adds that "the individual properties of each do not become plural, because they are not properties of two things. And conversely, that which is

sense. He does not claim direct knowledge of God or to sufficiently know or understand the divine essence. Rather, he confesses that

> I do not try, Lord, to attain Your lofty heights, because my understanding is in no way equal to it. But I do desire to understand Your truth a little, that truth that my heart believes and loves. For I do not seek to understand so that I may believe; but I believe so that I may understand.[22]

This classic statement presents Anselm's aim to know God, while admitting that whatever can be known by revelation or reason remains a mystery. God is one, indivisible, unified, and yet three, distinct, and plural. How these terms are parsed is guided by a doctrine of divine simplicity in order to avoid asserting or allowing any composition to be entailed or predicated of God.

PETER LOMBARD

Finally, book 1 of Peter Lombard's *Sentences* offers insight into the way divine simplicity was received in the twelfth century. Following Augustine in book 6 of *De Trinitate*, he writes that divine simplicity means "no diversity or change or multiplicity of parts, or accidents, or of any other forms."[23] It is the creature and creation that is manifold and therefore distinguished from the simple being of God. While God is certainly indivisible, Peter follows the tradition and notes that God is still described in many different ways. He comments that Augustine "does not say this because of a diversity of accidents or parts, but due to the diversity and multitude of names which are used about God."[24] These names refer to all that God is, meaning that "the simplicity and purity of this essence is such that there is nothing in it which is not itself."[25] All that is in God *is* God. Reaffirming the

---

common to both is a single unity, even though it belongs wholly to each individual" (Anselm, *Monologion* 43 [56]).

22. Anselm, *Proslogion* 1 (87).

23. Peter Lombard, *The Sentences*, book 1, *The Mystery of the Trinity*, trans. Giulio Silano, MST 42 (Toronto: PIMS, 2007), 8.3 (23). All citations come from this translation and contain the distinction and chapter (8.3) and page number in parenthesis.

24. Peter Lombard, *The Sentences* 8.5 (25).

25. Peter Lombard, *The Sentences* 8.8 (28). Peter Lombard relies heavily on Augustine, but also refers to Hilary, Boethius, and Isidore of Seville.

traditional statements of divine simplicity, he states that the being of God is not the result of participation or possession.

DIVINE SIMPLICITY IN THE THEOLOGY OF THOMAS AQUINAS

After Peter Lombard, the next major voice for the doctrine of divine simplicity is Thomas Aquinas.[26] His doctrine of God represents the height of classical theism.[27] Yet Karl Rahner argues that in Aquinas we encounter the beginnings of the separation between the oneness of God and the triunity of God. It appears "as if everything which matters for us in God has already been said in the treatise *On the One God*" with the result being that "the treatise becomes quite philosophical and abstract."[28] Because divine simplicity is treated immediately after the "five ways" and before the doctrine of the Trinity, it is naturally understood as a piece of philosophy, or natural theology, and linked with the problem of Aquinas's supposed preference for the

26. Thomas's views on divine simplicity develop after the events of the Council of Rheims (1148) and the Fourth Lateran Council (1215). The Council of Rheims is said to have condemned Gilbert de la Porre's views on the Trinity, although the events are not entirely clear. Emery writes that Gilbert saw "a difference between the divine person and his relative property, for instance, between the Father and his paternity. This idea elicited heated reactions, especially from Bernard of Clairvaux, who counterattacked in the name of God's *simplicity*. The theory would be rejected at the synod of Reims (1148), whose doctrinal decision was accepted by Gilbert. Whatever its accuracy with respect to Gilbert's actual thinking, the criticism which it addressed to him constituted the scholastic form of 'Porretanism,' as the kind of Trinitarian theology which Peter Lombard's *Sentences* characterized as 'heretical'" (Gilles Emery, *The Trinitarian Theology of Saint Thomas Aquinas*, trans. Francesca Aran Murphy [Oxford: Oxford University Press, 2007], 90). See also Nicholas M. Haring, "Notes on the Council and the Consistory of Rheims (1148)," *MS* 28 (1966): 39–59; Jaroslav Pelikan, *The Christian Tradition*, vol. 3, *The Growth of Medieval Theology* (Chicago: University of Chicago Press, 1980), 264–67. The Fourth Lateran Council made divine simplicity a dogma of the Roman Catholic Church and its teaching was reiterated at Vatican I (1869–1870).

27. On the story of classical theism, see Kevin Vanhoozer, *Remythologizing Theology: Divine Action, Passion, and Authorship*, CSCD (Cambridge: Cambridge University Press, 2010), 82–104, and H. P. Owen, *Concepts of Deity* (New York: Herder & Herder, 1971), 1–42. As it relates to divine simplicity, see Brian Davies, "Classical Theism and the Doctrine of Divine Simplicity," in *Language, Meaning, and God: Essays in Honour of Herbert McCabe*, ed. Brian Davies (London: Cassell, 1987), 51–74, and Eleonore Stump, *The God of the Bible and the God of the Philosophers*, AL (Marquette: Marquette University Press, 2016).

28. Karl Rahner, *The Trinity*, trans. Joseph Donceel, MCT (New York: Crossroad, 1997), 17. Anna Williams adds that "scholarly attention has so focused on its philosophical foundations and implications that the *Summa*'s other qualities have tended to recede into obscurity, creating the widely-held impression of Thomas as a hairsplitting philosopher" ("Mystical Theology Redux: The Pattern of Aquinas' *Summa Theologiae*," *ModTheo* 13 [1997]: 56–57).

unity of God. In this way, divine simplicity primarily speaks to God's oneness or unity and appears to be intolerant of distinctions of any kind.

A particular problem surfaces with this reading of Aquinas. It assumes that Aquinas structured his work according to importance, emphasis, or deduction. In other words, the treatise on the one God stands before the treatise on the Trinity because it should (or does) determine what must be said about the Trinity based on the issue of importance or reasoning via natural theology. But this reading misses the bigger picture and the point of Thomas's doctrine of God, giving the impression that he begins with natural theology (as a philosopher), or an abstract metaphysical concept of God, and moves toward a more Christian and personal view of God (as a theologian).[29]

This perspective misses the indication in Aquinas's prologue that the purpose of the work was to instruct beginners.[30] More specifically, "his *Summa theologiae* was not a university text, but was intended to serve the educational needs of the average Dominican friar, preparing him for the task of preaching and hearing confessions."[31] This is a work of theology, at least in intent, which is far from "philosophical and abstract." Its structure was meant to function pedagogically and was further designed to make up for the deficiencies Thomas saw in Peter's *Sentences*, making it "easy [for modern readers] to forget that the meticulously structured linearity of the *Summa* is in fact a solution."[32] Following the history of salvation and the progression of revelation, Thomas begins with what can be generally known about God and moves toward greater specificity, although this approach is something Rahner still believes is incorrect.[33]

29. Put differently, this reading assumes that Aristotle or philosophy in general is most important to Thomas and ignores the crucial influence of Augustine. For example, see Michael Dauphinais, Barry David, and Matthew Levering, eds., *Aquinas the Augustinian* (Washington, DC: Catholic University of America Press, 2007).

30. Rudi Te Velde rightly argues that "this remark [about beginners] should not be interpreted as a reference to any specific audience of (probably highly gifted) students just beginning the study of theology. It means that the order of the work is methodologically conceived from the standpoint of one who begins" (Rudi Te Velde, *Aquinas on God: The "Divine Science" of the Summa Theologiae*, ASHPT [Aldershot: Ashgate, 2006], 34n30).

31. Frederick Christian Bauerschmidt, *Thomas Aquinas: Faith, Reason, and Following Christ*, CTC (Oxford: Oxford University Press, 2013), 22. See also Denys Turner, *Thomas Aquinas: A Portrait* (New Haven: Yale University Press, 2013), 104–12; Thomas F. O'Meara, *Thomas Aquinas Theologian* (Notre Dame: University of Notre Dame Press, 1997), 51–53.

32. Turner, *Thomas Aquinas*, 29 (cf. 25).

33. In Velde's words, "What Thomas is doing in his treatment of God may be described as construing systematically, step-by-step, a complex concept of a simple God: an articulated con-

Reading the *Summa* as a text aimed at theological instruction for preaching changes the approach to its structure and content. I agree with Denys Turner, who sees Thomas as a pluralist "when it came to questions of systematic theological exposition." A brief look at the order of three texts—*Summa contra gentiles*, *Compendium theologiae*, and *Summa theologiae*—reveals three structures that are not only different from each other, but also from Peter's *Sentences*.[34] In this regard, Thomas's *Summa* aims more at aiding education than providing a final theological structure by which all doctrines can be deduced from natural reason. "In all of Thomas's intellectual activities, his single goal was at all times the Dominican task of preaching Jesus Christ and caring for souls so that human beings might attain beatitude."[35]

This issue may seem to distract from the discussion of divine simplicity, but such assumptions and conclusions regarding the purpose of the *Summa* often determines how one reads the text and understands his doctrine of divine simplicity. The *Summa* is not the only place Aquinas presents his doctrine of divine simplicity,[36] but I will engage this text for two reasons: First, this text is most frequently consulted to determine Thomas's doctrine of divine simplicity. Second, one might expect the project to attend to Thomas's biblical commentaries since the focus of this book is on divine simplicity and scripture.[37] However, to do so could still leave the impression

ceptual account of God according to the way in which the truth of God is accessible—negatively and indirectly—to human thought" (*Aquinas on God*, 70). To be fair to Rahner, he recognizes the "separation" of the one God and the triune God as "more a didactic than a fundamental problem," but he still finds it "incorrect to claim that this separation and sequence follow the course of revelation" (*The Trinity*, 20).

34. Turner, *Thomas Aquinas*, 26–27.

35. Bauerschmidt, *Thomas Aquinas*, 37.

36. For example, in *Summa Contra Gentiles*, vol. 1, Aquinas begins with the immutability of God and moves toward the doctrine of divine simplicity. From there, he examines God's other perfections. See *Summa Contra Gentiles*, trans. Anton C. Pegis (Notre Dame: University of Notre Dame Press, 1975), 1:22–23; Thomas Aquinas, *On the Power of God*, trans. Lawrence Shapcote (Westminster, MD: Newman Press, 1952); Thomas Aquinas, *Compendium of Theology*, trans. Richard J. Regan (Oxford: Oxford University Press, 2009).

37. For examples of Thomas's reference to divine simplicity in his commentaries, see his commentary on Psalm 4, 30; John 1, 6, 16; 2 Cor 11; Phil 2; or Heb 1. For more on Thomas's biblical commentaries, see Thomas Weinandy, Daniel Keating, and John Yocum, eds., *Aquinas on Scripture: An Introduction to His Biblical Commentaries* (London: T&T Clark, 2005); Michael Dauphinais and Matthew Levering, eds., *Reading John with St. Thomas Aquinas: Theological Exegesis and Speculative Theology* (Washington, DC: Catholic University of America Press, 2005); Christopher Baglow, *"Modus et Forma": A New Approach to the Exegesis of Saint Thomas Aquinas with an Application to the "Lectura Super Epistulam Ad Ephesios,"* Analecta Biblica Dissertationes (Rome: Gregorian & Biblical Press, 2002); Thomas Ryan, *Thomas Aquinas as Reader of Psalms*

that Thomas is doing natural theology (or philosophy) in the *Summa*, which is different from what he is doing in his commentaries. While they do represent different genres, Thomas is not doing natural theology in one and revealed or biblical theology in the other. "There is, in a strict sense, no natural theology in the *Summa*, even when the search for the intelligibility of what faith is about is carried out within the horizon of the Greek-metaphysical quest for the first principle."[38] On this basis, I will first clarify the context and content of Thomas's doctrine of divine simplicity in the *Summa*, noting the often ignored or missed connections to scripture. Second, I will present his theology of divine names as another element involved in the relationship between divine simplicity and scripture. And third, I will highlight Thomas's unique contributions to the doctrine of divine simplicity, noting the ways he extends the theological tradition.[39]

DIVINE SIMPLICITY IN THE *SUMMA THEOLOGIAE*

There have been a variety of dissertations, monographs, and essays that seek to directly describe Aquinas's doctrine of divine simplicity from both critical and laudatory standpoints.[40] Many of these

(Notre Dame: University of Notre Dame Press, 2000); Matthew Levering, *Paul in the "Summa Theologiae"* (Washington, DC: Catholic University of America Press, 2014); Matthew Levering and Michael Dauphinais, eds., *Reading Romans with St. Thomas Aquinas* (Washington, DC: Catholic University of America Press, 2012); Levering, *Scripture and Metaphysics: Aquinas and the Renewal of Trinitarian Theology*, CCT (Oxford: Blackwell, 2004). For his academic sermons, see Thomas Aquinas, *The Academic Sermons*, trans. Mark-Robin Hoogland (Washington, DC: Catholic University of America Press, 2010).

38. Velde, *Aquinas on God*, 68. He adds that "one can select topics, arguments and discussions from the *Summa* in order to construe a system of natural theology as a purely philosophical enterprise independent of Christian faith. But in doing this one is likely to miss the systematic unity as well as the spirit of Thomas' thought" (ibid.).

39. This section will not respond to Alvin Plantinga's influential account against Thomas. Plantinga was summarized in chap. 1, and there have been many responses that sufficiently expose the problems in his argument. For example, see Eleonore Stump, "Review of Does God Have a Nature? (The Aquinas Lecture: 1980) by Alvin Plantinga," *Thomist* 47 (1983): 616–22; Lawrence Dewan, "Saint Thomas, Alvin Plantinga, and the Divine Simplicity," *MSch* 66 (1989): 141–51.

40. See esp. Peter Burns, "The Status and Function of Divine Simpleness in *Summa theologiae* Ia, qq.2–13," *Thomist* 57 (1993): 1–26; Vincent M. Dever, "Divine Simplicity: Aquinas and the Current Debate" (PhD diss., Marquette University, 1994); W. Matthews Grant, "Aquinas, Divine Simplicity, and Divine Freedom," *PACPA* 77 (2003): 129–44; Juan José Herrera, *La simplicidad divina según santo Tomás de Aquino* (Salta, Argentina: Ediciones de la Universidad del Norte Santo Tomás de Aquino, 2011); Hughes, *Complex Theory*; J. Lamont, "Aquinas on Divine Simplicity," *Monist* 80 (1997): 521–39; Brian Leftow, "Aquinas, Divine Simplicity and

contributions primarily read Thomas as a philosopher and see his account in the *Summa* to be authoritative.[41] Yet again, as a work designed to educate beginners (or help students "begin"), it is structured to facilitate knowledge of God rather than an authoritative account of how theology must be done at all times and in all ways.

Thomas's doctrine of God is divided into three sections—the nature of God (1.2–26), the Trinity (1.27–43), and creation (1.44–119).[42] Yet they are often read independently of one another as distinct units. Taken as a whole, one could say that Thomas's doctrine of God is "phased,"[43] meaning that his "starting point" does not express the greatest importance, but where one must begin in order to cumulatively progress to the end. Thus "failing" to begin with the Trinity or Christ is not Thomas's way of saying that Jesus makes no difference for our understanding of God. Rather, the work is designed to help the student move from beginning to end, similar to the progression of revelation found in scripture. On this point, Rahner mistakenly identifies a "separation" between the one God and the triune God. Since Aquinas never intended such a separation (nor would he likely be unaware of such a blatant problem in his work), readers should seek to undertake his doctrine of God collectively.[44]

Divine Freedom," in *Metaphysics and God: Essays in Honor of Eleonore Stump*, ed. Kevin Timpe (New York: Routledge, 2009), 21–38; Joseph S. O'Leary, "The Simplicity of the Ultimate: East and West," in *Aquinas, Education and the East*, ed. Thomas Brian Mooney and Mark Nowacki (New York: Springer, 2013), 133–45; D. Stephen Long, *The Perfectly Simple God: Aquinas and His Legacy* (Minneapolis: Fortress Press, 2016), 3–115; Eleonore Stump, "Aquinas's Account of Divine Simplicity," in *Theologie Negative*, ed. Marco M. Olivetti (Casa Editrice Dott: Antonio Milani, 2002), 575–84; Stump, "Aquinas on Being, Goodness, and Divine Simplicity," in *Die Logik des Transzendentalen: Festschrift für Jan A. Aertsen zum 65. Geburtstag*, ed. Martin Pickave, Miscellanea Mediaevalia 30 (Berlin: de Gruyter, 2003), 212–25; Stump, "God's Simplicity," in *The Oxford Handbook of Aquinas*, ed. Brian Davies and Eleonore Stump (Oxford: Oxford University Press, 2011), 135–46; Stump, *God of the Bible*, 77–97; Peter Weigel, *Aquinas on Simplicity: An Investigation into the Foundations of His Philosophical Theology* (New York: Peter Lang, 2008); Thomas Joseph White, "Divine Simplicity and the Holy Trinity," *IJST* 18 (2016): 66–93 (esp. 71–82); White, "Nicene Orthodoxy and Trinitarian Simplicity," *ACPQ* 90 (2016): 727–50 (esp. 735–42).

41. In response, Kerr argues that "Thomas' God is not the perfect being of Greek metaphysics, the supreme entity at the top of a hierarchy of atomistically conceived substances. Rather, describing the biblical and liturgical experience of God in what is no doubt an extremely strange and even alienating language, Thomas offers a concept of God as substance activity/actuality: a triad of action-based subsisting relations." See Fergus Kerr, "God in the *Summa Theologiae*: Entity or Event," in *Philosophy of Religion for a New Century: Essays in Honor of Eugene Thomas Long*, ed. Jeremiah Hackett and Jerald Wallulis (Boston: Springer, 2004), 77.

42. Unless otherwise noted, all quotations of the *Summa* are from the Blackfriars edition.

43. Fergus Kerr, *After Aquinas: Versions of Thomism* (Oxford: Blackwell, 2002), 184.

44. As Karen Kilby points out, "Thomas does not, then, present the Trinity as a datum of rev-

Thomas seeks to establish the existence of God on the grounds of knowledge common to all.[45] Even so, this approach only provides a minimal and general understanding "that a certain thing exists," leaving one to wonder about "the way in which it exists."[46] This leads to the now famous statement that "we cannot know what God is, but only what he is not."[47] As we will see, Thomas's apophatic theology not only directs what is said about divine simplicity but also permits positive statements and positive knowledge of God. Overall, his apophatic theology points to "the intellectual form of our respect and adoration in confrontation with God's mystery."[48] Divine simplicity, which comes next in the *Summa*, is therefore a part of this negative theology.[49]

Thomas begins his discussion on "what God is not" by ruling out "everything inappropriate, such as compositeness, change, and the like."[50] Divine simplicity rules out composition, but what kind of composition? Eight articles structure the overall question of God's simplicity and provide the insights into what Thomas wants to deny and what must be affirmed. To be sure, he uses Aristotelian logic, terms, and concepts in order to make his points. However, what he ultimately does is attend to the issues raised by scripture, grappling with them from the angle of faith and not merely from reason alone.

Thomas's doctrine of divine simplicity begins with the question of whether scripture teaches that God has a body. He cites eight

elation which is awkwardly appended to a philosophical presentation of God, but deliberately and progressively develops a single treatment of God" (Kilby, "Aquinas, the Trinity and the Limits of Understanding," *IJST* 7 [2005]: 417). Emery adds that "there is no question of a 'one God' or of a 'tri-God,' but of God considered *under the aspect* of the essence and *under the aspect* of distinction. . . . The nuance is important, because the structure set forth by Thomas poses simply the opportunity for a double consideration or a double approach to the God confessed by Christian faith." See Gilles Emery, "Essentialism or Personalism in the Treatise on God in Saint Thomas Aquinas?," *Thomist* 64 (2000): 532.

45. *ST* 1a.2.

46. *ST* 1a.2.3.

47. *ST* 1a.2.3.

48. Jean-Pierre Torrell, *Saint Thomas Aquinas: Spiritual Master*, trans. Robert Royal (Washington, DC: Catholic University of America Press, 2003), 2:36.

49. Kevin Hector argues that Thomas's apophaticism is but one step among others toward making positive statements about God. See "Apophaticism in Thomas Aquinas: A Re-formulation and Recommendation," *SJT* 60 (2007): 377–93. Also in this regard, David Burrell and Brian Davies take a stronger apophatic approach to Thomas's doctrine of divine simplicity. See David B. Burrell, *Knowing the Unknowable God: Ibn-Sina, Maimonides, Aquinas* (Notre Dame: University of Notre Dame Press, 1992); Davies, "Classical Theism and the Doctrine of Divine Simplicity."

50. *ST* 1a.2.3.

different passages that would seem to naturally lead a reader to this question: Genesis 1:26, Hebrews 1:3, Job 11:8–9 and 40:4, Psalm 34:16 and 118:6, and Isaiah 6:1 and 3:13. If God has a body, how would a reader make sense of John 4:24, "God is spirit"? Aquinas proceeds to explain what must be affirmed of God if he has a body: God would be mutable, would have potential and not be actual, and would not be the most excellent of beings. In each instance it is not divine simplicity, but what "has been shown" or what "we have seen" or "what has been said" in the previous sections that help guide what may now be said. For example, Thomas refers his readers back to his discussion of scripture's use of bodily metaphors for God that "symbolize the extent of God's power."[51] The image of God spoken of in Genesis 1:26 refers to humanity's "intellect and reason, which are not bodily characteristics."[52] The heart of the issue is scripture and its interpretation even though it takes shape in Aristotelian and scholastic forms.

Articles 2–8 raise the questions of whether God is composed of form and matter (a. 2); whether he can be identified with his own essence (a. 3); if one can distinguish between God's essence and existence (a. 4); whether God is contained in a genus (a. 5); whether God is composed of essence and accidents (a. 6); whether God is "altogether simple" (a. 7); and whether God enters into composition with other things (a. 8).[53] The kinds of composition differ—physical, logical, metaphysical, and so on—but the point is that God is not composite in any sense of the word. If he was, then he would not be the unmoved mover, the uncaused cause, and so on.

If these forms of composition are what is inappropriately affirmed of God, then what does divine simplicity require that we *do* say? After summarizing the ways he denied composition to God in articles 1–6, Thomas provides four ways that God is altogether simple. First, "everything composite is subsequent to its components and dependent upon them; whilst God, as we have seen, is the first of all beings." Thomas, therefore, is concerned that if God is not simple then one must explain where his parts come from, in what order, and then accept that God is dependent on these parts to be who he is.

---

51. *ST* 1a.3.1.

52. Ibid.

53. For a more complete account of these models of composition, see James E. Dolezal, *God without Parts: Divine Simplicity and the Metaphysics of God's Absoluteness* (Eugene, OR: Pickwick, 2011), 31–66. He sums it up this way: "A composite being is a creature" (33).

Second, "everything composite is caused; . . . God however is not caused, as we have seen, but is himself the first cause." On this account, if God is made of parts then he was somehow combined. But how, and by whom? Third, "in any composite there is a realizing of potentialities," which entails that all of the parts reached their full potential and God, as a whole, was finally realized. But God is pure act, "sheer actuality," and has no potentialities and is in no need of actualization. Last, "in all composites there is some element not sharing a common predicate with the whole." In other words, "no part of a man is a man, and no part of the foot a foot."[54] However, God is "identical with his own godhead, with his own life and with whatever else is similarly said of him."[55]

If divine simplicity is taken to mean that there are no distinctions within God, or that all multiplicity and plurality is merely the result of human finite minds trying to grasp the infinite, then what need is there to discuss the divine perfections following Thomas's treatment of divine simplicity? Here, divine simplicity is not the reduction of God into an indistinguishable monad, but the recognition of his plentiful being, a point recognized by Jean-Pierre Torrell: "In starting with the divine simplicity, Thomas centers his exposition on the plentitude of God's Being and on the identification within him of Essence and Existence."[56] As plentiful, many names are required to even begin to describe who and what God is and is not. At this point, I will take up Thomas's account of the names of God in 1a q. 13.

THE NAMES OF GOD

After beginning with simplicity and stating what God is not (1 qq. 3–11), Thomas moves to the names of God.[57] "In this life we do not see the essence of God, we only know him from creatures; we think

---

54. *ST* 1a.3.7.

55. *ST* 1a.3.3.

56. Torrell, *Saint Thomas Aquinas*, 2:35.

57. For a longer treatment of Thomas's theology of divine names, see Gregory P. Rocca, *Speaking the Incomprehensible God: Thomas Aquinas on the Interplay of Positive and Negative Theology* (Washington, DC: Catholic University of America Press, 2008), 291–333. See also D. Stephen Long, *Speaking of God: Theology, Language, and Truth*, EES (Grand Rapids: Eerdmans, 2009), 163–80. See also James Dominic Rooney, "Being as Iconic: Aquinas on 'He Who Is' as the Name for God," *IJST* 19 (2017): 163–74; Scott R. Swain, "On Divine Naming," in *Aquinas Among the Protestants*, ed. Manfred Svensson and David VanDrunen (Oxford: Wiley-Blackwell, 2018), 207–27.

of him as their source, and then as surpassing them all and as lacking anything that is merely creaturely."[58] As the divine source of what is found in creatures, "God is good" cannot be the mere denial that he is evil (for example, Maimonides's view), but does refer to what God is even if it "fail[s] to represent adequately what he is."[59] Therefore, predicating goodness of God "means that what we call 'goodness' in creatures pre-exists in God in a higher way. . . . Goodness flows from him because he is good."[60] In other words, the names predicated of God must *first* be understood to flow from him as their source in a way that transcends their existence in creatures.

If the names of God are identical with his essence, then are the names predicated of him synonymous? On the one hand, Thomas answers negatively since "the words that signify what God is (although they do it imperfectly) also have distinct meanings."[61] Good does not mean the same thing as infinite. On the other hand, we rightly assert many names of God because "what pre-exists in God in a simple and unified way is divided amongst creatures as many and varied perfections. The many perfections of creatures correspond to one single source which they represent in varied and complex ways."[62] There is a certain similitude between what is named of God and the divine essence; yet the correspondence is imperfect and utterly fails to represent him adequately.

This view of the divine names leads Thomas to a clearer exposition of how God is named analogically. Univocal and equivocal language is rejected in order to properly express the imperfect and inadequate correspondence of the names for God.[63] Based on the understanding of God as source and as the transcendent preexistence of all divine names, words used of God and creatures must be properly ordered: God as source and creatures as image. This order also governs whether words are predicated primarily of God or creatures.[64] For Thomas, "The primary application of the word is to the central thing

58. *ST* 1a.13.1.

59. *ST* 1a.13.2.

60. Ibid.

61. *ST* 1a.13.4.

62. *ST* 1a.13.4.

63. On analogical language in Thomas, see Ralph M. McInerny, *Aquinas and Analogy* (Washington, DC: Catholic University of America Press, 1998); George P. Klubertanz, *St. Thomas Aquinas on Analogy: A Textual Analysis and Systematic Synthesis* (1960; repr., Eugene, OR: Wipf & Stock, 2009); Archie J. Spencer, *The Analogy of Faith: The Quest for God's Speakability*, SIET (Downers Grove, IL: IVP Academic, 2015), 94–141.

64. *ST* 1a.13.6.

that has to be understood first."[65] Metaphorical names (such as rock) demonstrate a parallel between God and a rock, but "rock" must first be understood on the creaturely end before understanding how it is being applied to God. On the other hand, nonmetaphorical names are said primarily of God (because they preexist in him transcendentally) and derivatively of creatures.[66]

Thomas then treats the issue of particular divine names. For example, the name "'God' signifies the divine nature," and its meaning is "something that is above all that is, and that is the source of all things and is distinct from them all."[67] Drawing from scripture and John of Damascus, He Who Is (qui est), the name found in Exodus 3:13–14, is "the most appropriate name for God" for two reasons:[68] First, because "it does not signify any particular form, but rather existence itself," and second, "because of its universality." Stated differently, all other divine names are too nuanced or insufficiently general. Thomas is not trying to be vague; rather, his point is that "the less determinate our names are and the more general and simple they are, the more appropriately they may be applied to God" since "any other name selects some particular aspect of the being of the thing, but He Who Is fixes on no aspect of being but stands open to all and refers to him as to an infinite ocean of being."[69] Qui est is an all-encompassing name that more clearly reflects the fact that we cannot know God as he is. More specific names, while still appropriate, create stricter limits of what is named of God and end up constraining our knowledge. They are also said, more importantly, to name God more imperfectly.

In some instances, He Who Is or God may be a more appropriate name than the other. However, "even more appropriate is the Tetragrammaton which is used to signify the incommunicable and, if we could say such a thing, individual substance of God."[70] Thomas references this name in Summa Contra Gentiles 4.7, but Torrell argues that

65. ST 1a.13.6.

66. ST 1a.13.6.

67. ST 1a.13.8.

68. ST 1a.13.11. On Thomas's understanding of Exod 3:14, see D. Stephen Long, The Perfectly Simple Triune God: Aquinas and His Legacy (Minneapolis: Fortress Press, 2016), 70–75.

69. ST 1a.13.11.

70. ST 1a.13.11. It seems that Thomas gained his understanding of this name through Maimonides, or Rabbi Moses, a Spanish Jewish philosopher. See Moses Maimonides, The Guide of the Perplexed, trans. Shlomo Pines (Chicago: University Of Chicago Press, 1963), 1.50–70 (esp. 60–62). Maimonides distinguishes between the Tetragrammaton and "I am who I am." Thomas rejected his much stronger apophatic (i.e., equivocal) view of language. See also Burrell, Knowing the Unknowable God; Mercedes Rubio, Aquinas and Maimonides on the Possibility of

the *Summa theologiae* is the first place that Thomas makes topical use of the name.

> This is a serious shift, because Thomas situates himself not only in the perspective of the name's origin, but in the reality that the same was meant to signify. The name revealed to the believer is preferred to the name arrived at by the philosopher. Entirely singular, this is truly the name above every other name, and it refers only to God.[71]

This name is the truly incommunicable and personal name of God, and this recognition begins to illustrate the progressive nature of Thomas's doctrine of God. On the one hand, moving from creatures (what we know) to God, one must recognize that all divine names are applied analogically, are not synonymous with one another, and truly but imperfectly name what God is. On the other hand, these names (or predicates) preexist in God transcendently, meaning that what is named of God is first found in him in its pure, albeit analogical form. As we recognize these two united but distinct poles, we can begin to better grasp Thomas's approach to the divine names in relation to his doctrine of divine simplicity.[72]

How does Thomas's account of the divine names and divine simplicity relate to scripture? Matthew Levering helpfully describes the biblical character of Aquinas's understanding and explanation of the names of God. In his account,

---

the *Knowledge of God: An Examination of the* Quaestio de attributis, ASJP (Dordrecht, Netherlands: Springer, 2010).

71. Torrell, *Saint Thomas Aquinas*, 2:46. Armand Maurer adds that "the *Summa Theologiae* is the only work of St. Thomas, to my knowledge, that recognizes a divine name that is in a sense more suitable than 'He who is'" ("St. Thomas on the Sacred Name 'Tetragrammaton,'" *MS* 34 [1972]: 62). Thomas's preference for the revealed and personal name of God points to fact that his discussion of the existence, attributes, and names of God is not separable from the revelation of Israel's God as YHWH. Put differently, "however charged with metaphysical language, the questions on the one God have to do with the God of Abraham, Isaac, and Jacob, who will send Christ, not the god of Aristotle's *Physics*" (Kerr, *After Aquinas*, 321).

72. The movement from creatures to God and God to creatures—with God remaining primary—clarifies the relation of God's simplicity and our knowledge of his simplicity: "Our minds do not understand simple forms as they are in themselves, but as though they were concrete things in which there is duality of the thing and the form that it has. In this way we treat simple forms as though they were subjects to which something can be attributed" (*ST* 1a.13.12). Furthermore, "when our minds understand the simple things superior to them we understand them in our own way, that is on the model of composite things; not that we understand the simple things to be composite, but that composition is involved in our way of understanding them. Thus the fact that our statements about God are composite does not make them false" (*ST* 1a.13.12). Cf. *ST* 1a.32.2.

Aquinas' approach unifies metaphysical and scriptural naming. The divine names found in Scripture cannot be understood apart from metaphysical analysis, but nonetheless it is the biblical narrative of salvation that governs the task of divine naming in Aquinas' treatise on God in his oneness.[73]

This unified naming is because "Aquinas developed his entire theology on the basis of a close and direct reference to scripture," and "it is a matter of fact that Scripture was both the source and the measure of Aquinas' theology."[74] Contrary to some modern receptions of Aquinas's theology, scripture plays an important role in both the structure and content of his theology.[75]

THOMAS'S CONTRIBUTIONS

If we recall, Thomas ruled out that God was composed of essence and existence. James Dolezal calls this "his most important contribution to the doctrine of divine simplicity."[76] Thomas first argues that God is identical with his own essence (*ST* 1a.3.3), but he inquires as to whether God's existence differs from his essence. He notes that if "the existence of a thing is to be other than its nature, that existence must either derive from the nature or have an external cause."[77] But, as he already demonstrated, God does not derive from anything nor is he caused since he is the first cause. Second, he states that "when a nature is not itself existence, then, it must be potential of existence," yet "God does not contain potentialities" since it is "God's very nature

73. Levering, *Scripture and Metaphysics*, 52. He adds that "metaphysical analysis clearly can be undertaken apart from Scripture, but Aquinas' metaphysical probing in the *Summa Theologiae* belongs to *sacra doctrina*" (ibid., 52n15). For a more in-depth treatment of Aquinas and scripture, see Wilhelmus Valkenberg, *Words of the Living God: Place and Function of Holy Scripture in the Theology of St. Thomas Aquinas*, PTUNS 6 (Louvain: Peeters, 2000).

74. T. Prügl, "Thomas Aquinas as Interpreter of Scripture," in *The Theology of Thomas Aquinas*, ed. R. Van Nieuwenhove and J. Wawrykow (Notre Dame: University of Notre Dame Press, 2005), 405. Thomas's theology is also influenced by Denys. For more on Thomas's commentary on Denys's text, see Sammon, *The God Who Is Beauty*, 259–88. For a view in contrast to Sammon's, see John D. Jones, "(Mis?)-Reading the Divine Names as a Science: Aquinas' Interpretation of the Divine Names of (Pseudo) Dionysius Areopagite," *SVTQ* 52 (2008): 143–72.

75. For a more detailed account of Thomas's doctrine of divine simplicity in relation to scripture and his moral theology, see Tyler R. Wittman, "'Not a God of Confusion but of Peace': Aquinas and the Meaning of Divine Simplicity," *ModTheo* 32 (2016): 151–69.

76. Dolezal, *God without Parts*, 62.

77. *ST* 1a.3.4.

to exist."[78] Last, things that exist are either existence itself or partakers of existence, but we cannot say that God partakes of existence. He is not only his own essence, but his own existence as well.

What is the significance of this argument? For Thomas, every created thing contains a real distinction between its essence and existence. Following the three points above, all created things are caused, have potency, and are partakers of existence. God's essence and existence is identical, and God is the only one who can account for himself. If he were made of parts or composed in any way, those parts would account for the whole and God would therefore be said to derive his being, existence, or identity from somewhere other than himself. This view surely has similarities with Augustine's and Anselm's doctrines of divine simplicity, for example, but Thomas moves beyond them to greater clarity and depth in light of the available scholastic methods, terms, and concepts.

Thomas also clarifies what was left undeveloped in Augustine—namely, whether the names or predicates used of God are identical in the sense that they are synonymous. Augustine stated that "to be" and "to be wise" are identical in God, leaving some scholars to interpret this as though distinctions do not exist in either human language or in God himself. As seen above, Thomas rejects this entailment and denies that a single reference requires a singular meaning of each divine name. Two points are important here: (1) We may use Frege's well-known example of the morning and evening star. They differ in sense (that is, different names), yet both refer to one and the same thing (that is, Venus). In the same way, each divine name carries a different sense while always referring to the same reality: what God is. (2) Thomas's point about analogy is crucial. There is something in or about God that is analogous to power, analogous to wisdom, and so on, even though all of these names refer to the same thing. Therefore, when the criticism is raised that Augustine's or Aquinas's doctrine of divine simplicity entails an undifferentiated monad because everything in God is identical and indistinguishable, one must remember that Thomas is not talking about real and identical properties that exist or are possessed by God in a univocal sense.

The arguments offered by Thomas are certainly different from the ones encountered in patristic theology. However, the degree of discontinuity is minimal and is primarily the result of a new context

---

78. *ST* 1a.3.4.

that includes the rise of universities, new methods, translations of previously unavailable works, and so forth. Through Lombard and many others, Thomas sees divine simplicity as a key component of the tradition he inherits, and his work seeks to develop its content in new terms and concepts that still maintain the core of what divine simplicity means. In Thomas we find a strong doctrine of divine incomprehensibility, not making God unknowable or nameless, but keeping strict limits on what knowledge can be claimed and how it is claimed. His exposition of divine simplicity originates in scripture and, in one sense, is the result of a hermeneutical difficulty. Nowhere does Thomas claim to derive divine simplicity from exegesis or from a "prooftext." Instead, he believes divine simplicity arises from scripture and is a teaching that must be affirmed in order to read scripture accurately.[79] This point is seen most clearly in his theology of divine names, which is drawn from both scripture and Denys, but also in continuity with earlier theologians covered in the previous section on patristic theology.[80] Divine simplicity, therefore, is a concept that originates in questions about scripture's broad presentation of God's many names. What does it mean to call God light, love, King, and He Who Is?

CONCLUSION

This chapter has attempted to clarify the way some medieval representatives understood the relationship between divine simplicity and scripture. After Augustine, simplicity develops less in response to false teaching and more in terms of clarification and for the purpose of explanation and education. Two biblical themes begin to emerge: the divine name(s) and the doctrine of inseparable operations.[81] From Basil to Thomas Aquinas, these themes receive varied attention but seem to provide the necessary biblical grounding for a doctrine of divine simplicity. The following chapters will add clarity to this point

---

79. As Long points out, scripture "is the overwhelming authority in the first forty-three questions of the *De Deo*" (*The Perfectly Simple Triune God*, 69).

80. The best work on Thomas and Denys remains Fran O'Rourke, *Pseudo-Dionysius and the Metaphysics of Aquinas* (Notre Dame: University of Notre Dame Press, 2005).

81. Scripture played an important role, even in the supposed "speculative" period of medieval scholasticism. As Marcia L. Colish points out, "There is no doubt that medieval Christian thinkers saw the Bible as the book of books and its study as the discipline of disciplines." See Marcia L. Colish, *Peter Lombard* (Leiden: Brill, 1994), 1:155.

and will ultimately lead to chapter 5, on the biblical roots of divine simplicity.[82]

In seeking clarity, the content has been primarily historical, descriptive, and analytical by trying to explain what divine simplicity meant, how it developed, and why it continued to be maintained. It is another question to ask whether each theologian was correct in his perspective on divine simplicity. However, there appears to be sufficient reason to at least give divine simplicity the benefit of the doubt after seeing its continuity in the West and East and across hundreds of years. In the next chapter, I will continue this approach by outlining theologians during the Reformation who assume divine simplicity and do not reject it, even in light of their emphasis on *sola scriptura*. I will then turn to Francis Turretin, John Owen, and Herman Bavinck before arriving at the often-neglected voice of Karl Barth. Oddly, his view has been ignored in the majority of the literature on divine simplicity, and it will be one of my aims to determine whether he can help move the dialogue forward while avoiding many of the criticisms, most notably the issue of divine simplicity and scripture.

---

82. One issue that also becomes clear is that the medieval period does not present one view of divine simplicity. This has much to do with the kind of distinctions drawn between the divine attributes and between the attributes and the divine essence. This means that there is no "traditional account" of divine simplicity, and therefore any account requires greater specificity. Nevertheless, there is greater continuity than discontinuity in trying to express what it means for God to be without parts. On Aquinas, Scotus, and Ockham, see Marilyn McCord Adams, *William Ockham* (Notre Dame: University of Notre Dame Press, 1987), 903–60. In *Medieval Trinitarian Thought from Aquinas to Ockham* (Cambridge: Cambridge University Press), Russell L. Friedman argues that the fourteenth century included "one main theological motivation" that he calls "The Search for Simplicity" (98). The thirteenth century's approach to trinitarian theology can be understood according to the category of "explanation." As Friedman points out, "in order to explain something we need to draw distinctions" and the thirteenth-century theologians Friedman analyzes "all thought that the types of distinctions that they were positing in order to explain certain facts about the Trinity were fully compatible with divine simplicity" (ibid., 99–100). However, in the fourteenth century "a group of theologians to all intents and purposes claim that divine simplicity is more important than trinitarian explanation" (ibid., 100). Therefore, "theologians who followed the search for simplicity judged that it was better to leave matters unexplained than to posit the distinction in God that would be required in order to explain them" (ibid.). For an assessment of Friedman's narrative, see Richard Cross, review of *Medieval Trinitarian Thought from Aquinas to Ockham*, by Russell Friedman, *Notre Dame Philosophical Reviews* (2010).

4.

Divine Simplicity from the Reformation to Karl Barth

Following the patristic and medieval conceptions of divine simplicity, the Reformation and post-Reformation mark a time of significant change. Yet does this mean that the doctrine of divine simplicity itself changed? Surely, it was not at the center of the Reformation debates, but that does not mean that it received little or no attention from the Reformation to the early modern periods. In this chapter, I will begin with a brief overview of the Reformation and early modern approaches to God and divine simplicity. Next, I will continue the approach of previous chapters—choosing representative theologians who espouse the doctrine of divine simplicity—and will look at John Calvin, John Owen, Francis Turretin, Charles Hodge, Herman Bavinck, and finally Karl Barth. I will also continue with the aim of seeing how each theologian incorporates scripture into their understanding of divine simplicity, if at all.

REFORMATION AND POST-REFORMATION APPROACHES TO GOD AND DIVINE SIMPLICITY

The Reformed orthodox approach to the doctrine of God has been helpfully researched and presented by Richard Muller and more recently by Dolf te Velde.[1] They both note that there is continuity

---

1. Richard A. Muller, *Post-Reformation Reformed Dogmatics*, vol. 3, *The Divine Essence and*

and discontinuity between the Reformation and medieval scholasticism, as well as the Reformation and post-Reformation. Although aspects of Muller's project have been critiqued,[2] both works remain a reliable and helpful starting point to paint a broad picture of the context and motivation for a doctrine of divine simplicity in the Reformation period.[3] Therefore, in this section, I will present some of these general approaches to the doctrine of God. After this, I will give a brief overview of the names of God, the content of divine simplicity, the importance of distinctions, and the place of scripture.

GENERAL FEATURES OF THE DOCTRINE OF GOD

The Reformation doctrine of God does not mark a completely new teaching or approach. Rather, it has great continuity with medieval scholasticism and the early patristic tradition when it comes to the content. Where they differ is in their particular approach to this content, specifically in the scholastic use of philosophical and metaphysical tools in relation to the doctrine of God. In contrast, Reformation thought represents a "distrust for philosophical speculation and a high degree of concern for the biblical basis of theology."[4] Therefore, the rejection of scholasticism was not wholesale, but rather "involved the rejection of speculative excesses of a method and the rejection of certain doctrinal conclusions, particularly concerning the doctrines of salvation and the church."[5] As Muller concludes, "The underlying assumptions governing the doctrine of God during the eras of the

---

Attributes, 2nd ed. (Grand Rapids: Baker Academic, 2003). Hereafter, PRRD and volume number. See also Dolf te Velde, The Doctrine of God in Reformed Orthodoxy, Karl Barth, and the Utrecht School: A Study in Method and Content, SRT (Leiden: Brill, 2013). This first section is indebted to Muller's and Velde's work.

2. For example, see Douglas Kelly, "A Rehabilitation of Scholasticism? A Review Article on Richard A. Muller's Post-Reformation Reformed Dogmatics, Vol. 1, Prolegomena To Theology," SBET 6 (1988): 112–22; Martin I. Klauber, "Continuity and Discontinuity in Post-Reformation Reformed Theology: An Evaluation of the Muller Thesis," JETS 33 (1990): 467–75.

3. For "Aquinas's legacy among the reformers," see D. Stephen Long, The Perfectly Simple God: Aquinas and His Legacy (Minneapolis: Fortress Press, 2016), 119–70.

4. Muller, PRRD, 3:31. For more on the use of philosophy in theology during this time, see Richard A. Muller, Post-Reformation Reformed Dogmatics, vol. 1, Prolegomena to Theology, 2nd ed. (Grand Rapids: Baker Academic, 2003), 360–405. For more on Muller's presentation of the medieval background, see 53–58, 70–76.

5. Muller, PRRD, 3:85.

Reformation and Protestant orthodoxy are very little different from those governing the discussion during the Middle Ages."[6]

Although there may be differences in the use of philosophy, this does not mean that the Reformers ignored or rejected philosophy altogether. It was possible, for example, for metaphysics to serve theology. As Velde points out, "Metaphysical truth must be maintained when investigating the implications of biblical statements."[7] Even in the seventeenth century, a time often understood to be highly metaphysical, the Reformed orthodox works "reflected arguments found in the natural theologies and the metaphysics of the era—but in the context of a use of Scripture as the primary source for the doctrine of essence and attributes."[8] Most treatments of God addressed five topics—namely, the divine names, being, attributes, works, and persons of God.[9] By not rejecting metaphysics and instead subordinating it to scripture, the Reformed orthodox maintained many traditional doctrines even when their approach and defense of them varied from their precursors. Within a time that sought to return to scripture and challenge aspects of tradition, it is telling that divine simplicity remained "a governing concept in the doctrine of God . . . throughout the orthodox era and on into the early eighteenth century."[10] At this stage, it is important to understand how the Reformed orthodox arrived at their doctrine of divine simplicity.

THE NAMES OF GOD

A "major mark of continuity" between the Reformation and orthodoxy was the divine names in relation to scripture. This "was not, typically, a pattern reminiscent of the medieval scholastic systems . . . [and] must be understood as an indication of the importance of the text of Scripture."[11] Because of the significance of scripture, the names of God act as the "primary source" with regard to the doctrine of God. This "fundamental biblicism" produces an exegetical motive

6. Ibid., 3:97.

7. Velde, *The Doctrine of God*, 109.

8. Muller, *PRRD*, 3:169.

9. Velde, *The Doctrine of God*, 111.

10. Muller, *PRRD*, 3:217. Velde writes that "all Reformed orthodox theologians believe in the simplicity of God" (Velde, *The Doctrine of God*, 131).

11. Muller, *PRRD*, 3:98–99. While the divine names may not be a typical pattern for medieval scholasticism in general, the previous chapter did advance the point that the names of God were important for Thomas's account of divine simplicity.

that results in an interest in the divine names in order to "offer a primary way of approach to the identity of God."[12] The great majority of Reformed orthodox theologians followed this approach, treating "the names of God immediately prior to and as a ground of the discussion of the individual attributes of God," giving them a "natural point of contact between the biblical language of God and a more strictly philosophical discussion."[13] Overall, the starting point with the biblical divine names provides the Reformed orthodox with a biblical basis for their doctrine of God and the divine attributes. Yet, how does this approach affect their doctrine of divine simplicity?

DIVINE SIMPLICITY

Muller's research led him to the conclusion that "divine simplicity was held by virtually all of the orthodox theologians of the sixteenth and seventeenth centuries," and that "from the time of the fathers onward, divine simplicity was understood as a support of the doctrine of the Trinity and as necessarily defined in such a manner as to argue the 'manifold' as well as the non-composite character of God."[14] The universal support for this doctrine was related to the biblical nature of the teaching. For anyone to protest that divine simplicity "might not be easily rooted in the text of Scripture . . . was never taken particularly seriously . . . given . . . that the alternative to the doctrine of divine simplicity is so bizarre as to be neither amenable to any exegetical result nor acceptable to reason."[15] This is because composite beings have both a beginning and an end and therefore have potential. To have parts means that a person is separable, divisible, or was at one time not the whole that they are now. In contrast, scripture teaches that God is eternal—even if this is not understood as timelessness—having always existed and being immortal by nature.

This does not mean, however, that divine simplicity was without its opponents. As we have seen in the previous chapter, divine simplicity has both developed and been maintained in relation to false teachings throughout various generations. During the time of the Reformation, both Vorstius and the Socinians were staunchly

12. Ibid., 3:246.
13. Ibid., 3:248. For a longer assessment of the Reformation approach to the individual names of God, see 248–70.
14. Ibid., 3:275, 276.
15. Ibid., 3:276.

opposed to divine simplicity, specifically in relation to the Trinity.[16] However, the orthodox theologians saw divine simplicity and the Trinity as two "interdependent" doctrines that nevertheless were stated in different ways: "Simplicity with respect to essence, trinity with respect to persons."[17] Both statements must be affirmed, although in their own particular ways.

Aside from the opposition to the Trinity and simplicity, the Reformed orthodox recognized that divine simplicity could not be stated in such a way that ignores or even rejects distinctions within God. There *are* distinctions, but it is the *kind* of distinctions that is important. In fact, "the entire force of the Reformed scholastic argument is to deny in God *only* those distinctions that imply composition, namely, real distinctions and, therefore, to point toward the *proper* distinctions that do subsist among the attributes and between the attributes and the divine essence."[18] A deeper understanding requires greater clarity regarding which distinctions were found unacceptable and which ones were discovered to be necessary.

DISTINCTIONS WITHIN GOD

The orthodox theologians sought to avoid the error of nominalism. As it relates to divine simplicity, nominalism essentially teaches that any distinction between God's essence and his attributes (or among the attributes) exists in God's revelation *ad extra* or merely in the human conception of his attributes. It rejects, therefore, the belief that these distinctions exist *ad intra*, and so any human speech about God is recognized to be true in name *only* and not true of God's immanent life. To avoid this error, the orthodox theologians took up a number of traditional views on the distinctions within God.

First, there are real distinctions. Distinction exists between one essence and another essence, and therefore cannot be applied to God. Second, there are formal, modal, eminent, and virtual distinctions that can be asserted *in* things. They do not cause the thing to be viewed as composite, but one can recognize differentiation within the thing. Thus, "in the case of the trinitarian relations and divine attributes,

---

16. See ibid., 3:276–83.
17. Ibid., 3:282, 283. Muller's words come from Francis Turretin.
18. Ibid., 3:278 (emphasis original).

such distinctions can and do apply to God."[19] Third, there are rational distinctions "by reason of analysis (*ratio ratiocinata*) founded in the thing" and "purely rational (*ratio rationans*) distinctions." The latter is nearer to nominalism by locating the distinction more so in the mind than in a thing. Even in light of the diversity of views on these distinctions, Muller concludes that "all of the Reformed ortho-dox assume the simplicity of the divine essence, and all understand the attributes as in some sense distinct."[20] Such a discussion of the distinctions in relation to divine simplicity illustrates the willingness among the Reformed orthodox to make use of philosophy as a tool for doing theology. Yet the crucial question in this project is how the doctrine of divine simplicity relates to scripture, the primary source and authority for Reformation teaching.

SCRIPTURE AND DIVINE SIMPLICITY

This issue naturally requires a return to the biblical names of God. "The divine names present a biblical point of entry into the rather abstruse and necessarily metaphysical discussion of the essence and attributes."[21] The subject of the divine names demonstrates how the plurality and diversity of divine names raises the questions of how these are predicated of God. How are they related to his essence? How are they related to each other? Are they truly distinct? These questions were brought forth by revelation in scripture and explained with the aid of philosophy and traditional conceptions. At the same time, it must be noted that "the Reformation . . . did very little to revise the dogmatic content of the doctrine of God." What it did offer was, first, a doctrine that was "built far more consistently and profoundly on the text of Scripture." Second, the doctrine of God was presented not with initial reflection on the divine essence, but by starting with the divine names in scripture and only then discussing the divine essence and traditional attributes. Third, they would "insist on relating each doctrinal topic to the Christian life."[22] One might expect that if divine simplicity were lacking an exegetical footing that it would be dropped as a teaching full of cold, speculative, and meta-physical elements when compared to any other time in the history

19. Ibid., 3:286.
20. Ibid., 3:296.
21. Ibid., 3:248.
22. Ibid., 3:134.

of theology. Instead, this doctrine was upheld throughout this period and even defended in light of the attacks from Vorstius and various Socinians. After giving this brief overview, it is now important to take a more detailed look at how certain theologians understood divine simplicity as a biblical teaching.

JOHN CALVIN

Muller's and Velde's overviews provide a helpful starting point, but their claims must be confirmed and extended through examples. Calvin is well known for his preference for brevity, but he is also known for his distaste for speculation. One would expect, therefore, that he would have no patience for a supposed metaphysical doctrine of divine simplicity with little to no relation to scripture. Calvin did view late medieval theology as a speculative enterprise, causing him to disagree with a number of theological issues, yet this does not mean that he completely parted ways with all late medieval theology. Writing on the doctrine of angels, Calvin pauses to remind his readers of a general principle when approaching Christian doctrine:

> Let us remember here, as in all religious doctrine, that we ought to hold to one rule of modesty and sobriety: not to speak, or guess, or even to seek to know, concerning obscure matters anything except what has been imparted to us by God's Word. Furthermore, in the reading of Scripture we ought ceaselessly to endeavor to seek out and meditate upon those things which make for edification. Let us not indulge in curiosity or in the investigation of unprofitable things. And because the Lord willed to instruct us, not in fruitless questions, but in sound godliness, in the fear of his name, in true trust, and in the duties of holiness, let us be satisfied with this knowledge.[23]

This concern for speculation also applies to the doctrine of God: "[It] is not for us to attempt with bold curiosity to penetrate to the investigation of his essence, which we ought more to adore than meticulously to search out."[24] Of course, Calvin affirms that a person can

---

23. John Calvin, *Institutes of the Christian Religion*, ed. John T. McNeill, trans. Ford Lewis Battles, LCC 20–21 (Philadelphia: Westminster, 1960), 1.14.4. All quotations of Calvin are from this translation. On the relationship of Calvin and scholasticism, see Richard A. Muller, *The Unaccommodated Calvin: Studies in the Foundation of a Theological Tradition* (New York: Oxford University Press, 2001), 44–58.

24. Calvin, *Institutes* 1.5.9.

have knowledge of God even though God's essence is an impenetrable mystery that is beyond human knowledge. Even so, Calvin prohibits speculation, curiosity, and imagination that go beyond the teachings of scripture.[25] Yet, does this mean that Calvin limits theology to the words and concepts of scripture alone? If this is the case, then again, it seems Calvin would be inclined to reject divine simplicity on the grounds that it is a speculative teaching with little or no basis in scripture.

Elsewhere in the *Institutes* Calvin argues that "we ought to seek from Scripture a sure rule for both thinking and speaking" and relates this to the terminology used to express the doctrine of the Trinity. Such terms were not "rashly invented" but became "especially useful when the truth is asserted against false accusers."[26] These terms may be foreign to scripture, but they add clarity in response to false teaching and aid the proper interpretation of scripture. Rather than being a source of speculation or curiosity, the terms actually draw the reader into scripture and toward the edifying truth found in God's revelation of himself.

Calvin may have an aversion to speculation and a desire to limit Christian teachings to the Word, but this does not mean that he expects mere repetition of scripture, especially in the face of false teaching. However, even if this is granted, it does not mean that Calvin should be expected to find significance in the doctrine of divine simplicity. He may, instead, find sufficient reason to reject the teaching. Yet in the *Institutes* Calvin displays a clear and consistent belief that even though we can never truly know the essence of God, it must be asserted that it is simple and undivided.[27]

In his section on the Trinity, Calvin states that "the essence of God

---

25. As Warfield notes, "*Reverence* for God was the great thing for Calvin. . . . His doctrine of God has the *practical* end of serving the needs of his fellow-believers." See B. B. Warfield, "Calvin's Doctrine of God," in *Calvin and Calvinism*, ed. Samuel G. Craig (New York: Oxford University Press, 1931), 141.

26. Calvin, *Institutes* 1.13.3–5.

27. Calvin's denial of the knowledge of God's essence stems from his distinction between knowledge of the *quid* and knowledge of the *quails*—knowledge of what God is in himself and knowledge of what he is toward us. For Calvin, we only know God as he is toward us, but this should not be taken as a form of nominalism. We know God by virtue of his attributes, which "are true determinations of the divine nature and truly reveal to us the kind of a person [God] is; he is only refusing to speculate on what God is apart from His attributes. . . . He is refusing all *a priori* methods of determining the nature of God" (Warfield, "Calvin's Doctrine of God," 152–53). In other words, Calvin's avoidance of speculation is his "refusal to go behind the attributes" and search for a deeper knowledge than we have already been given (ibid, 155).

is simple and undivided," meaning that God "contains all in him-self, without portion or derivation, but in integral perfection."[28] As it pertains to the three divine persons, they do not result in "a dis-tinction of essence, which it is unlawful to make manifold."[29] Such a distinction would violate divine simplicity; however, this does not mean that the divine essence lacks distinctions. It is here that Calvin puts forth a helpful rule when considering divine simplicity and the Trinity: there is "a distinction, not a division."[30] A division implies not only three Gods but also multiple parts that make up the divine essence. However, a distinction is not a division, but still allows and even requires plurality even within the simple, ontological oneness. Furthermore, in response to false teachings on the Trinity, Calvin implores his readers: "If we hold fast to what has been sufficiently shown above from Scripture—that the essence of the one God is sim-ple and undivided, and that it belongs to the Father, the Son, and Spirit . . . , the gate will be closed not only to Arius and Sabellius but to other ancient authors of errors."[31] Calvin does not provide a prooftext for divine simplicity, but he does not find the teaching to be speculative or beyond the teachings or implications of scripture.

Finally, in the last chapter of book 1, Calvin teaches that God's will is a unity. At this point, divine simplicity functions as a teaching that helps him read scripture accurately. Some object that "if nothing happens apart from God's will, [then] there are in him two contrary wills." After citing a number of passages to the contrary, Calvin con-cludes, "Yet, God's will is not therefore at war with itself, nor does it change, nor does it pretend not to will what he wills. But even though his will is one and simple, it appears manifold to us." Why? "Because, on account of our mental incapacity, we do not grasp how in divers ways it wills and does not will something to take place."[32] This distinction between the Creator and creature, between the infinite and finite, grounds Calvin's understanding of our diverse

---

28. Calvin, *Institutes* 1.8.2. Calvin's commentaries mention divine simplicity in passing, but it is merely assumed and does not receive the same form of explanation as found in the *Insti-tutes*. For one example, see Calvin's comments on Ps. 77:9. The main reason for this brevity is likely Calvin's tendency in the *Institutes* to explain loci and arguments inherent in scripture. Cf. Muller, *The Unaccommodated Calvin*, 24–38, 140–58.

29. Calvin, *Institutes* 1.8.2.

30. Calvin, *Institutes* 1.8.17.

31. Calvin, *Institutes* 1.8.22.

32. Calvin, *Institutes* 1.18.3. See also John Calvin, *Calvin's Calvinism : Treatises on "The Eternal Predestination of God" and "The Secret Providence of God,"* trans. Henry Cole (Grand Rapids: Reformed Free, 1987), 307.

experience in relation to God's simple unity. Even "God's wisdom appears manifold," and yet we would never "dream that there is any variation in God himself" and therefore must "recall our mental incapacity."[33] For God to "will" what he "forbids" is beyond our understanding, but Calvin believes it is clearly taught in scripture and that God's will cannot be divided into two contradictory or conflicting wills since his will is one and simple.[34]

JOHN OWEN

In his examination of Socinianism, John Owen responds to John Biddle's rejection of the Trinity and divine simplicity.[35] Specifically, Owen is responding to Biddle's argument that God "is limited, and of us to be comprehended; his essence and being consisting of several principles, whereby he is in a capacity of being what he is not."[36] This leads Owen to clarify the teaching of divine simplicity in relation to scripture and other doctrines. God is a "simple act," and this is meant to "deny him to be compounded of diverse principles, and assert him to be always actually in being, existence, and intent operation." God's name, I AM, refers to his "simple being, existing in and of itself," and this means that he cannot be "compounded with anything whatever."[37]

Owen's doctrine of divine simplicity is worked out in relation to other teachings and with further support from scripture. First, divine simplicity is true of God only if we understand his "absolute independence and firstness in being and operation."[38] God's "firstness" is derived from Isaiah 44:6, Revelation 1:8, and Romans 11:35–36. God was not caused by anything, and nothing existed prior to him. However, this would not be true if God is said to be *composed* of parts. The very idea of composition, for Owen, implies the existence of these

33. Calvin, *Institutes* 1.18.3.
34. The confessions of the Reformation period also present an inherited doctrine of divine simplicity. For representative examples, see the Augsburg Confession (1530), Belgic Confession (1561, rev. 1619), Thirty-Nine Articles (1563), Second Helvetic Confession (1566), Westminster Confession (1646), and the Savoy Declaration (1658).
35. See John Owen, *Vindiciae Evangelicae: The Mystery of the Gospel Vindicated and Socinianism Examined*, WJO 12 (Edinburgh: Banner of Truth, 1966), 70–73. See also Carl R. Trueman, *John Owen: Reformed Catholic, Renaissance Man* (Aldershot: Ashgate, 2007), 38–39.
36. Owen, *Vindiciae Evangelicae*, 71.
37. Ibid.
38. Ibid.

parts alongside God or before God. In this sense, God is not truly first, independent, superior, or simple.

Second, Owen argues that God is "perfectly one and the same, and nothing differs from his essence in it."[39] Drawing God's oneness from Deuteronomy 6:4 and God's sameness from Psalm 102:27, he asserts that "where there is an absolute oneness and sameness in the whole, there is no composition by an union of extremes."[40] He further supports this view from Exodus 3:14–15 and Revelation 1:8, which characterize God as one who cannot truly be "all that he is in himself" if he is composed of parts, accidents, or principles.

Third, the divine attributes are all "essentially the same with one another" and "the same with the essence of God itself." This has been a traditional element of the doctrine of divine simplicity going back to Aquinas and, with less detail, as far back as Augustine. Owen arrives at this view through two forms of reasoning: (1) scripture speaks of the attributes together, such as God's "eternal power" (Rom 1:20) or "faithful love" (Ps 13:5); (2) the attributes are either infinitely perfect or are finite. To deny this last statement is problematic, for "if they are not the same with God, there are more things infinite than one, and consequently more Gods," and it also implies that "God knows not himself, for a finite wisdom cannot know perfectly an infinite being."[41]

Finally, God must be understood to be a "simple act." To say otherwise is to acknowledge some form of potentiality in God. Owen further links God as simple act to divine immutability, noting that "every composition whatever is of power and act; which if it be, or might have been in God, he could not be said to be immutable."[42] If divine simplicity is rejected, then divine immutability must be rejected as well. Overall, Owen's biblical and theological arguments for divine simplicity are rather traditional, but are, as many before him, also in response to false teaching.

FRANCIS TURRETIN

Francis Turretin's presentation of divine simplicity shows many similarities to Owen, but Turretin goes into greater detail. Some of this

39. Ibid., 72.
40. Ibid.
41. Ibid.
42. Ibid.

is surely due to Turretin's systematic treatment of theology in his *Institutes of Elenctic Theology*. In this work, Turretin begins with the unity of God and moves on to discuss God's incommunicable name, Jehovah. It is only from there that he presents his doctrine of divine simplicity and the other divine attributes, all of which leads to his exposition of the Trinity. Similar to Owen, Turretin responds to various Socinians, who seek to weaken the doctrine of the Trinity by finding composition in God and denying "that simplicity can be attributed to God according to the Scriptures."[43] Not only do the Socinians believe that divine simplicity causes problems for the Trinity, but they also do not believe it is scriptural.

Turretin first draws a distinction between two senses of divine simplicity: absolute and relative. Absolute simplicity means that "every kind of being excludes composition," whereas relative simplicity is the idea that "excludes [composition] only with respect to some."[44] For example, angels and souls are simple in relation to bodies. Nevertheless, they still represent a form of composition since there is a real distinction between their essence and existence. God's simplicity "is his incommunicable attribute by which the divine nature is conceived by us not only as free from all composition, but also as *incapable* of composition and divisibility."[45] Similar to Owen, Turretin starts to prove God's simplicity by arguing from God's independence, unity, perfection, and his activity as pure act.[46] However, Turretin goes on to define composition with greater clarity than Owen. Turretin states that the removal of composition from God's essence includes any composition that is physical, of quantitative parts, subject or accident, logical, metaphysical act and power, or essence and existence.[47] All of these forms of composition break down to the fact that, at their essence, "there is more than one real entity."[48]

---

43. Francis Turretin, *Institutes of Elenctic Theology*, ed. James T. Dennison Jr., trans. George Musgrave Giger (Phillipsburg, NJ: P&R, 1992), 3.7.1 (1:191). Further quotations of Turretin are from this edition, with volume and page numbers in parentheses. Turretin also attributes the denial of divine simplicity to Vorstius and the Remonstrants. Readers concerned that Turretin's doctrine of God amounts to mere metaphysical reasoning should consult Sebastian Rehnman, "Theistic Metaphysics and Biblical Exegesis: Francis Turretin on the Concept of God," *RelS* 38 (2001): 167–86.

44. Turretin, *Institutes* 3.7.2 (1:191).

45. Turretin, *Institutes* 3.7.3 (1:191, emphasis added).

46. Turretin, *Institutes* 3.7.4 (1:191).

47. Turretin, *Institutes* 3.7.5 (1:192).

48. Turretin, *Institutes* 3.7.8 (1:192).

This statement cannot be said of God, whether regarding the divine persons or his divine attributes.

Turretin also anticipates the objections related to the incarnation and the Trinity. Regarding the incarnation, Turretin clarifies that the Son is "God-man (*theanthropos*) not by composition properly so-called, but by hypostatic union," meaning that "the human nature did thence receive perfection, but nothing was added by it to the divine nature."[49] He also clarifies that the three divine persons do not *compose* the divine essence since they "are modes distinguishing indeed the persons, from each other, but not composing because they are not real entities concurring to the composition of some fourth thing." He summarizes it in this way: "Simplicity in respect to essence, but Trinity in respect to persons."[50] Turretin certainly believes that divine simplicity is a teaching stemming from scripture that supports, rather than hinders, the doctrine of the Trinity and the incarnation.

Turretin also follows the tradition by drawing particular distinctions between the relationship of the divine essence and attributes. He defines attributes in two ways: (1) as "the essential properties by which [God] makes himself known to us" and (2) as "those which are attributed to him according to the measure of our conception."[51] The latter definition leads Turretin to point to the fact that the attributes represent God's nature "only inadequately." This is because our finite minds fail to adequately conceive of God's essence in totality, therefore requiring that we divide the concepts so that we can at least understand some aspect. "Thus omnipotence is the divine essence itself apprehended as free from every obstacle in acting; eternity is the essence of God as without limit in duration; and so of the rest."[52] Naturally, these statements lead to the need to understand how the attributes relate to God's essence and each other if they are in some sense finite conceptions of the whole of God's essence.

Contrary to the Socinians, who find a real distinction between God's essence and attributes, Turretin argues that they must be distinguished virtually and eminently. This distinction must be admitted because it "is evident from the diversity of conceptions."[53] The

---

49. Turretin, *Institutes* 3.7.7 (1:192).

50. Turretin, *Institutes* 3.7.8 (1:193). Turretin also clarifies the relationship between divine simplicity, the divine decrees, and God's relation to the world (3.7.10–13 [1:193]).

51. Turretin, *Institutes* 3.5.1 (1:187).

52. Turretin, *Institutes* 3.5.3 (1:188).

53. Turretin, *Institutes* 3.5.8 (1:188).

distinction is neither real, nor formal, but nor does this result in a form of nominalism. The diversity of conceptions is on the human end, but its foundation is in the divine essence rather than the human mind. Consequently, Turretin can reason that "the properties are many on the part of the object and end (or of the operations and effects), but not on the part of the subject or principle, which is one and perfectly simple."[54] This view has many parallels to Calvin's, especially when Turretin summarizes that "distinction is not composition."[55] Turretin's understanding of divine simplicity follows fairly traditional notions and places him with the majority of other Reformed scholastic theologians.[56]

MODERN PERSPECTIVES ON DIVINE SIMPLICITY

Having surveyed the various arguments for divine simplicity in Calvin, Owen, and Turretin, it is becoming increasingly evident that divine simplicity maintains its significance for any understanding and presentation of the divine attributes, and that it is recognized as a biblical teaching even if such a view is assumed rather than demonstrated. Part of the reason for its assumption is, as Muller and Velde point out, because divine simplicity as a teaching of scripture seemed obvious and did not warrant the need for repeated arguments since other doctrines were facing heavier opposition and therefore deserved more time and space. Other theologians could be included between the times of Turretin and Hodge such as Jonathan Edwards,[57]

---

54. Turretin, *Institutes* 3.5.14 (1:189).

55. Turretin, *Institutes* 3.7.16 (1:194).

56. Peter van Mastricht argued in his *Theoretic-practica theologia* (1655) that John 4:24 is the biblical foundation for a doctrine of divine simplicity. See Adriaan C. Neele, *Petrus van Mastricht (1630–1706), Reformed Orthodoxy: Method and Piety*, BSCH (Leiden: Brill, 2009), 221–44. Others followed his lead—e.g., see Dolf te Velde, ed., *Synopsis Purioris Theologiae / Synopsis of a Purer Theology: Latin Text and English Translation: Disputations 1–23*, trans. Riemer Faber, SMRT (Leiden: Brill, 2014).

57. For example, Jonathan Edwards could have been included in this analysis. I have not included him because his particular doctrine of divine simplicity has rarely been followed or imitated by theologians after him, perhaps because it stands further outside of the tradition. Furthermore, Edwards does not offer an extended or detailed discussion of divine simplicity in his works (nor does he relate divine simplicity to scripture). This, and other reasons, has caused an ongoing debate as to whether Edwards's doctrine of divine simplicity is compatible with his doctrine of divine excellency and the Trinity. For those who believe Edwards did not hold to divine simplicity, see Amy Plantinga Pauw, *"The Supreme Harmony of All": The Trinitarian Theology of Jonathan Edwards* (Grand Rapids: Eerdmans, 2002); Plantinga Pauw, "'One Alone Can-

Friedrich Schleiermacher,[58] or Isaak Dorner,[59] but it remains important to also understand how divine simplicity was received in America, through Hodge, and how it was more thoroughly exposited in the Dutch Reformed tradition through Herman Bavinck.

---

not be Excellent': Edwards on Divine Simplicity," in *Jonathan Edwards: Philosophical Theologian*, ed. Paul Helm and Oliver Crisp (Aldershot: Ashgate, 2003), 115–25; Michael J. McClymond, "Hearing the Symphony: A Critique of Some Critics of Sang Lee's and Amy Pauw's Accounts of Jonathan Edwards' View of God," in *Jonathan Edwards as Contemporary: Essays in Honor of Sang Lee* (New York: Peter Lang, 2010), 67–92; Gerald McDermott, "Jonathan Edwards and God's Inner Life: A Response to Kyle Strobel," *Themelios* 39 (2014): 241–50; Michael J. McClymond and Gerald R. McDermott, *The Theology of Jonathan Edwards* (Oxford: Oxford University Press, 2012). For those who believe Edwards had a doctrine of divine simplicity, see Oliver D. Crisp, "Jonathan Edwards on Divine Simplicity," *RelS* 39 (2003): 23–41; Crisp, "Jonathan Edwards's God: Trinity, Individuation, and Divine Simplicity," in *Engaging the Doctrine of God: Contemporary Protestant Perspectives*, ed. Bruce L. McCormack (Grand Rapids: Baker Academic, 2008), 83–106; Crisp, *Jonathan Edwards on God and Creation* (Oxford: Oxford University Press, 2012); Stephen R. Holmes, "Does Jonathan Edwards Use a Dispositional Ontology? A Response to Sang Hyun Lee," in *Jonathan Edwards: Philosophical Theologian*, ed. Paul Helm and Oliver Crisp (Aldershot: Ashgate, 2003), 99–114; Kyle C. Strobel, *Jonathan Edwards's Theology: A Reinterpretation*, SST (Bloomsbury T&T Clark, 2013). Even though these scholars agree that Edwards held to divine simplicity, they still find many problems with his particular understanding of the teaching. For example, see Crisp's essay on the "Edwardsian Dilemma" in Oliver Crisp, "On the Orthodoxy of Jonathan Edwards," *SJT* 67 (2014): 304–22.

58. For examples, see Friedrich Schleiermacher, *Christian Faith*, ed. Catherine L. Kelsey and Terrence N. Tice, trans. Terrence N. Tice, Catherine L. Kelsey, and Edwina Lawler (Louisville: Westminster John Knox, 2016), §50–56, §79–85, §167–69. Schleiermacher is clear that "the doctrine of God, as set forth in the totality of the divine attributes, can only be completed simultaneously with the whole system" (§31.2). In this sense, he does not have an independent doctrine of divine simplicity, but deploys the concept throughout *Christian Faith*, albeit with a different form and content from the tradition. On his view of the divine attributes and divine simplicity, see Gerhard Ebeling, "Schleiermacher's Doctrine of the Divine Attributes," in *Schleiermacher as Contemporary*, ed. Robert W. Funk (New York: Herder & Herder, 1970), 125–75; Richard R. Niebuhr, "Schleiermacher and the Names of God," in Funk, *Schleiermacher as Contemporary*, 176–215; B. A. Gerrish, "Theology within the Limits of Piety Alone: Schleiermacher and Calvin's Notion of God," in *The Old Protestantism and the New: Essays on the Reformation Heritage* (Chicago: University of Chicago Press, 1982), 196–207; Bruce L. McCormack, "Not a Possible God but the God Who Is: Observations on Friedrich Schleiermacher's Doctrine of God," in *The Reality of Faith in Theology: Studies on Karl Barth (Princeton-Kampen Consultation 2005)*, ed. Bruce L. McCormack and Gerrit Neven (Bern: Peter Lang, 2007), 111–39; Daniel J. Pedersen, "Schleiermacher and Reformed Scholastics on the Divine Attributes," *IJST* 17 (2015): 413–31.

59. See Isaak A. Dorner, *Divine Immutability: A Critical Reconsideration*, TMT (Minneapolis: Fortress Press, 2000), 137–61. Dorner redefines divine simplicity, allowing for immanent distinctions in God. He also argues for love as the primary attribute amid the other divine attributes, a view similar to Schleiermacher's, even though Dorner understands this notion as an ethical rather than a metaphysical concept. On the connection of Dorner to Schleiermacher, see Robert Sherman, "Isaak August Dorner on Divine Immutability: A Missing Link between Schleiermacher and Barth," *JR* 77 (1997): 380–401.

CHARLES HODGE

Hodge is a unique figure based on his reception of the doctrine of divine simplicity. He discerns a distinction between the divine attributes and predicates (indicating God's relation to creatures), properties (particular to the divine persons), and accidents (qualities that do not belong to the divine essence). True attributes of God are those "without which He would cease to be God."[60] How do the divine attributes relate to the divine essence? Here, Hodge wants to avoid two extremes: the "realists" of the Middle Ages who ascribed genuine existence to the attributes, thus making God composite, and the "nominalists" who understood the attributes as "mere words" and therefore confounded the attributes, "making them all mean the same thing, which is equivalent to denying them all together."[61] Hodge argues that the Lutheran and Reformed theologians did not successfully avoid the nominalist extreme, teaching that God lacks any kind of composition and that the attributes only differ in conception.

In light of the failed Lutherans and Reformed attempts to describe the divine attributes' relation the divine essence, Hodge strongly criticizes any form of nominalism. To say that the attributes "differ only in name" is to "destroy all true knowledge of God."[62] Claiming that the attributes are identical (for example, Augustine and Aquinas) still results in nominalism. "If in God eternity is identical with knowledge, knowledge with power, power with ubiquity, and ubiquity with holiness, we are using words without meaning when we attribute any perfection to God."[63] Such a view, for Hodge, is ultimately "derogatory to God."[64]

Although Hodge rejects both the realist and nominalist distinctions between the divine attributes, he argues that "there should be a real distinction between the divine attributes" because "there is in God a reason why we think of Him as possessing these diverse perfections."[65] Despite his use of "real distinction," Hodge clarifies his view, arguing that "the divine attributes differ neither *realiter* [really], nor

60. Charles Hodge, *Systematic Theology* (Peabody, MA: Hendrickson, 2003), 1:369.
61. Ibid. Hodge does not name any of the realists, but labels Ockham and Biel as nominalists.
62. Ibid., 1:371.
63. Ibid., 1:372.
64. Ibid. Hodge also argues that causality is to be rejected. This view argues that "when we say God is just, we mean nothing more than that He causes misery to follow sin," or that it must be said that "God is not holy, He is only the cause of holiness" (1:373).
65. Ibid., 1:372, 373.

nominaliter [nominally], but *virtualiter* [virtually]."[66] It is true that God is wise, omnipotent, and good, but it is here that Hodge reveals his underlying concern: "We are not to give up the conviction that God is really Himself what He reveals Himself to be, to satisfy any metaphysical speculations as to the difference between essence and attribute in an infinite Being."[67] Nominalism empties God's self-revelation of its content and trustworthiness, leading a person to question whether their knowledge of God is true of who God really is. Hodge aligns himself with Turretin's virtual distinction, but he fails to realize that this is the same distinction drawn by Thomas as well as many Lutheran and Reformed theologians. Hodge's view is similar if not identical to those he criticizes in the tradition. In terms of scripture, Hodge assumes a biblical basis for divine simplicity and does not explicitly express his reasons for maintaining the teaching.

HERMAN BAVINCK

Bavinck offers a much richer account of divine simplicity that is undoubtedly Reformed, but is also catholic in its use of sources, argumentation, and terms. After discussing the names of God in scripture, he follows with the incommunicable-communicable classification often found in Reformed theology. However, simplicity is not located as the first attribute, nor does it function as any kind of governing concept over all other Christian doctrine. Instead, Bavinck places it at the end of his discussion of the incommunicable attributes, following God's independence, immutability, infinity (and eternity and omnipresence), and unity. At the same time, he does include divine simplicity in his presentation of the divine names, specifically in relation to the way the names relate to God's essence and attributes.

Bavinck begins with the names of God, not because of a desire to keep within the tradition, but because of his conviction that "all we can learn about God from his revelation is designated his Name in Scripture."[68] This singular name "is divisible for us in a great many names" and is also "identical with the attributes or perfections that

---

66. Ibid., 1:373.

67. Ibid., 1:374.

68. Herman Bavinck, *Reformed Dogmatics*, vol. 2, *God and Creation*, ed. John Bolt, trans. John Vriend (Grand Rapids: Baker Academic, 2006), 97.

[God] exhibits in and to the world."[69] In God's name, we encounter his many names, and in his many names we are still dealing with his one name. However, primacy is given to the one name since it "is the foundation of all the names by which we address him."[70]

The many names of God serve the function of revealing God to us, but they also must be recognized as anthropomorphisms (this also includes accommodation). In fact, for Bavinck, scripture "is anthropomorphic through and through."[71] What he means is that "all of [the names] are expressions that first of all apply to creatures and are then transferred to God by way of eminence." Even the incommunicable attributes are anthropomorphic since they are found in scripture as "forms and expressions derived from the finite world and are therefore stated negatively."[72] Bavinck illustrates these points by listing a number of examples of scripture that speak of God's soul, body, emotions, actions, offices, and so forth. He sums up his point with the statement that "the entire creation, all of nature with all its [diverse] kingdoms, but especially the human world, is mined in Scripture for the description of the knowledge of God. Almost no limit is set to the use of anthropomorphic language."[73]

The establishment that the names of God are anthropomorphic naturally leads to the issue of how the names can be predicated of God. For Bavinck, "The reason can only be this: the whole creation, though as creature it is infinitely far removed from God, is still God's handiwork and related to him."[74] This is not a panentheistic understanding of the Creator-creature relationship, but is an extension of the Reformed understanding of divine accommodation. God descends to humanity's level and reveals his name through creation. The names are in and of themselves accommodations, meaning that "we cannot name him as he is within himself," yet "this does not make them untrue, a product of human imagination."[75] Human knowledge is already "finite and limited, but not for that reason impure or untrue."[76]

69. Ibid., 99, 98. Bavinck says this because "in Scripture, 'to be' and 'to be called' are two sides of the same thing" (ibid., 99).

70. Ibid., 99.

71. Ibid.

72. Ibid., 100.

73. Ibid., 101.

74. Ibid., 104. He later calls this relation the "kinship" between God and creatures (ibid., 128).

75. Ibid., 106. "If God were to speak to us in divine language, not a creature would understand him" (ibid., 100).

76. Ibid.

Knowledge of God may be finite, but it remains true because it is the result of God's self-revelation in the accommodated form of divine names. These names are drawn from God's works, presented in scripture, yet they are also known from the created order or at least somehow related to it. One might expect the accommodated names to raise questions about their capacity to mediate genuine knowledge of God. However, it is here that Bavinck presents the significance of the order of knowing and being. For the human intellect, God's names are first derived from the world before they are applied eminently to him. However, they exist first in God before they are known in his creatures.

> It is true: we first apply to creatures the names by which we speak of God because we know them before we know God. But materially they first apply to God and then to creatures. All perfections are first in God, then in creatures. He possesses them because they belong to his essence; we possess them only by participation.[77]

Bavinck finds this view in scripture, that humanity's origin derives from God and therefore reflects him, leading him to the conclusion that human knowledge of God through the divine names (and in general, including theology) is ectypal or analogical.

After linking the divine name(s) to God's attributes and describing the nature and limits of human knowledge of God, Bavinck outlines the relationship of the divine names to divine simplicity. After all, Bavinck argues, "it remains the calling of theology, following the example of Scripture, to honor equally all the attributes of God."[78] Following the Augustinian logic, Bavinck states that God "*is* what he *possesses*" and that "all his attributes are identical with his being. . . . Whatever God is, he is that completely and simultaneously."[79] The goal of divine simplicity is to avoid "splitting God's attributes from his essence and of making them more or less independent from, and opposed to, his essence," a problem that can be found in polytheism, Plato's philosophy, Gnosticism, and Arianism.[80] The same can be said of Gilbert Porretan, Duns Scotus, and Socinianism.

A number of other theologians failed to understand or offer an acceptable distinction between the divine attributes, including

77. Ibid., 107.
78. Ibid., 118.
79. Ibid. (emphasis original).
80. Ibid.

Eunomius, Ockham, the Palamites, and Schleiermacher. Bavinck argues "against this view of the names of God" "on the basis of God's revelation," noting that "though every attribute is identical with the divine being, the attributes are nevertheless distinct."[81] The attributes are not synonymous, and Bavinck agrees with the Reformed understanding that the attributes differ "in thought." However, he goes beyond this distinction to assert that "this diversity is rooted in God's revelation itself" (*ratio ratiocinata*).[82] The attributes are identical without being synonymous, meaning that "each attribute expresses something special" and therefore should not, and cannot, be conflated.[83]

Do the distinctions or diversity of attributes cause a problem for divine simplicity? Rather than being a problem, divine simplicity is actually the basis for a proper understanding of the need for many divine names.

> This diversity of attributes, moreover, does not clash with God's simplicity. For that simplicity does not describe God as an abstract and general kind of being; on the contrary, it speaks of him as the absolute fullness of life. It is for this very reason that God reveals himself to finite creatures by many names. The divine essence is so infinite and profusely rich that no creature can grasp it all at once. Just as a child cannot picture the worth of a coin of great value but only gains some sense of it when it is counted out in a number of smaller coins, so we too cannot possibly form a picture of the infinite fullness of God's essence unless it is displayed to us now in one relationship, then in another, and now from one angle, then from another.[84]

It is almost as though God must be "broken down" into parts in order for human finite minds to understand him. However, such composition speaks to human need rather than divine ontology, especially as it relates to divine accommodation and the anthropomorphic nature of scripture's testimony.

At this point, Bavinck begins to classify the divine names according to two groups: first, God's proper names of address, where he

81. Ibid., 125. He claims to be following Basil and Gregory on this point. The crucial question is what kind of distinction Bavinck draws between the divine attributes.

82. Ibid., 127.

83. Ibid., 126.

84. Ibid., 127. Elsewhere, Bavinck comments that "in God holiness and mercy may be the same in essence, yet our understanding of these two attributes, formed from God's self-revelation, differs. There is no name capable of expressing God's being with full adequacy. Given that reality, many names serve to give us an impression of his all-transcending grandeur" (ibid., 128).

focuses on El, Elohim, El Shaddai, Yahweh, Yahweh Sabaoth, and Father; second, the unique properties that pertain to the divine persons. He notes that "between these two groups is a large space for the attributes that describe God's being," and he goes on to follow the classical Reformed categories of communicable and incommunicable.[85] It is at this point that Bavinck moves from the divine names to a more specific doctrine of divine simplicity.

Bavinck's presentation of the incommunicable attributes should not indicate that he has left the realm of the divine names or scripture. From the beginning, he points out that God's "whole identity was wrapped up in the name: 'I will be what I will be.' All God's other perfections are derived from this name."[86] This reiterates what Bavinck has been said before. Divine simplicity is an element of God's unity or oneness, both distinct from God's unity of singularity (monotheism), but also inseparable from it. Together, they form a strong bond that seeks to express scripture's teachings on God's unity and the implications it has for one's understanding of God.

Scripture uses both adjectives and substantives "to denote the fullness of the life of God,"[87] and so we encounter many descriptions of God from a variety of viewpoints. This should be understood to convey the point that "every attribute of God is identical with his essence."[88] Bavinck points out that this teaching has existed since Irenaeus and found further expression in the Cappadocians and Augustine. Those who rejected or criticized divine simplicity include Eunomius, the Anthropomorphites, Arabian philosophers, nominalists, Socinians, the Remonstrants, and pantheists. The final result is that "the attribute of God's simplicity almost totally disappeared from modern theology," a fact that still remains to this day.[89]

Bavinck sees things differently. Divine simplicity is incredibly important, for "it is not only taught in Scripture (where God is called 'light,' 'life,' and 'love') but also automatically follows from the idea of God and is necessarily implied in the other attributes."[90] Far from being a metaphysical abstraction, divine simplicity is a recognition of the fullness of divine life. The human mind can only grasp one aspect of God and from one angle, but this does not mean that the

85. Ibid., 135.
86. Ibid., 151.
87. Ibid., 173.
88. Ibid., 171.
89. Ibid., 175.
90. Ibid., 176.

knowledge is untrue or that God is composed of such parts. However, neither does divine simplicity mean that God is not truly named with many names. "This simplicity of being does not exclude the many names ascribed to him, as Eunomius thought, *but demands them.* God is so abundantly rich that we can gain some idea of his richness only by the availability of many names."[91]

Bavinck's account of divine simplicity is biblically grounded in the divine names in scripture. He assumes there is no reason to reject the traditional view that these names are identical with God's attributes and essence. Furthermore, in scripture the names are drawn from the created world, and most uniquely from humanity, and this is justified by the fact that such perfections preexisted first in God. The kinship between God and creation recognizes the complete ontological otherness of God without neglecting divine accommodation and the anthropomorphic nature of scripture. God descends to humanity, using and welcoming its language to describe himself, yet only according to an ectypal or analogical pattern that respects both God's transcendence (he is beyond the names) and immanence (yet the names are still true of him). In all of this, divine simplicity recognizes the richness of God's life, which warrants and also insists on the plurality of divine names to describe him. This may be summarized as Bavinck's "unity in diversity" theme,[92] and it is here that we come to a better understanding of Bavinck's account of divine simplicity and its relation to scripture.

KARL BARTH

Barth may appear as an unexpected addition to this survey since he is, after all, highly averse to natural theology, general metaphysics, or any sense of a general being of God. He is also concerned that theology remain faithful to God's self-revelation as the triune God and most importantly in the person of Jesus Christ. How could Barth ever maintain a doctrine of divine simplicity if he opposes natural theology and his theology is deeply trinitarian and christological? This is where Barth becomes an interesting voice in the discussion, particularly in relation to the contemporary theological rejections of

---

91. Ibid., 177 (emphasis added).
92. See ibid., 300, 331. See also James Eglinton, *Trinity and Organism: Towards a New Reading of Herman Bavinck's Organic Motif*, SST (London: T&T Clark, 2012), 104–14.

divine simplicity. Ironically, Barth's doctrine of divine simplicity has been neglected by most scholars, with the exception of direct expositions of his account of the divine perfections in *Church Dogmatics* II/1.[93] Works that directly engage Barth's doctrine of divine simplicity have been primarily historical,[94] comparative,[95] or have related his view to other disciplines, such as ethics.[96] While these approaches are certainly beneficial, they tend to ignore the biblical and theological underpinnings that form the basis of Barth's position. This is significant since Barth stands with one foot inside the tradition and one foot in a new location. As we will see, Barth desires to account for the intent of simplicity without being tied to its supposedly accompanying metaphysics.[97]

Barth on Natural Theology and Knowledge of God

In order to establish the uniqueness of Barth's account, it is crucial to at least summarize his distaste for natural theology and the ways he understands divine revelation in relation to knowledge of God. On one level, Barth sees natural theology as "the doctrine of a union

93. For general expositions of Barth's doctrine of the divine perfections that include divine simplicity, see Robert B. Price, *Letters of the Divine Word: The Perfections of God in Karl Barth's Church Dogmatics*, SST (London: T&T Clark, 2011); Cornelis Van Der Kooi, *As in a Mirror: John Calvin and Karl Barth on Knowing God*, trans. Donald Mader, SHCT (Leiden: Brill, 2005); Christopher R. J. Holmes, *Revisiting the Doctrine of the Divine Attributes: In Dialogue with Karl Barth, Eberhard Jüngel, and Wolf Krötke*, IST (New York: Peter Lang, 2006); Claus-Dieter Osthövener, *Die Lehre von Gottes Eigenschaften bei Friedrich Schleiermacher und Karl Barth*, Theologische Bibliothek Töpelmann 76 (Berlin: de Gruyter, 1996); Velde, *The Doctrine of God*, 259–477; Todd Pokrifka, *Redescribing God: The Roles of Scripture, Tradition, and Reason in Karl Barth's Doctrines of Divine Unity, Constancy, and Eternity*, PTM (Eugene, OR: Pickwick, 2010); Jay Wesley Richards, *The Untamed God: A Philosophical Exploration of Divine Perfection, Immutability, and Simplicity* (Downers Grove, IL: InterVarsity Press, 2003); Colin E. Gunton, *Becoming and Being: The Doctrine of God in Charles Hartshorne and Karl Barth* (Oxford: Oxford University Press, 1978).

94. Rinse H. Reeling Brouwer, "The Conversation between Karl Barth and Amandus Polanus on the Question of the Reality of Human Speaking of the Simplicity and the Multiplicity in God," in McCormack and Neven, *The Reality of Faith in Theology*, 51–110.

95. Christopher A. Franks, "The Simplicity of the Living God: Aquinas, Barth, and Some Philosophers," *ModTheo* 21 (2005): 275–300.

96. Stephen Pickard, "Barth on Divine Simplicity: Some Implications for Life in a Complex World," in *Karl Barth: A Future for Postmodern Theology?*, ed. Geoff Thompson and Christiaan Mostert (Hindmarsh: Australian Theological Forum, 2000), 210–23.

97. Barth makes use of Cremer's work on the divine attributes in *CD* II/1, and Cremer's influence can be seen in Barth's desire to start with God's revelation and with Jesus. See Hermann Cremer, *The Christian Doctrine of the Divine Attributes*, ed. Helmut Burkhardt, trans. Robert B. Price (Eugene, OR: Pickwick, 2016).

of man with God existing outside God's revelation in Jesus Christ."[98] Barth's problem is that

> this attempt certainly cannot end in any other way than with the affirmation that even apart from God's grace, already preceding God's grace, already anticipating it, [man] is ready for God, so that God is knowable to him otherwise than from and through Himself.[99]

Knowledge of God cannot be grounded elsewhere, especially when God's self-revelation is an act of grace and is properly seen in Jesus Christ. Barth's phrase "God reveals God" means that God's revelation is a free decision, that this revelation stems from God's initiative and capacity since humanity has no independent capacity for revelation, and that revelation is God's *self*-revelation and not a mere communication of information about the divine. In Barth's mind, nothing about this is natural.

Ruling out natural knowledge of God or the mere transference of information, Barth argues that in revelation we come to know God himself not just as he is toward us, but as he is in himself. However, he qualifies this point by noting that that it is not as though "God gives Himself to be known by us only in part" as if "we have to do only with a limited quantity of His being and not, or not yet, with some other quantity." This option does not exist, for "He is known in his entirety or He is not known at all. There is no existence of God behind or beyond this entirety of His being."[100] This is not simply due to the limitations inherent in humanity's finite knowledge and struggle with sin, but it is due to God himself, who "exists in this entirety of His being and therefore not in any kind of parts. . . . A separable being of this kind or one part of such a separable being would have nothing whatever to do with the being of God."[101] Because revelation is God's self-revelation, his being as the inseparable triune God determines human knowledge of him, rather than human finitude determining the boundaries of divine revelation.

At the same time, Barth does not ignore that although God reveals himself entirely and not in part (nothing remains behind his

---

98. *CD* II/1, 168. All references are drawn from Karl Barth, *Church Dogmatics*, ed. Geoffrey Bromiley and Thomas F. Torrance, trans. G. W. Bromiley et al., 4 vols in 14 parts (Edinburgh: T&T Clark, 1936–1977).

99. *CD* II/1, 135.

100. *CD* II/1, 51.

101. *CD* II/1, 52.

revelation), this does not mean that we have complete or exhaustive knowledge of God. Surely, "there is of course a limitation—in revelation—we cannot think of it as quantitative. The fact that God gives to us only a share in the truth of His knowledge of Himself cannot mean that He does not give Himself to be known by us as the One He is."[102] Yet, even in this limitation, we have true knowledge of God's entire being because "He lets Himself to be known in truth as the One He is, yet not at all as He knows Himself."[103]

This brief look at Barth's view of natural theology and knowledge of God would appear to cause serious problems for divine simplicity. After all, is not divine simplicity the result of a natural theology that reasons from creatures to the Creator? Is not divine simplicity a speculative and abstract view of God that is ultimately determined by some form of metaphysics? Contemporary theology argues that the answer to such questions is yes (see chapter 1), but in Barth there is a somewhat traditional, yet revised, doctrine of divine simplicity that is not the product of natural theology, general metaphysics, or speculation. Instead, he locates divine simplicity in a trinitarian and christological context and finds it to be drawn from scripture's presentation of God's trustworthiness. In the following sections, I will present Barth's doctrine of divine simplicity as it develops from the *Göttingen Dogmatics* and as it is found in *Church Dogmatics* II/1.

Divine Simplicity in the Göttingen Dogmatics

Barth's treatment of the divine attributes and divine simplicity is fairly traditional in its content and terminology. From the beginning, he takes up the crucial question of whether the distinctions and juxtapositions of the divine attributes are true of God himself or are only true of our knowledge of God. The possibility of nominalism is serious, doing "violence to revelation," ultimately making God unknowable. "Where we can only see one color, we can see nothing. Where we can hear only one sound, it is as if we were deaf."[104] The rejection of nominalism, in turn, poses three questions that Barth must answer: (1) "Are the attributes of God something other in him than his nature,

102. Ibid.

103. *CD* II/1, 61. On the differences between Barth's view of God's self-revelation and Calvin's view of God's revelation as God is toward us, see Kooi, *As in a Mirror*.

104. Karl Barth, *The Göttingen Dogmatics: Instruction in the Christian Religion*, ed. Hannelotte Reiffen, trans. Geoffrey W. Bromiley (Grand Rapids: Eerdmans, 1991), 1:378. Hereafter *GD*.

and if so, does not this mean that in part he is not God?" (2) "Does not the multiplicity of his attributes negate his unity or simplicity?" (3) "Is not God hereby subsumed under higher general concepts such as infinity, truth, and righteousness?"[105] These questions guide Barth's presentation of the divine attributes and specifically divine simplicity.

In answer to the first question, Barth affirms that in God there are not accidents, for "God is all things essentially" and without them "God cannot exist."[106] Therefore, the attributes of God are nothing other than himself. Yet, does their multiplicity negate God's simplicity? Barth answers this second question negatively, stating that the attributes "differ neither from [God's nature] nor among themselves," and that "each attribute is the total essence of God."[107] However, Barth will not allow this claim to result in any form of nominalism. The truthfulness of both the multiplicity and unity of the divine attributes forms a dialectic. "For the many are an expression of the revelation of the one. . . . We cannot speak about God without speaking about the many even as we remember the one."[108] Both, for Barth, must be equally affirmed as a dialectic and not a contradiction.[109] Finally, Barth again answers negatively to the third question, arguing that our concepts first originate in God and are always subordinate to his revelation.

Barth later treats divine simplicity in relation to God's uniqueness and under the broader category of God's unity. Following Heidegger's definition, Barth comments that "the whole series of divine attributes is thus set in a circle behind one another, and between each of them there is a sign of equality, and God's nature is not the sum of them, but their being ineffably one and the same."[110] This claim causes no problems for the Trinity since we do not speak of three essences, nor three parts, but three persons who equally share in all of the divine attributes. Neither does this cause problems for

---

105. Ibid., 1:379.

106. Ibid., 1:381, 382.

107. Ibid., 1:382.

108. Ibid., 1:383.

109. As Pokrifka puts it, "Barth's dialectic here is different from Hegel's. There is no 'third term,' no synthesis of the thesis and antithesis. As such, the opposites that form the two sides of his dialectic remain in an unresolved tension with each other. This is typical of Barth's use of dialectic (as in the dialectic between love and freedom) and is indicative of his Trinitarian and Chalcedonian thought-patterns" (Pokrifka, *Redescribing God*, 305n8).

110. Barth, *GD*, 1:428.

the incarnation, since the hypostatic union rules out the possibility of "mutual permeation of the divine and the human."[111]

Barth may positively endorse the concept of divine simplicity, but he also recognizes that it can be taken too far. Taken "to the end, we naturally come dangerously close to a spiritualistic pantheism, to what is called panentheism."[112] This problem is brought about by reversing the statement "God is simple" and attempting to say that the simple is God, illustrating a failure of thinking that "God is *one*" rather than "*God* is one"[113] and derives from a general concept of unity rather than the particular form of unity in God's uniqueness and simplicity that is found in his self-revelation.

Divine Simplicity in Church Dogmatics II/1

Barth's account of the divine attributes, now called the divine perfections in the *Church Dogmatics*, revises traditional presentations of the perfections by treating them in terms of love and freedom. In fact, his whole doctrine of the divine perfections can be summed up in "The Being of God as the One Who Loves in Freedom."[114] In the sphere of divine love, these perfections communicate God's will to be "for us," whereas the sphere of divine freedom represents the fact that even in his self-revelation God remains the same as he is in himself. While the two can be distinguished in presentation, neither is separable from the other since the aim is to present them holistically and as indivisible perfections of God.

Barth includes divine simplicity under the aspect of divine freedom. Similar to the *Göttingen Dogmatics*, he links simplicity with God's uniqueness and under the more extensive perfection of God's unity.[115] God's unity is unique (*Einzigkeit*; *singularitas*) and simple (*Einfachheit*; *simplicitas*), and both manifest the divine freedom. In this sense, "if we understand it rightly, we can express all that God is by saying that God is One."[116] As Barth will later explain, this divine unity is christological and trinitarian, and each one has implications

111. Ibid., 1:429.
112. Ibid., 1:430.
113. Ibid., 1:432 (emphasis original).
114. *CD* II/1, §28 (257).
115. Stead finds this distinction as far back as Tertullian (Christopher Stead, *Divine Substance* [Oxford: Clarendon, 1977], 182).
116. *CD* II/1, 442.

for the way divine simplicity must be understood. In order to understand Barth's doctrine of divine simplicity, it is important to first understand how he received its traditional forms. In this way, we will better see how Barth situated himself in relation to previous theologians, and we will have a better sense of views or aspects of the tradition that he finds problematic or unhelpful.

Barth does not identify any problems with divine simplicity in the early church. On the contrary, he seems to believe that the doctrine of divine simplicity was initially handled well.

> The early battle for a recognition of the simplicity of God was the same as for the recognition of the Trinity and of the relation between the divine and human natures in Jesus Christ. We can put it equally well both ways. The Church clarified its mind about the simplicity of God by means of the essential unity of the Son and the Holy Spirit with the Father, and the undivided but unconfused unity of the divine with the human nature in Jesus Christ. But it also clarified its mind about the *homoousia* of the Son and the Holy Ghost in the one divine being, and the unity of the two natures in Jesus Christ, by means of the simplicity of God. Properly considered, the two things are one. The unity of the triune God and of the Son of God with man in Jesus Christ is itself the simplicity of God.[117]

Barth does not elaborate on the historical claim, and I will set aside the question of its accuracy since this project does not depend on it. His point, however, is that divine simplicity was properly located in a trinitarian and christological framework and operated similarly to the teaching of *homoousios*. The difficulties in articulating the unity and distinction among the three divine persons and Jesus's two natures appears to be similar to the complicated nature of affirming both the simplicity and multiplicity of God's perfections. In fact, earlier in his discussion of the perfections of God, Barth states that "we have an exact parallel to the concern of the doctrine of the Holy Trinity."[118]

---

117. *CD* II/1, 446.

118. *CD* II/1, 326. I will draw out the significance of this claim in chapter 6. Here, Barth adds that "in this doctrine the one God in His three modes of being corresponds to the Lord of glory. As it is of decisive importance to recognise the three modes of being, not only economically as modalism does, but, according to the seriousness of the divine presence and power in the economy of His works, as modes of being of the one eternal God Himself, so it is equally important to understand that God in Himself is not divested of His glory and perfections, that He does not assume them merely in connexion with His self-revelation to the world, but that they constitute His own eternal glory. Again, as it is of decisive importance not to dissolve the unity of the Godhead tritheistically into three gods, but to understand the three modes of being

George Hunsinger takes this statement to mean that "Barth sees the distinctions among God's perfections as real for God and not merely for us. In scholastic terminology, they are therefore *distinctionae formales* and not merely *distinctionae rationis ratiocinatae*. In other words, these distinctions are not merely mental conveniences, but inherent in the being of God."[119] However, Barth never identifies his view as a formal distinction, and thus there is need for greater clarity on this point. What is clear is that Barth's understanding of the development of divine simplicity in the early church is positive; yet his view grows more critical and worrisome as he evaluates how the teaching develops from the early medieval period onward.

Barth begins to find problems in Augustine's and Anselm's theology, specifically "a purely logical and metaphysical kind."[120] He does not specify the problems he finds, but adds that "the older Protestant orthodoxy, too, usually adopted much the same arguments and explanations when it placed and expounded the simplicity of God first among the divine attributes."[121] It becomes clear that Barth is concerned about the importance given to divine simplicity. The problem becomes greater, as Barth elaborates:

> There could be no objection to the logic, metaphysics and mathematics of these lines of thought if they had been used only to perform the service of explanation. . . . But we cannot read these things in the older writers with unmixed joy. The trouble is that they are put at the head, and not, as we are trying to do here, in their proper turn. They thus give the impression that what is argued and considered is the general idea of an *ens vere unum* [being truly one] and not the God of the doctrine of the Trinity and of Christology. . . . [Furthermore], it leads to an underlying nominalism or semi-nominalism. . . , [and so] we will have to give it a more distinctly biblical and therefore Christian basis than it had in

strictly as the modes of being of the one God with whom we have to do in all His works, so it is of equal importance to interpret God's glory and perfections, not in and for themselves, but as the glory of the Lord who alone is able to establish, disclose and confirm them as real glory" (ibid., 326–27). Although Barth points out the trinitarian parallel, he does not clarify the effects this has for a doctrine of divine simplicity.

119. George Hunsinger, "*Mysterium Trinitatis*: Karl Barth's Conception of Eternity," in *Disruptive Grace: Studies in the Theology of Karl Barth* (Grand Rapids: Eerdmans, 2000), 196n11.

120. *CD* II/1, 446. For one assessment of Barth's view of "classical theism," see Don Schweitzer, "Karl Barth's Critique of Classical Theism," *TJT* 18 (2002): 231–44. For Barth's views on philosophy, see Kenneth Oakes, *Karl Barth on Theology and Philosophy* (Oxford: Oxford University Press, 2012).

121. *CD* II/1, 447. On Barth's relation to post-Reformation orthodoxy, see Rinse H. Reeling Brouwer, *Karl Barth and Post-Reformation Orthodoxy*, BS (Burlington, VT: Ashgate, 2015).

the early Church [Augustine onward], the Middle Ages and Protestant orthodoxy.[122]

This statement indicates four problems: (1) the use of metaphysics and logic to argue for divine simplicity; (2) its theological location; (3) beginning with a general concept of God; (4) the inevitable result of various forms of nominalism.

Two of these problems deserve additional attention due to their consistent presence throughout Barth's other critiques—namely, nominalism and a general concept of God. The *Göttingen Dogmatics* made it clear that nominalism is a major failure that Barth wants to avoid. He continues this warning in *Church Dogmatics* II/1, but divides nominalism into two aspects: strict or extreme nominalism, and seminominalism. The strict nominalists, initially represented by Eunomius, William of Ockham, and Gabriel Biel, argued for a "pure simplicity" in which the distinction between attributes existed only in the human mind and not in God himself. Barth admits that "there is no desire simply to abandon and deny the attributes of God, but actually to assert them."[123]

Nevertheless, the problem is that the "properties" of God were affirmed as neither qualities nor accidents, but were strictly identified with the divine essence. On one level, there was nothing wrong with this claim, but it eventually led to God's properties losing their reality since they were rooted not in God's essence but in his relation to humanity. This view led to further problems. Barth is worth quoting in full at this point.

> The fact that the life of God was identified with the notion of pure being, the fact that the idea of God was not determined by the doctrine of the Trinity, but that the latter was shaped by a general conception of God (that of ancient Stoicism and Neo-Platonism), was now avenged at the most sensitive spot. Starting from the generalized notion of God, the idea of the divine simplicity was necessarily exalted to the all-controlling principle, the idol, which, devouring everything concrete, stands behind all these formulae. As a result it was impossible to make proper use of what Augustine had so happily indicated with his phrase *multiplex simplicitas* or *simplex multiplicitas*: the triumphant unity in God of the Lord with glory and of glory with the Lord. From this starting point we can speak only hesitantly about the reality of the divine perfections. On this

122. *CD* II/1, 447.
123. *CD* II/1, 328.

basis, when we speak of God, we must mean essentially only the simplicity and not the richness, at best the simplicity of the richness, but at bottom only the simplicity. We may try to specify, but in the last resort we can intend and demonstrate only the barrenness of *nuda essentia* [bare essence].[124]

Nominalism not only causes problems for revelation but also neglects the richness of God in the simplicity and multiplicity of his essence.[125] This can also be said of partial nominalism, which Barth locates in Thomism and the orthodox Protestants.[126] Instead, Barth praises nineteenth-century German theologians F. H. R. Frank, G. Thomasius, and I. A. Dorner for recognizing the true diversity of God's perfections.[127]

In response to a nominalist and seminominalist view, Barth offers three propositions on the divine perfections that form a crucial aspect of his doctrine of divine simplicity. First, the "multiplicity, individuality and diversity of the divine perfections are those of the one divine

124. *CD* II/1, 329.

125. Later on in the *Church Dogmatics*, Barth writes about another false view of divine simplicity: "We must not be led astray at this point by a false conception of the simplicity of the divine essence. This simplicity has not to be explained as the simplicity of the absolute as compared with the relative, or of the general as compared with the particular, or of the digit 1 as compared with its multiplications and divisions, or of the concept as compared with its perception. It is the simplicity of the God who is eternally rich in His threefold being: 'May God in His eternal riches always give us in our lives a cheerful heart and noble serenity.' It is simplicity as opposed to divisibility and separability, as opposed to inward disloyalty and inconstancy, as opposed to all forms of self-contradiction. But it is the simplicity of the One who in Himself as Father, Son, and Holy Ghost is love, who in Himself does not merely exist but co-exists, who in Himself has space and dimension, who in Himself has life (Jn 5:26). It is the simplicity of the One who in His own being is not nowhere but everywhere, not never but always; of the One who is therefore omnipresent before and above and after all space, and eternal before and above and after all time: who at one and the same time is distant and near, yesterday, today and tomorrow. It is this God, who is not poor in Himself but rich, who works together with the creature. He does not do it uniformly or monotonously or without differentiation, for He is not uniform or monotonous or undifferentiated in Himself. If He were to do it in this way He would be doing violence to His own nature; He would not be God" (*CD* III/3, 138).

126. On Barth and Thomas Aquinas, see Franks, "The Simplicity of the Living God"; Bruce L. McCormack and Thomas Joseph White, eds., *Thomas Aquinas and Karl Barth: An Unofficial Catholic-Protestant Diaologue* (Grand Rapids: Eerdmans, 2013); Eugene F. Rogers, *Thomas Aquinas and Karl Barth: Sacred Doctrine and the Natural Knowledge of God* (Notre Dame: University of Notre Dame Press, 1995). Franks argues that Barth "is truly the modern heir to Thomas's understanding of divine simplicity." What he means is that "while not at all identical to Thomas's [doctrine of divine simplicity], [it] stands on the same lessons about God's causality" (Franks, "The Simplicity of the Living God," 277) meaning that both Barth and Thomas recognize an ontological difference between Creator and creature that is not affirmed by Stump, Kretzmann, and other philosophers.

127. On Dorner's influence on Barth, see Sherman, "Isaak August Dorner on Divine Immutability."

being and therefore not those of another divine nature allied to it."[128] In other words, the perfections and God's being are inseparable, and despite the plurality of the perfections, they do not constitute another essence or nature alongside God's being. Barth speaks here of God's "abundance" and "variety" along with his multiplicity and diversity. Moreover, this multiplicity does "not arise simply from His relation to the world, but are those of His own being as He who loves in freedom."[129] God is not multiple from our perspective or only to this world, but is multiple in his very being. Barth draws this insight from God's self-revelation, specifically in the Trinity.[130]

Second, this "multiplicity, individuality, and diversity of the perfections of God are those of His simple being, which is therefore not divided and then put back together again. In God multiplicity, individuality and diversity do not stand in any contradiction to unity."[131] The term "unity" implies that distinctions must exist, but this distinction does not destroy the unity between God's perfections and his essence or between the perfections themselves.

> Every individual perfection in God is nothing but God Himself and therefore nothing but every other divine perfection. It means equally strictly on the other hand that God Himself is nothing other than each of His perfections in its individuality, and that each individual perfection is identical with every other and with the fullness of them all.[132]

This comes back to Barth's view of the richness of God, leading him

128. *CD* II/1, 331.

129. *CD* II/1, 332.

130. As Adam Johnson states, "The specific unity in multiplicity of the Trinity justifies and necessitates the distinct but related form of the unity and multiplicity of the divine perfections." See Adam Johnson, *God's Being in Reconciliation: The Theological Basis of the Unity and Diversity of the Atonement in the Theology of Karl Barth*, SST (London: T&T Clark, 2012), 101.

131. *CD* II/1, 332.

132. *CD* II/1, 333. It is important to notice that Barth uses the traditional language, found most prominently in the West, stating that "each individual perfection is identical with every other." He later writes that "each of the divine perfections is materially identical with each of the others" (*CD* II/1, 335). For all of Barth's talk of genuine "multiplicity," it is surprising that he retains the language of "identical attributes." Robert Jenson argues that Barth means something different by this language: "Even as God's attributes are each identical with his essence, and therefore identical with each other—as the standard maxim has it—this is not to be taken as the tradition, in Barth's judgment, too often has. For each divine perfection is identical with each other perfection *and* with all the others taken not identically but *together*, precisely in their distinction from one another. Thus in himself, and not merely in relation to us, God is, for example, *both* merciful and just, and both of these things must individually be said to be speaking of the one godly essence" ("Karl Barth on the Being of God," in McCormack and White, *Thomas Aquinas and Karl Barth*, 50).

to affirm that "God's being transcends the contrast of *simplicitas* and *multiplicitas*." These terms are not exclusive, but inclusive, and must be equally predicated of God.[133]

Finally, Barth writes that "the multiplicity, individuality and diversity of God's perfections are rooted in His own being and not in His participation in the character of other beings."[134] God's being is plentiful, and he is in need of nothing from the outside. God does not need to become anything by entering into relation with another being. This, again, is part of Barth's desire to do justice not only to the unity of God but to his multiplicity as well, believing that both are required in order to avoid the problems he found throughout the tradition.

These three propositions direct Barth to a fundamental question: "To what extent do these many individual and various perfections of God exist?"[135] He recognizes the temptation toward a total or partial nominalism. At the same time, to affirm a real distinction at this point would be similar to saying that each individual perfection has an existence independent from the others. Put differently, each perfection would be its own essence. Barth does not give a sufficient answer. As it stands, it appears "more important to affirm *that* the God of Scripture (a) has both multiple perfections and (b) is one than it is to affirm *how* (a) and (b) are logically consistent with each other."[136] Barth does not conclude that the distinctions are real, but we can also recall how everything that has been said up to this point comes to bear on his answer to this question.

Barth consistently rejects any form of nominalism. This error must be taken seriously because it divides God *ad intra* and *ad extra*. As Todd Pokrifka points out, "Barth's main concern is to ensure that God 'remains himself' rather than being a divided and potentially self-contradictory self."[137] God only appears to be just without being true to who he is in himself. Stated differently, Barth worries about a "God behind God" where God appears to humanity in one way, but in reality is different than he appears. Barth believes that "He is known in his entirety or He is not known at all. There is no existence of

133. *CD* II/1, 333.
134. Ibid.
135. *CD* II/1, 335.
136. Pokrifka, *Redescribing God*, 174.
137. Ibid., 165n15.

God behind or beyond this entirety of His being."[138] And, as Barth has been arguing, God's being is his multiplicity, individuality, and diversity of divine perfections that are truly united in God's essence and to each other in their simple multiplicity.

After identifying the problems that Barth finds in the tradition and clarifying his understanding of the simplicity and multiplicity of the divine perfections, it still remains to describe Barth's doctrine of divine simplicity. For Barth, simplicity means that "in all that He is and does, He is wholly and undividedly Himself. At no time or place, then, is He divided or divisible."[139] Aside from lacking composition, divine simplicity also means that "nothing can affect Him, or be far from Him, or contradict or withstand Him, because in Himself there is no separation, distance, contradiction or opposition." Finally, God remains distinct from his creation since for the world to identify with God (or God with the world) would imply a combination or mixing of God and the world.

This is not a general view of composition or simplicity, but is derived primarily from God's own being. "The relation between subject and predicate is an irreversible one when it is a matter of God's perfections," meaning that "we must say that God is the absolutely One, but we cannot say that the absolutely one is God."[140] God is one, but this is not based on any general reflection or definition of oneness that is then applied to God. Reversing the order—not beginning with God's self-revelation—would mean beginning with a general concept of oneness, simplicity, or composition and risk predicating a concept of God that is not true of him (that is, idolatry).

A better way to understand the simplicity of God is to give sufficient attention to the way scripture describes him. Barth begins by noting that the divine perfections

> all have their existence and their essence, not outside of Him, but absolutely in Him. The One who is all this, and in whom all this is, is God Himself. And He is simple, i.e., He is all this indivisibly, indissolubly, inflexibly. The reason for this is that He is Himself indivisible, indissoluble, inflexible.[141]

138. *CD* II/1, 51.

139. *CD* II/1, 445. "God is simple without the least possibility of either internal or external composition" (ibid., 447). This traditional language marks a degree of continuity between Barth and the tradition, but he certainly takes the concept in new directions.

140. *CD* II/1, 448.

141. *CD* II/1, 458.

If God himself is these things, then his simplicity "is not to be looked for in any other place than that in which the prophets and apostles found it, . . . God's self-demonstration, given by Him in His Word and work."[142]

Barth understands divine simplicity to be connected to scripture's presentation of God's trustworthiness. Robert Price views this connection as a "loose" conceptual link,[143] but Barth sees it as the basis of divine simplicity according to the prophets and apostles.

> According to the testimony of the Bible (which refers us to His revelation as to Him Himself), the simplicity of God consists in the trustworthiness, truthfulness and fidelity which He is Himself, and in which, therefore, He also is what He is, and does what He does. If He were divisible, dissoluble, or flexible, He would not be trustworthy. But the God of the prophets and apostles is trustworthy. And He is not merely casually or accidentally trustworthy, so that He could also be untrustworthy. On the contrary, He is trustworthy in His essence, in the inmost core of His being.[144]

Pokrifka recognizes three conceptual relationships in Barth's statement. First, Barth "*equates* simplicity with trustworthiness, or vice versa." Second, Barth argues that "trustworthiness is *dependent upon* simplicity, or, in other words, simplicity is the *basis of* trustworthiness." Third, "simplicity is *dependent upon* trustworthiness; trustworthiness is the *basis of* simplicity."[145] What Pokrifka takes this to mean is that "the dogmatic statement 'God is simple' provides the necessary and sufficient (ontological) condition for the biblical statement that 'God is faithful.'"[146] For Barth, God could not be faithful in his revelation and actions if he were divided or experienced inner conflict among his perfections. However, because God is simple—or indivisible—he remains faithful and trustworthy since he "remains the same, single person (or subject) in all his diverse ways of being and acting."[147]

Barth continues by stating that "His simplicity is what the Bible so often calls Him, the 'rock,' the unshakable foundation, on which

---

142. *CD* II/1, 459.
143. Price, *Letters of the Divine Word*, 112.
144. *CD* II/1, 458.
145. Pokrifka, *Redescribing God*, 182–83 (emphasis original).
146. Ibid., 193.
147. Ibid., 194.

is based not only the doctrine of God but all the doctrines, and not only these but the whole life of the Christian Church, all Christian life, and finally all human life as a whole, and the promise of eternal life."[148] His simple nature means that his actions are true and trustworthy because they spring forth from his trustworthy essence. In addition, God's inner unity comes forth in his unified acts:

> It involves the unity of His promise and His command, of the Gospel and the Law, and in such a way that the Gospel is the fulfilling of the Law, while the Law is the form of the Gospel. It involves the unity of the election and calling of the sinful people Israel and of the Church of Jews and Gentiles sanctified by grace. It involves the unity of grace and holiness, mercy and righteousness, patience and wisdom, in the total work of His love. It is in this way that God confirms Himself, that He is One and the same. And everywhere that this takes place, even at the points where at first we may think we see difference, opposition, or contradiction, but later find unity, He attests Himself and gives Himself to be known by faith in His simplicity.[149]

Because God's essence and perfections are indivisible, his self-revelation and his works are trustworthy. God's actions, in all their plurality and diversity, are trustworthy and true.

Barth demonstrates a strong commitment to the doctrine of divine simplicity from the *Göttingen Dogmatics* through the first part of the second volume of the *Church Dogmatics*.[150] His aim is to frame the

---

148. *CD* II/1, 459.

149. *CD* II/1, 460.

150. McCormack argues that "those who would make exclusive and uncritical use of *Church Dogmatics* II/1, in their efforts to elaborate Barth's doctrine of God fail to see that his doctrine of election had ontological implications which brought Barth's thinking into conflict with elements of his exposition of that doctrine in II/1." See McCormack, "The Actuality of God," 240. McCormack does not specify which elements come into conflict, but it is not clear that divine simplicity is one of them. First, Barth still affirms simplicity in *CD* III/3, 138. In *CD* IV/1 and IV/2 there is no explicit denial of divine simplicity. In fact, he seems to maintain some form of his views from *CD* II/1 when he writes that "he is absolute, infinite, exalted, active, impassible, transcendent, but in all this He is the One who loves in freedom" (*CD* IV/1, 187). Furthermore, "In Him there is no paradox, no antinomy, no division, no inconsistency, not even the possibility of it" (*CD* IV/1, 186). In another place, Barth seems to have a concept of divine simplicity without mentioning the term: "The totality of the divine—for there is no obvious necessity why we should cautiously make reservations and instead of speaking of the totality speak only of certain properties of God which are addressed to the human and confronted with it in Jesus Christ. Nor is it very obvious how such a division is even possible. Is not each perfection of God itself the perfection of his whole essence, and therefore in any modification [*Modifikation*] the sum and substance of all others? How can some of these perfections be separated off from others? Would it be the divine essence of the Father, Son and Holy Spirit if such separations

doctrine in a trinitarian and christological context, making sure to place it within his dogmatic structure in such a way that it avoids being the result of a general concept of being or an abstract metaphysics. Furthermore, Barth works to maintain a dialectic, or perhaps better, simultaneity, between the simplicity and multiplicity of God's indivisible essence. Neither one takes precedence, and each one must be equally affirmed to uphold scripture's presentation of the many perfections of God and his invariable unity. Last, Barth ties his concept of simplicity with the biblical teaching of God's trustworthiness and faithfulness. For God to be simple means that he is one in his multiplicity such that he is not divided against himself in any way. Because God is indivisible, because there is no inner conflict or priority of certain perfections, God is trustworthy and remains faithful to his promises.

CONCLUSION

This chapter has sought to continue the survey of representative theologians on the doctrine of divine simplicity in relation to scripture. What has become clear is that divine simplicity is not tied to a particular passage of scripture. Nevertheless, its biblical nature is often assumed by theologians or at least assumed to be part of other biblical teachings. We saw in Calvin that he undoubtedly held to divine simplicity and did so despite his serious concerns about theological speculation. Furthermore, as a Reformation theologian, one would expect that his doctrine of *sola scriptura* would move him to correct a teaching like divine simplicity if it were truly foreign to scripture. Instead, Calvin maintained divine simplicity, assumed it, and referred to it throughout the *Institutes* and his commentaries.

John Owen demonstrated, once again, a response to critics of divine simplicity. Owen believed scripture taught the "firstness" of God where nothing could be prior to God (that is, no parts) and therefore be responsible for his being. Moreover, he understood that in scripture the divine attributes were essentially the same as all the others. This was not a form of nominalism where there are no real divine attributes, but was the belief that they are not separated from

---

were to take place in it?" (*CD* IV/2, 86). One of the main questions in *CD* IV/1 is whether obedience and humility are essential perfections of the Son alone, or whether these are predicated of the Son in terms of appropriation.

the essence or from each other in any way that would imply a divine essence distinct from each attribute.

Francis Turretin also sought to defend divine simplicity in the face of opposition—namely, the Socinians and Vorstius. He followed others from the tradition who asserted a virtual distinction among God's attributes, the diversity of which is seen in our conception, although it is grounded in God's essence rather than merely in our conception. Turretin saw no reason to reject divine simplicity since it not only was unproblematic for the Trinity and incarnation but also actually supported and safeguarded these teachings.

Charles Hodge voiced a serious concern regarding the nominalist understanding of the divine attributes, seeing that an extreme form of divine simplicity could easily result in this view and that it would have serious repercussions for divine revelation. At the same time, he wanted to avoid an extreme realist position where the divine attributes are understood to exist as real properties, therefore resulting in composition in God. Avoiding both extremes, Hodge followed Turretin and others by affirming a virtual distinction among the divine attributes.

Herman Bavinck served as a prominent example of the importance of the divine names to divine simplicity. His connecting of the divine names to divine simplicity gives simplicity a stronger biblical grounding. The many names are actually *required* in order to begin to express the fullness of God's being, and neither do they contradict God's simplicity. Bavinck also sees God's accommodation to humanity in the names, pointing to the anthropomorphic nature of scripture, which gives us true knowledge of God while never being exhaustive or complete. Our knowledge remains finite and analogical, based on God's true revelation, but never attaining the kind of knowledge that he has of himself. Divine simplicity is ultimately a recognition of the fullness of divine life.

Finally, in Barth one might expect to find a serious rejection of divine simplicity due to his objections to natural theology, general metaphysics, and any general notion of God. Instead, Barth finds some of these problems within the tradition, but this does not stop him from retrieving the doctrine and giving it renewed life within a trinitarian and christological framework. Barth also saw the need for a dialectic between God's multiplicity and simplicity, which affirmed the simplicity of God's essence while also acknowledging the reality of God's many perfections attested throughout scripture. Last, Barth believed that the biblical home of God's simplicity was his trustworthiness and faithfulness found in scripture. God is faithful and trustworthy because his perfections are not in conflict and cannot be divided.

Based on the previous chapters, the picture has become clearer that divine simplicity has been consistently affirmed and maintained from as early as Irenaeus to as recently as Barth. Yet it cannot be said that each understanding and expression of divine simplicity was identical, as though there were one monolithic version of divine simplicity throughout the tradition. There were differences between East and West, between Aquinas and Scotus, and new emphases in the theology of Barth. Although there were diverse expressions of the doctrine, there remained a stable core in which each theologian sought to express the nature of God as simple: His attributes are not parts of his nature; they are not in conflict with one another; they are not mixed together; and so forth. These claims were not the conclusion of a purely apophatic or negative account of God, but developed in response to combat oppositions and misinterpretations of scripture. Many of the theologians went back to scripture and the received tradition in order to provide corrections to their opponents, offering a better reading of scripture via the divine name(s) or the indivisible operations of the Trinity.

At this point, it must also be acknowledged that it is one thing to argue that these theologians understood the doctrine of divine simplicity to stem from scripture. It is another thing to argue that they were correct. However, it is beyond the scope of this project to assess each theologian's arguments in sufficient detail. At the same time, my argument does not depend on the correctness or assessment of any one theologian. While I do believe that the accounts of divine simplicity presented in these chapters differ from the understanding of many contemporary critics presented in chapter 1, the aim of these historical chapters has been to clear the ground for a reconsideration of the relationship between divine simplicity and scripture. If the contemporary rejections of divine simplicity represent misreading of the tradition, then this opens up new avenues for retrieving the best of the tradition in order to help clarify the relationship between divine simplicity and scripture. In the next chapter, I will draw out these biblical connections more clearly, and in the final chapter I will offer my own constructive proposal for divine simplicity.

5.

Biblical Roots of Divine Simplicity

We cannot prove the truth of the dogma that is not as such in the Bible merely from the fact that it is a dogma, but rather from the fact that we can and must regard it as a good interpretation of the Bible.

—Karl Barth, *Church Dogmatics*

The goal of the previous historical chapters was both to hear and to describe the ways in which various theologians articulated the doctrine of divine simplicity in relation to scripture. There was no burden to argue that some or even all examples were truly biblical in their portrayals. Rather, it was found that these theologians understood divine simplicity to be compatible with scripture and therefore made use of the doctrine in their teachings and writings. Even so, this does not fully release them from the charges brought against them (or the doctrine itself) by contemporary critics. It is easy to claim to be biblical and much harder to demonstrate this in actual practice.

What does it mean to say that divine simplicity is biblical? K. Scott Oliphint represents one example, connecting simplicity to aseity and concluding that "simplicity, therefore, is a biblical doctrine; it follows from God's aseity."[1] Jay Wesley Richards admits that "there is no proof text for [divine simplicity] in Scripture," but he still argues that "we might see divine simplicity as a philosophical extension of

---

1. K. Scott Oliphint, "Simplicity, Triunity, and the Incomprehensibility of God," in *One God in Three Persons: Unity of Essence, Distinction of Persons, Implications for Life*, ed. Bruce A. Ware and John Starke (Wheaton, IL: Crossway, 2015), 221.

the biblical concept of God's holiness."[2] F. G. Immink is clearer that divine simplicity "is not revealed by Scripture but is used to secure God's aseity and otherness, and this aseity and otherness is certainly taught by Scripture."[3] What is missing from these kinds of conclusions is an explicit connection between divine simplicity and scripture. To be clear, the doctrine does not rely on a series of prooftexts since an exposition of its relationship to scripture is more complicated and requires extended discussion of key biblical texts.

This chapter will provide a partial synthesis of the preceding chapters by including and analyzing the most prominent biblical connections to divine simplicity. However, this chapter is not entirely a work of retrieval. Although traditional accounts of divine simplicity were described first in this project, scripture provides the final word and norm on matters relating to Christian doctrine. If divine simplicity has a biblical basis in any sense, then its origins in scripture must be clarified with greater detail than has been done in the past.

Two particular biblical teachings stand out from the historical chapters. First, the name(s) of God in scripture consistently guided the tradition's speech and thought about God. The many names do not divide God into parts, nor do they merely describe the human experience of God apart from his real existence. Instead, they adequately describe his nature without claiming to fully capture all that he is. Second, the teaching of inseparable operations played an important role. If the works of the Father, Son, and Holy Spirit are undivided, then it seemed to these theologians that God's being must also be undivided—not only in terms of the three divine persons, but also in terms of the unity of the divine attributes shared among them.

I argue that these two insights should have served as the biblical origins of the doctrine of divine simplicity, but they were implicit or assumed throughout the tradition and therefore are in need of greater clarification. If divine simplicity is to remain a viable Christian teaching, then its technical expressions must function as an abbreviation of what is already found in the Old and New Testaments. Furthermore, its chief source must be revelation rather than natural theology, philosophy, or "classical theism." Therefore, in this chapter I will establish that divine simplicity has roots in scripture and that these two

2. Jay Wesley Richards, *The Untamed God: A Philosophical Exploration of Divine Perfection, Immutability, and Simplicity* (Downers Grove, IL: InterVarsity Press, 2003), 215.

3. F. G. Immink, *Divine Simplicity* (Utrecht: J. H. Kok, 1987), 35.

roots are the divine name(s) and the indivisible operations of the three divine persons.

BIBLICAL ROOTS AND CHRISTIAN THEOLOGY

Does the doctrine of divine simplicity impose an already defined framework or concept onto scripture? Put differently, is it possible for a doctrine of divine simplicity to be found in scripture, or does a right reading of scripture require a doctrine of divine simplicity? Must the concept, language, or framework be found within the biblical canon? These questions speak to the struggle of understanding the relationship between doctrine and scripture. In this sense, if divine simplicity is a truly Christian teaching, then it must be an extension of what is already found in scripture.

David Yeago's essay "The New Testament and Nicene Dogma" has been widely cited by those working in the area of theological exegesis or theological interpretation of scripture and has the potential to be a key resource for divine simplicity.[4] He analyzes Philippians 2:6–11 and argues that "the ancient theologians were right to hold that the Nicene *homoousion* is neither imposed *on* the New Testament texts, nor distantly deduced from the texts, but, rather, describes a pattern of judgments *in* the texts, in the texture of scriptural discourse concerning Jesus and the God of Israel."[5] To support this claim, Yeago investigates Paul's use of Isaiah 45:21–24 in Philippians 2 and concludes that "within the thought-world of Israel's scriptures, no stronger affirmation of the bond between the risen Jesus and the God of Israel is possible."[6] How does this work? Yeago argues that we must "distinguish between *judgments* and the *conceptual terms* in which those judgments are rendered."[7] As Michael Allen paraphrases,

Judgments are the material claims made by any given communicator, while concepts are the particular and contingent forms used to express that judgment. Importantly, judgments may be rendered by a variety of

4. David S. Yeago, "The New Testament and Nicene Dogma: A Contribution to the Recovery of Theological Exegesis," in *The Theological Interpretation of Scripture: Classic and Contemporary Readings*, ed. Stephen E. Fowl (Oxford: Blackwell, 1997), 87–100. This essay was originally published in *ProEccl* 6 (1997): 16–26. Further citations come from the former source.

5. Ibid., 88. For a related proposal, see Thomas F. Torrance, *The Christian Doctrine of God: One Being Three Persons* (London: T&T Clark, 1996), 88–107.

6. Yeago, "The New Testament and Nicene Dogma," 90.

7. Ibid., 93.

concepts, and concepts can be employed to express a number of judgments. In other words, categories and metaphors are tools.[8]

Returning to Philippians 2 and Isaiah 45, this means that "the judgment about Jesus and God made in the Nicene Creed—the judgment that they are 'of one substance' or 'one reality'—is indeed 'the same,' in a basically ordinary and unmysterious way, as that made in a New Testament text such as Philippians 2:6ff."[9] In this way, doctrines can be faithful to scripture's judgments even if they use concepts or terms that are not found in scripture itself. Concepts and terms are meant to be a faithful translation of the same judgment(s) found in scripture. Scripture does not have to use the same terms and concepts for a doctrine—like the Trinity—to be found within it. The issue under question is not the sameness of concepts, but the sameness of judgments.

According to Yeago's distinction, it is true that scripture never uses the language of Trinity, *hypostasis*, *homoousios*, and so on. The absence of these terms is why Gordon Fee calls Paul a "latent trinitarian" who was "presuppositionally an ontological trinitarian as well."[10] Or, as Richard Hays explains, "Paul's understanding of God is proto-trinitarian . . . , [and] the later doctrine of the Trinity is an attempt to describe and analyze the way in which Jesus Christ and the Spirit had 'become intrinsic to Paul's way of referring to God.'"[11] The later teaching of the Trinity is therefore a fruit of theological reflection and biblical reasoning, which has its roots in scripture.

Christoph Schwöbel makes a related point in his discussion of theological ontology and divine-human relations. He writes that "whenever Christian theology is challenged to lay open the resources in which the activity of doing theology is rooted, it will ultimately

---

8. R. Michael Allen, *Justification and the Gospel: Understanding the Contexts and Controversies* (Grand Rapids: Baker Academic, 2013), 62.

9. Yeago, "The New Testament and Nicene Dogma," 94. At this point Yeago criticizes James D. G. Dunn's *Christology in the Making* (Grand Rapids: Eerdmans, 1996) for ignoring the distinction between judgments and concepts (95–97).

10. Gordon D. Fee, "Paul and the Trinity: The Experience of Christ and the Spirit for Paul's Understanding of God," in *The Trinity: An Interdisciplinary Symposium on the Trinity*, ed. Stephen T. Davis, Daniel Kendall, and Gerald O'Collins (Oxford: Oxford University Press, 2002), 51, 71. See also C. Kavin Rowe, "Biblical Pressure and Trinitarian Hermeneutics," *ProEccl* 11 (2002): 295–312.

11. Richard B. Hays, "The God of Mercy Who Rescues Us from the Present Evil Age: Romans and Galatians," in *The Forgotten God: Perspectives in Biblical Theology*, ed. A. Andrew Das and Frank J. Matera (Louisville: Westminster John Knox, 2002), 141. Hays's comment is in reference to Francis Margaret Young and David F. Ford, *Meaning and Truth in 2 Corinthians* (Grand Rapids: Eerdmans, 1987).

have to return to Scripture."[12] Failing to make this return results not only in theological errors but also in confusion, since "the whole range of [theology's] form of expression and the whole scope of its content would not make sense without understanding the roots in the biblical witness."[13] Yeago's call to clearly understand and identify the "judgments" of scripture is similar to Schwöbel's argument that theology must depend on an understanding of its biblical roots. Scripture governs theological discourse and, if a dogmatic concept is to be a legitimate theological expression, it must have and rely on its biblical roots so that the judgment(s) in scripture are faithfully communicated in the concept.

As it relates to divine simplicity, the question is whether the judgments inherent in the concept of divine simplicity correspond to the same judgments found in scripture. Is it a philosophical concept forced on the text? Is the concept of simplicity a faithful rendering of a series of judgments found in scripture? These are significant questions, and this chapter will clarify the biblical roots of divine simplicity—or, in Yeago's terms, its judgments—in order to better understand the doctrine as a conceptual elaboration of two biblical teachings, specifically the divine name(s) and the indivisible operations of the Trinity.[14]

12. Christoph Schwöbel, "God as Conversation: Reflections on a Theological Ontology of Communicative Relations," in *Theology and Conversation: Towards a Relational Theology*, ed. J. Haers and P. De Mey (Leuven: Leuven University Press, 2003), 46. Or, as John Webster comments, "Scripture is the place to which theology is directed to find its subject matter and the norm by which its representations are evaluated." See John Webster, *The Domain of the Word: Scripture and Theological Reason* (London: Bloomsbury T&T Clark, 2012), 128–29.

13. Schwöbel, "God as Conversation," 46. Another way of looking at this is to see that the biblical texts exercise "pressure" on its readers to construct Christian doctrine in light of biblical teachings. Returning to the Trinity as an example, C. Kavin Rowe states that "Scripture exerts a pressure upon its interpreters to understand the God of the entire Bible as the Trinity and . . . this pressure is felt most acutely at the point of the intersection of the Old and New Testaments" (Rowe, "Biblical Pressure and Trinitarian Hermeneutics," 311). What are the pressures in scripture that press readers to understand God as simple? Are they in the text, or are they forced on it from the outside?

14. Kevin Vanhoozer calls this move from scripture to doctrine a "conceptual elaboration." See Kevin J. Vanhoozer, *Remythologizing Theology: Divine Action, Passion, and Authorship*, CSCD (Cambridge: Cambridge University Press, 2010), 105, 408. Webster calls it a "conceptual representation" or "summary concept." See Webster, *Domain of the Word*, 130–31. One thing must be made clear: such concepts—whether elaborations, representations, or summaries—should never be said to be improvements on the language and concepts of scripture. The biblical judgments remain the norm, and therefore any expression of them by a chosen concept can be judged according to whether it faithfully "represents" or "elaborates" such biblical judgments. Concepts may vary according to a particular culture, time, language, or other needs. Their function is to provide abbreviations, or shorthand descriptions, that briefly summarize a number of inherent details and claims.

THE DIVINE NAME(S)

Names are indispensable for communication and identifying people, places, events, and nearly any other thing. They "particularize" in that they refer to a particular person, place, or event and not another. However it is framed, what a name communicates or refers to (attributes, a person, history) and how a name is used (to identify, distinguish, express authority) are significant factors of human life and identity. These issues are no less important in a discussion of the divine name(s) found throughout scripture. While the modern Western world tends to see names as mere labels, scripture displays a strong relationship between a name and the person who bears that name.

Adam named Eve, meaning "living," "because she was the mother of all living" (Gen 3:20). God also gives names to people that describe their role in redemptive history: Abram, "exalted father," was later changed to Abraham, "father of a multitude" (Gen 17:5). Name changes also take place in the event of life transformations such as Jacob's being renamed Israel (Gen 32:28). When speaking of God, names come in the form of adjectives (compassionate or gracious, Exod 34:6–7),[15] self-identified names (jealous, Exod 34:14), or images and titles (Shepherd of Israel, Ps 80:1). Scripture also joins divine names with particular actions or specific narratives: "I am the Lord your God, who brought you out of the land of Egypt, out of the house of slavery" (Exod 20:2; Ps 81:10).[16] Summarizing these examples, it may be said that names are "inextricably connected to the very nature of that which is named. Hence, to know the name is to know something of the fundamental traits, nature, or destiny of the name's bearer."[17] Names are crucial not only in labeling or identifying but also in describing a person's character and even their very nature.[18]

15. These adjectives are what often go under the label of "attributes."

16. As I will later show, the divine name Yahweh is bound to the name Jesus as well as Father, Son, and Holy Spirit.

17. Karl G. Bohmbach, "Names and Naming in the Biblical World," in *Women in Scripture: A Dictionary of Named and Unnamed Women in the Hebrew Bible, The Apocryphal/Deuterocononical Books, and the New Testament*, ed. Carol Meyers (Boston: Houghton Mifflin, 2000), 33.

18. This statement recalls the way names function in the Old Testament. For example, "Let not my lord regard this worthless fellow, Nabal, for as his name is, so is he. Nabal is his name, and folly is with him" (1 Sam 25:25). A number of Old and New Testament theologies also make this point as well. For example, see Brevard S. Childs, *The Book of Exodus: A Critical, Theological Commentary*, OTL (Philadelphia: Westminster, 1974), 596; Bruce K. Waltke and Charles Yu, *An Old Testament Theology: An Exegetical, Canonical, and Thematic Approach* (Grand

Throughout the tradition one of the most noteworthy passages was Exodus 3:14, a traditional "prooftext" for the doctrine of divine simplicity. For example, Matthew Levering explains how Thomas saw the name He Who Is (*qui est*) as the most proper expression of God's divinity. This name signifies "being and nothing more. It conveys God's simplicity" while also pointing to his "sheer presence." On this basis, this "ensures both God's transcendence and his active immanence."[19] Étienne Gilson has famously called this the "metaphysics of Exodus."[20] I am sympathetic to traditional interpretations of this passage, but I do not see how I AM is capable of referring to "being" in the way that Thomas or others describe this term. This does not mean that there can be no ontological interpretation of this passage.[21] Rather, it cannot bear the weight of divine simplicity on its own. Exodus 3 is in need of Exodus 33 and 34 and other passages to fill out its meaning and relation to divine simplicity. As I will point out below, the connection between Yahweh and I AM THAT I AM reveals a future reference which indicates that Yahweh would reveal more about his name at a later time.

If prooftexts or particular names cannot form the basis for divine simplicity, neither can grammatical and etymological discussions provide sufficient access to the meaning of God's name. As Michael P. Knowles suggests,

> The "meaning" of God's name is, so to speak, ultimately no great mystery. It is revealed neither by grammatical nor by mystical speculation any more than it can ultimately be safeguarded by holy fear. Rather, it is both disclosed and guaranteed by the nature of God's relationship

Rapids: Zondervan, 2007), 359; Michael P. Knowles, *The Unfolding Mystery of the Divine Name: The God of Sinai in Our Midst* (Downers Grove, IL: IVP Academic, 2012), 29; Charles H. H. Scobie, *The Ways of Our God: An Approach to Biblical Theology* (Grand Rapids: Eerdmans, 2003), 108; C. Kavin Rowe, "Romans 10:13: What Is the Name of the Lord?," *HBT* 22 (2000): 159.

19. Matthew Levering, *Scripture and Metaphysics: Aquinas and the Renewal of Trinitarian Theology*, CCT (Oxford: Blackwell, 2004), 63. This also calls into question the identity of the "divine name." Throughout scripture it appears to be Yahweh since it is the most widely used name in the Old Testament. However, Thomas refers to I AM as the "most proper name" and as the name that implies divine simplicity.

20. Étienne Gilson, *The Spirit of Mediaeval Philosophy*, trans. A. H. C. Downes (New York: Charles Scribner's Sons, 1940), 94, 147. For a contemporary metaphysical reading of Exodus 3:14 in the Thomist tradition, see Thomas Joseph White, *Exodus*, BTCB (Grand Rapids: Brazos, 2016), 39–44, 292–304.

21. For an exegetical and theological reading of Exodus 3 that also takes an ontological interpretation seriously, see Andrea Saner, *"Too Much to Grasp": Exodus 3:13–15 and the Reality of God*, JTISup (Winona Lake, IN: Eisenbrauns, 2015).

with Israel (and, indeed, with the whole of creation). God's "name" is expounded by God's acts, revealing this God to be, indeed, [who he is in Exod 34:6–7].[22]

I would add, and will demonstrate below, that God's name is revealed not only in his acts but also in scripture's statements about God (e.g., "The Lord our God is holy" in Ps 99:9) and God's revelation of himself ("I am holy" in Lev 11:44–45). Therefore, in this section I will illustrate the use of God's name by focusing on the significance and meaning of it first, in Exodus, and second, in the Psalms. While this chapter does not allow sufficient space for a comprehensive study of the divine name,[23] these examples will demonstrate that (1) the divine name is God himself in his self–revelation; (2) there is no conflict among God's attributes (e.g., mercy and justice); and (3) the language used to describe God's attributes is mutual.

IDENTIFYING GOD'S NAME

The first major insight into the divine name is found in Exodus 3. God appears to Moses at the burning bush and, prior to revealing his personal name, identifies himself by three other divine names: "the God of Abraham, the God of Isaac, and the God of Jacob" (Exod 3:6). God has seen the suffering of the Israelites and heard their cries, telling Moses that he will send him to Pharaoh to deliver the Israelites and lead them out of Egypt. Hesitant to defy Pharaoh and lead the Israelites, Moses raises the question "Who am I that I should go to Pharaoh, and bring the Israelites out of Egypt?" and receives God's promise: "I will be with you" (Exod 3:11–12). Even still, Moses worries that after telling them that the "God of your fathers" sent him

22. Knowles, *Unfolding Mystery of the Divine Name*, 47. Paul Ricoeur raises a related point as to whether the narrowly exegetical discussions of Exod 3:14 severely limit its meaning due to the constraints not only of the Hebrew language but also because of the tools used to study it. See Paul Ricoeur, "From Interpretation to Translation," in *Thinking Biblically: Exegetical and Hermeneutical Studies*, trans. David Pellauer (Chicago: University of Chicago Press, 1998), 331–61. See also Saner's critique of etymological and religio-historical approaches in *Too Much to Grasp*, 13–58.

23. For a helpful summary, see Stephen G. Dempster, "LORD," in *The Routledge Encyclopedia of the Historical Jesus*, ed. Craig A. Evans (New York: Routledge, 2008), 375–80; Christopher Seitz, "The Divine Name in Christian Scripture," in *Word without End: The Old Testament as Abiding Theological Witness* (Grand Rapids: Eerdmans, 1998), 251–62; R. Kendall Soulen, *The Divine Name(s) and the Holy Trinity: Distinguishing the Voices*, vol. 1 (Louisville: Westminster John Knox, 2011), esp. part 2.

that they will ask for his name. God answers Moses with the famous I AM WHO I AM.[24] As many commentators point out, this response is vague and difficult to interpret. I am what? W. Ross Blackburn and others see within the text a "future orientation [in the divine name], opening the possibility, even expectation, of further revelation. Any 'definition,' or understanding, of the name would become clearer as God makes himself known in rescuing Israel from Egypt."[25] This points to the importance of verse 15 for the first deepening of this revelation: it is "the Lord, the God of your fathers, the God of Abraham, the God of Isaac, and the God of Jacob" who is I AM, and that "this is my name forever."[26]

Verse 16 further deepens the meaning of God's answer to Moses's initial question, telling him to "Go and gather the elders of Israel together and say to them, 'The Lord, the God of your fathers, the God of Abraham, of Isaac, and of Jacob, has appeared to me" (Exod 3:16). The "God of your fathers" is the Lord, Yahweh. Yahweh is the divine name given to Moses and is used most often throughout the Old Testament.[27]

24. Other translation options exist, but note that my argument does not depend on one particular translation. On the history of interpretation of this verse, see Cornelis Den Hertog, *The Other Face of God: "I Am That I Am" Reconsidered* (Sheffield: Sheffield Phoenix, 2012), chaps. 4–5; Scott M. Langston, *Exodus: Through the Centuries*, BBC (Oxford: Wiley-Blackwell, 2005), 61–63; Childs, *Book of Exodus*, 84–87; Dennis J. McCarthy, "Exodus 3:14: History, Philosophy, and Theology," *CBQ* 40 (1978): 311–22. For a philosophical history, see J. W. Gericke, "Philosophical Interpretations of Exodus 3:14—A Brief Historical Overview," *Journal for Semitics* 21 (2012): 125–36.

25. W. Ross Blackburn, *The God Who Makes Himself Known: The Missionary Heart of the Book of Exodus*, NSBT (Downers Grove, IL: IVP Academic, 2012), 37. Austin Surls translates Exod 3:14 as "I will be whoever I will be" partly due to the connection between YAHWEH and I AM in which there is "a verbal phonetic complement that contains a future reference in the *yiqtol* conjugation." This claim leads him to conclude that the connection between "I will be whoever I will be" and Yahweh "communicates that *YAHWEH would reveal the meaning of his name in the future.*" See Austin Surls, "Finding the Meaning of the Divine Name in the Book of Exodus: From Etymology to Literary Onomastics" (PhD diss., Wheaton College, 2014), 87–88 (emphasis original).

26. I agree with Terence Fretheim, who argues that this is not a matter of God holding back his name. See Terence E. Fretheim, *Exodus*, IBC (Louisville: Westminster John Knox, 2010), 64.

27. Surls notes that I AM "could not function as the divine name because its morphology as a first-person verbal form would be immediately transparent" and because it is "arguably never used as the proper name of Israel's God outside of [Exod 3:14]" (Surls, "Finding the Meaning," 86). He is aware of the possibility of finding I AM in Hos 1:9 but remains unconvinced. Saner disagrees, arguing that I AM is God's name for himself, whereas Yahweh is the name given to Moses and is the name God's people are to use for him. See Saner, *Too Much to Grasp*, 125–29. For history and background on the use of this name, see Robert J. Wilkinson, *Tetragrammaton: Western Christians and the Hebrew Name of God; From the Beginnings to the Seventeenth Century*,

With that said, the name Yahweh in Exodus 3 cannot be understood in isolation. As stated above, there is a future orientation inherent within the connection of I AM THAT I AM and Yahweh. The meaning and significance can only be located by paying attention to its explanation and use throughout the rest of scripture. As R. W. L. Moberly puts it, "The meaning of the name is the meaning it was given in Hebrew thought and usage as reflected in Exod 3:14, 33:19, 34:14 and everywhere, and not some 'basic' meaning derived from the verb *hyh*."[28] Within scripture's own language and concepts, the use of Exodus 3:14–15 as a reference to being, immutability, aseity, or simplicity is a misrepresentation of the text.[29] These verses cannot support the burden of these claims, nor should they function as proof-texts as though such weighty doctrines could be justified by these verses alone. Having said that, this does not mean that Exodus 3 is not a significant starting point for a doctrine of divine simplicity. Beginning with the divine name in Exodus 3, readers must continue to listen to the rest of scripture in order to hear and see the unfolding of its meaning. In what follows, I will briefly outline the remainder of the key passages in Exodus that shed light on the richness of the divine name.

GOD'S MANY NAMES

After the revelation of the name Yahweh to Moses in Exodus 3:1–22, the text continues to give further insights into the meaning of the divine name.[30] For example, Exodus 6 contains a declaration and deepening of God's presence and identity. The patriarchs knew Yahweh as "God Almighty," the one who made a covenant with them, and this was the same God who revealed himself to Moses as Yahweh

SHCT (Leiden: Brill, 2015); Geurt H. van Kooten, ed., *The Revelation of the Name YHWH to Moses: Perspectives from Judaism, the Pagan Graeco-Roman World, and Early Christianity*, Themes in Biblical Narrative 9 (Leiden: Brill, 2006).

28. R. W. L. Moberly, *At the Mountain of God: Story and Theology in Exodus 32–34*, JSOTSup (Sheffield: Sheffield Academic, 1983), 79.

29. On this point I agree with Seitz and others that these verses are not directly referring to the divine essence or, stated differently, were not written as a definitive statement of God's being. See Seitz, "Divine Name in Christian Scripture," 35–36. However, I am sympathetic to the "traditional" reading of Exod 3:14–15 due to the influence of the LXX and Vulgate. Last, even if this passage is not a direct statement about God's being this does not mean that an ontological interpretation of it is impossible or unwarranted.

30. Recall that I use the term "divine names" in a traditional sense to refer not only to God's proper names but also to attributes of all kinds (absolute, relative, metaphorical).

and promised to deliver them out of Egypt. The statement "I am the Lord" brackets Exodus 6:6–8, "suggesting that what falls between . . . lends further definition to the declaration."[31] Yahweh is the one who will "bring you out," "deliver you," and "redeem you." Most importantly, "I will be your God. You shall know that I am the Lord your God, who has freed you from the burdens of the Egyptians" (6:7). Their God, the Lord, is this same God who will do all these things. This is who he is and who he will be shown to be.

Exodus 33:12–23 deepens the significance and meaning of the divine name even more. Israel has broken their covenant with Yahweh by making and worshiping the golden calf. Their sin brings about God's anger, and he tells Moses that "I will not go up among you, or I would consume you on the way" (Exod 33:3). Moberly rightly points out that, rather than a problem of metaphysics or identity, the problem in this passage is a "moral problem of how a holy God can abide with a sinful people."[32] Because of this, Moses intercedes for Israel and seeks to restore Yahweh's presence with his people (Exod 33:12–17). However, the possibility remains that such a renewed presence will inevitably result in further judgment in relation to any future sin. Therefore, Moses seeks "something further," and it "is nothing less than a deeper and fuller revelation of the character of Yahweh as a God whose very nature it is to be gracious and merciful (33:19, 34:6f.)."[33]

This deeper and fuller revelation transpires when Moses asks Yahweh to "show me now your ways, so that I may know you" (Exod 33:13) and this eventually leads to a request for Yahweh to "show me your glory" (v. 18). Yahweh responds as follows:

> I will make all my goodness pass before you, and will proclaim before you the name, "The Lord"; and I will be gracious to whom I will be gracious, and will show mercy on whom I will show mercy. But," he said, "you cannot see my face; for no one shall see me and live." And the Lord continued, "See, there is a place by me where you shall stand on the rock; and while my glory passes by I will put you in a cleft of the rock, and I will cover you with my hand until I have passed by; then I

31. Blackburn, *The God Who Makes Himself Known*, 46.

32. Moberly, *At the Mountain of God*, 67. This is not to say that an ontological itnerpretation of this passage would be wrong. Rather, the context of this passage is not first of all concerned with making ontological statements about God.

33. Ibid., 68.

will take away my hand, and you shall see my back; but my face shall not be seen. (vv. 19–23)[34]

Many observations and questions arise from this text. First, crucial to the interpretation of this passage is noticing that Yahweh "will proclaim before you the name, 'The Lord'" (33:19) and what follows is "a commentary on the meaning of the divine name."[35] The divine name represents God as one who is free to be gracious and merciful, and it is his character that forms the basis of the renewed covenant. Readers should also see that God's goodness, glory, back, and face are all related to the proclamation of his name.

These points lead to the second observation, that the distinct names mean different things (e.g., glory is not the same as goodness), but that they all refer to Yahweh. Moses asks to see God's ways (v. 13)[36] and glory (v. 18).[37] In response, Yahweh tells Moses that he will "make all my goodness pass before you" (v. 19). However, Moses cannot see his face (v. 20), but can see his glory pass by while Moses stands in the cleft of the rock (v. 22). Once this happens, Yahweh will take away his hand, Moses will see his back,[38] but he still will not be able to see Yahweh's face. Moberly suggests that "the variety of terminology—glory, goodness, name, face—represents an attempt to express the inexpressible, the experience of God."[39]

Each name reveals God himself from one particular perspective. The glory (*kabod*) of God "appears again in v. 22 where it is effectively synonymous with God himself. . . . Moses thus asks to see Yahweh himself." [40] God's goodness (*tub*) is used differently, but there remains "a certain synonymity between 'goodness' and 'glory' . . . by

---

34. C. Houtman translates 33:19 as "I will make all my attributes pass before your eyes." See C. Houtman, *Exodus*, HCOT (Kampen: Peeters, 1999), 3:701.

35. James Plastaras, *The God of Exodus: The Theology of the Exodus Narratives* (Milwaukee: Bruce, 1966), 243.

36. Moberly comments that "'ways' often denotes a person's character or the course of behaviour that he adopts, and so the request would appear to be to know God's character" (*At the Mountain of God*, 73).

37. Fretheim sees that "glory *for Moses* refers to the face/presence of God no longer enveloped by the cloud (cf. 16:10; 40:34) or the fire (see 24:17)" (*Exodus*, 299 [emphasis original]).

38. Moberly points out that "back" (*ahor*) "is not the usual term for 'back' in the physical or anatomical sense (*gaw, gew*), but more vaguely means 'hinder part,' thus conveying the idea of a view from behind, while being less explicit about exactly what is seen" (Moberly, *At the Mountain of God*, 82).

39. Ibid., 76. This point is made through Saner's work *Too Much to Grasp*.

40. Moberly, *At the Mountain of God*, 76.

the parallelism between v. 19 . . . and v. 22."[41] Andrea Saner identifies a similar point, arguing that "the goodness of YHWH is not here described as a part of YHWH's character, but as the whole of it, as the proclamation of the divine name."[42] Knowles believes this "suggests that God's 'goodness' and God's 'name' are in fact the essence of God's 'glory.'"[43] He adds that God's ways, goodness, grace, mercy, and glory—"all are expressions of the same divine character. As such, they are all summed up in the meaning of God's 'name'—soon to be articulated more fully in Exodus 34:6–7."[44] If they all describe God's character, then not only is God good and gracious, but also his grace is good and his goodness is gracious. The same could be said about the other descriptions said of God in these passages. This does not mean that God's goodness, back, or glory are identical or synonymous. God's grace does not describe God in exactly the same way as his goodness or glory. The divine name is singular, but Exodus 33 sheds light on the inner richness of God's name, capable of being expressed through other divine names. God's goodness, back, and glory do not have the same meaning, but they are also nothing other than Yahweh.

The climax of the meaning and significance of the divine name is found in Exodus 34:6–7.[45] Moses's intercession results in further revelation of the divine name as well as Yahweh's commitment to show grace and mercy to Israel even in light of their sin. The outcome of this covenant renewal is, as Brueggemann states, "an astonishing disclosure of God, which tells Moses (and us) as much about the God of the Bible as any verse can."[46] Descending in a cloud, he says the following to Moses:

> The Lord, the Lord, a God merciful and gracious, slow to anger, and abounding in steadfast love and faithfulness, keeping steadfast love for the thousandth generation, forgiving iniquity and transgression and sin,

41. Ibid., 76–77.

42. Saner, *Too Much to Grasp*, 159.

43. Knowles, *Unfolding Mystery of the Divine Name*, 37. Here, "name" refers to Yahweh.

44. Ibid., 39.

45. Other passages ascribe multiple names or attributes to God (e.g., 2 Chr 5:13; Ps 106:1; Dan 2:20; Isa 5:16; 1 Cor 1:24), but Exodus 34 is unique not only in the number of descriptions given of God but also in terms of how God describes himself and how significant this passage is throughout the rest of the biblical canon (e.g., Num 14:18; Neh 9:17, 31; Ps 103:8; Jer 32:18–19; Joel 2:13; Jonah 4:2). For more on this issue, see Nathan C. Lane, *The Compassionate, but Punishing God: A Canonical Analysis of Exodus 34:6–7* (Eugene, OR: Pickwick, 2010).

46. Walter Brueggemann, "Exodus," in *The New Interpreter's Bible*, vol. 1, *Genesis to Leviticus*, ed. Leander Keck (Nashville: Abingdon, 1994), 947.

yet by no means clearing the guilty, but visiting the iniquity of the parents on the children and the children's children, to the third and the fourth generation. (Exod 34:6–7)

Moberly calls this "an account of the nature of God, from God's lips" and sees it as "the fullest statement about the divine nature in the whole Bible."[47] Terence Fretheim sees this as "a virtual exegesis of this [i.e., the divine] name,"[48] and Walter Brueggemann agrees.[49]

What does this passage add to the understanding and meaning of the divine name? One option is to follow Brueggemann, who finds "a profound, unacknowledged, and unresolved contradiction" since Yahweh is said to both forgive *and* punish.[50] This contradiction indicates that "God does deal with violators of the covenant in two very different ways that cannot be logically or in practice harmonized" and that "it is inadmissible to resolve the tension programmatically or systematically."[51] If this is true, then the conflicting nature of God's mercy and justice causes serious problems for divine simplicity. Mercy and justice represent not merely distinct expressions of God's simple nature, but a divided nature in tension with itself.

Yet is this "contradiction" truly representative of Exodus's account of who and what God is? Brueggemann is correct that Exodus 34:6–7 is an explanation of the divine name and therefore Yahweh's character.[52] However, it is not necessary that the resulting tension be expressed as a contradiction, nor must any clarification be considered a programmatic or systematic harmonization. Moberly helpfully explains that "the point is not that the people either experience wrath or mercy, but that both wrath and mercy are in the character of God though it is his mercy which is ultimately predominant in

47. R. W. L Moberly, *Old Testament Theology: Reading the Hebrew Bible as Christian Scripture* (Grand Rapids: Baker Academic, 2013), 192.

48. Fretheim, *Exodus*, 301. He adds that "it thus constitutes a kind of 'canon' of the kind of God Israel's God is" (302).

49. Brueggemann, "Exodus," 946.

50. Ibid., 947. See also his *Theology of the Old Testament: Testimony, Dispute, Advocacy* (Minneapolis: Fortress Press, 2005), 227.

51. Brueggemann, "Exodus," 947.

52. Surls adds that "Exodus 34:6 offers the only biblical example of YHWH speaking his own name twice. The repetition of human proper names is rhetorically emphatic. YHWH repeated the names of his servants to make unambiguous reference to them while indicating their special status (Gen 22:11; Exod 3:4; 1 Sam 3:10). Thus, the repetition of the name YHWH not only made unambiguous reference, it also indicated that the descriptions to follow would be predicated to this name alone" (Surls, "Finding the Meaning," 215).

his dealings with his people."[53] Rather than finding a contradiction between mercy and justice, both names reveal the nature of Yahweh and the meaning of his name. God punishes his people (e.g., Exod 32:5) and shows mercy through the renewal of the covenant.[54]

As an "exegesis of the divine name," Exodus 34:6–7 describes Yahweh as merciful, gracious, slow to anger, abundant in steadfast love (*hesed*) and faithfulness. He forgives, but will not fail to be just. All of these names, ranging from mercy to justice, are part of God's declaration of his name to Moses as promised in Exodus 33. As Austin Surls wisely summarizes, "Without these descriptive statements . . . , YHWH would remain unknown; without the proper name, the descriptions could be misapplied."[55] One might say that the revelation of the name Yahweh, without further explanation, would be confusing. Yet trying to explain God without reference to the name Yahweh would be meaningless.[56]

THE DOXOLOGICAL ELEMENT OF THE DIVINE NAME(S)

The divine name plays a crucial role in the book of Exodus and the Old Testament as a whole,[57] but it functions differently outside of

53. Moberly, *At the Mountain of God*, 87. I am hesitant to embrace Moberly's statement that God's mercy is predominant if he means that mercy is somehow greater or stronger than other attributes of God. Scripture may contain more accounts of God showing grace and mercy than judgment and wrath, but this does not mean that God's mercy is predominant. We do not always know why God chooses to be merciful nor to whom he will show mercy (Exod 33:19).

54. See also Ezek 20:13–17. Here, Yahweh recounts this narrative and says that he "acted for the sake of my name." He could have destroyed them, for he will show grace and mercy to whom he chooses (Exod 33:19), but "spared them" on the basis of his own character. For a lengthier engagement of each characteristic mentioned in Exod 34:6–7, see Knowles, *Unfolding Mystery of the Divine Name*.

55. Surls, "Finding the Meaning," 314.

56. On the loss and significance of the divine name(s) in scripture and theology, see D. Stephen Long, *Speaking of God: Theology, Language, and Truth* (Minneapolis: Fortress Press, 2009), 180–92. For a somewhat different reading, see Soulen, *Divine Name(s)*. Bavinck is also instructive on this point, stating that "the revealed name is the foundation of all the names by which we address him," and that "the *one* name of God, which is inclusive of his entire revelation both in nature and in grace, is divisible for us in a great many names. . . . It is the one name, the full revelation and to that extent the very being of God himself, with which we are dealing in all those names" (Herman Bavinck, *Reformed Dogmatics*, vol. 2, *God and Creation*, ed. John Bolt, trans. John Vriend [Grand Rapids: Baker Academic, 2006], 99).

57. For example, Seitz, Zimmerli, Feldmeier, and Spieckermann see the divine name as central for Old Testament theology. See Seitz, "Divine Name in Christian Scripture"; Walther Zimmerli, *Old Testament Theology in Outline*, trans. David E. Green (Louisville: John Knox, 1978); Reinhard Feldmeier and Hermann Spieckermann, *God of the Living: A Biblical Theology*, trans. Mark E. Biddle (Baylor, TX: Baylor University Press, 2011), 23.

Exodus as it finds expression in new contexts. Walther Eichrodt represents one way, referring to what he calls the "hypostatic character" of the divine name where the name is treated as a person who can be described with various traits or attributes.[58] Of course, it is not a person, but the point is that the divine name is capable of being described just as God is described elsewhere. The Psalms provide one of the clearest illustrations, presenting not only the "hypostatic character" of the divine name but also what I call the doxological element of the divine name(s). What will become clear is that God cannot be praised for being faithful or holy if these terms do not actually describe who and what he is.

Throughout the Psalms the divine name is described and treated in a variety of ways. God's name is loved (5:11; 69:36; 119:132), great (6:1), and awesome (99:3). Hearers are called to "ascribe to the Lord the glory due his name" (29:2; cf. 66:2; 72:19; 79:9; 86:9, 12; 96:8), to trust in his name (20:7; 33:21), and be patient for his name is good (52:9). "And those who know your name put their trust in you" (9:10) since God's name reflects his faithful character. God's name is also holy (33:21; 103:1; 105:3; 106:47; 111:9) and everlasting (135:13). This "name" being referred to is the Lord, Yahweh (68:4; 83:18), first revealed to Moses in Exodus 3 and further revealed throughout the rest of scripture. This has led some theologians to declare that God's name actually has divine attributes.[59]

The hypostatic character of the divine name is prevalent throughout the Psalms, but the same terms are also used of Yahweh himself. For example, various psalms refer to those who love God's name, but also to those who love the Lord (31:23; 97:10). Not only is God's name good, but so is the Lord (52:9; 135:3). Hearers are called to "ascribe to the Lord the glory due his name; worship the Lord in the splendor of holiness" (29:2). There is a call to trust in God's name, but also to trust in the Lord (4:5; 20:7; 26:1; 33:21; 115:9) because the Lord is great (48:1), holy (99:9), and everlasting (117:2). Identical terms are used of the divine name and Yahweh himself, leading to the conclusion that the name that is revealed in many names is *Yahweh himself in his self-revelation.*[60]

58. See Walther Eichrodt, *Theology of the Old Testament*, trans. J. A. Baker (Philadelphia: Westminster, 1961), 41–43.

59. See John Frame, *The Doctrine of God*, A Theology of Lordship (Phillipsburg, NJ: P&R, 2002), 348.

60. I add "in his self-revelation" in order to emphasize that this revelation is true, but only

If the divine name is Yahweh himself in his self-revelation, then whatever is said of God's name is equally said of God. To say that "his name is great" (Ps 76:1) is the same as saying that Yahweh is great (Ps 99:2). Furthermore, similar to the mutual nature of terms in Exodus 33, scripture speaks of God's identity in different ways, and yet the descriptions refer to the same thing: God himself. To illustrate, the divine name is said to be holy (Ezek 39:7), but God himself is also called the Holy One (Isa 43:15). Scripture also speaks of *his* holiness (Ps 29:2) or "my [God's] holiness" (Ezek 38:23). To speak of the holiness of God's name, God as the Holy One, or *God's* holiness is to speak of the same thing in three different ways: what God is.

Why is it important to recognize that what scripture says of God's name is said of God himself? Why is it significant to observe that the various descriptions are often seen as mutual and integrative, all meaning something different and yet all being said of Yahweh alone? Because these descriptions indicate that God is praised not only for what he has done but also for who and what he is, and this is what I call the doxological element of the divine name(s). Once again, the Psalms are full of examples. "Exalt the Lord our God and worship at His footstool; Holy is He" (99:5). "Praise the Lord! Oh give thanks to the Lord, for he is good, for his steadfast love endures forever!" (106:1). "Praise the Lord, for the Lord is good; sing to his name, for it is pleasant" (135:3). "Great is the Lord, and greatly to be praised, and his greatness is unsearchable" (145:3), or even "Praise him for his mighty deeds; praise him according to his excellent greatness" (150:2). One of the most common statements about the divine name in the Psalms is that its hearers are to sing praise to it (7:17; 9:2; 18:49; 61:8; 66:4; 68:4; 69:30; 74:21; 92:1; 113:1; 135:1, 3).

How can God and his name be praised for being good, great, or even for his works if these "things" being praised are not somehow himself? As I have shown above, there is good reason to believe that God's name, and all the names ascribed to it, is nothing other than himself in his self-revelation. Therefore, if God is praised for being holy, but his holiness is something other than God himself, or he

partial. God's name is himself, but the entirety of God remains beyond his name. He both transcends his name and yet descends and accommodates himself in his name. In reference to Rom 10:13, C. Kavin Rowe seems to agree, commenting that "there is no disjunction between the divine name and the divine being" ("What Is the Name of the Lord," 159). He admits that some passages seem to separate God's name and God himself (e.g., Isa 30:27–28), but that "these slightly ambiguous texts should be read in light of the overwhelming witness of the rest of the OT" (ibid., 159n73).

is holy according to a standard other than himself, then something other than God is being praised. The result would be a serious charge of idolatry, the worship of someone or something else as if it was Yahweh. Rather, in scripture the praise of God's name, his holiness, or his mighty deeds are all ways of praising who and what Yahweh *is*.[61]

THE DIVINE NAME(S) AND THE LORD JESUS

The New Testament represents both a continuation and development in the use and meaning of the divine name(s). The divine name is present, but in a different form: *kyrios* (Lord). The Septuagint translates the Hebrew *Adonai* as *kyrios*, which eventually leads to its use as a substitute for Yahweh, occurring over six thousand times in the Old Testament. In the New Testament the revelation of the divine name continues through statements regarding its nature. But, most significantly, it presents the personification of the divine name in Jesus. In relation to this development, this section will focus on three main points: (1) that "Yahweh" in the Old Testament and "Lord" in the New Testament refer to the same God; (2) that Jesus is Yahweh himself; (3) what is said of the name Yahweh is now said of the name Jesus.

The first point is already demonstrated by the fact that the Septuagint translates Old Testament references to Yahweh with the Greek word *kyrios*. This is evident from the LXX renderings of Exodus 3:14–15 and 34:6–7, Deuteronomy 6:4, Psalm 11:7, or the multitude of other examples. In the New Testament, Paul refers to Joel 2:32 (3:5) in Romans 10:13: "Everyone who calls on the name of the Lord shall be saved."[62] Or consider the use of Psalm 110:4 in Hebrews 7:21: "The Lord has sworn and will not change his mind, 'You are a priest

---

61. Gavin Ortlund and Pui Him Ip see the task of divine simplicity as leading toward doxology and worship of the Trinity. See Gavin Ortlund, "Divine Simplicity in Historical Perspective: Resourcing a Contemporary Discussion," *IJST* 16 (2014): 441–43; Pui Him Ip, "Re-imagining Divine Simplicity in Trinitarian Theology," *IJST* 18 (2016): 282–88. I agree with their arguments and see the "doxological element" as a way of locating a biblical root of their statements. On the relation of doxology and trinitarian theology, see Fred Sanders, *The Triune God*, NSD (Grand Rapids: Zondervan, 2016), 25–35.

62. Hebrew: *yhwh*; LXX: *kyrios*; Greek: *kyrios*.

forever.'"[63] The New Testament follows the lead of the Septuagint in using *kyrios* in the place of the Old Testament use of Yahweh.

Second, the New Testament provides a number of examples that demonstrate that Jesus is identified with Yahweh.[64] Returning to the use of Joel 2:32 in Romans 10:13, C. Kavin Rowe comments that "the theological medium is that of overlap and resonance such that the conjunction of the text of Joel 3:5 [EV 2:32] with Rom. 10:13 produces the conceptual space wherein the resonating identification between YHWH and Jesus occurs." This identification leads him to conclude that "the name which *is* the God of Israel alone (*kyrios*) is now the name which *is* Jesus (*kyrios*)."[65] Rowe provides other examples from John 20:28, 2 Corinthians 3:17, Galatians 4:4–6, and Romans 8:9–11. But the "pressure" of the texts, as he calls it, leads the reader to see both the identity of Yahweh and Jesus, as well as the distinctness of the Father and Jesus. The Father is Yahweh just as Jesus is Yahweh, yet the New Testament is clear that the Father is not the Son and the Son is not the Father. Rowe's conclusion is that "YHWH is not the Father alone. There is a differentiation into Father and Son within the unity of the one Lord (*kyrios heis* in Deut 6:4)."[66]

Perhaps most significantly, Jesus is given "the name that is above every name, so that at the name of Jesus every knee should bow, in heaven and on earth and under the earth, and every tongue confess that Jesus Christ is Lord, to the glory of God the Father" (Phil 2:9–10). Paul's words echo Isaiah 45:23–25, a passage that proclaims universal submission to Yahweh. Although Paul does not explicitly specify which name is given to Jesus, many argue that it is the name *kyrios* from verse 11.[67] What is said of Yahweh in Isaiah 45 is now

---

63. Hebrew: *yhwh*; LXX: *kyrios*; Greek: *kyrios*.

64. See also Larry W. Hurtado, *Lord Jesus Christ: Devotion to Jesus in Earliest Christianity* (Grand Rapids: Eerdmans, 2003); Richard Bauckham, *Jesus and the God of Israel: God Crucified and Other Studies on the New Testament's Christology of Divine Identity*, 2nd ed. Grand Rapids: Eerdmans, 2008); Gordon D. Fee, *Pauline Christology: An Exegetical-Theological Study* (Peabody, MA: Hendrickson, 2007).

65. Rowe, "Biblical Pressure and Trinitarian Hermeneutics," 301–2. See also Fee, *Pauline Christology*; Bauckham, *Jesus and the God of Israel*, 186–232; Rowe, "What Is the Name of the Lord"; Rowe, *Early Narrative Christology: The LORD in the Gospel of Luke* (Grand Rapids: Baker Academic, 2009).

66. Rowe, "Biblical Pressure and Trinitarian Hermeneutics," 303.

67. Bauckham is confident: "There can be no doubt that 'the name that is above every name' (v. 9) is YHWH: it is inconceivable that any Jewish writer could use this phrase for a name other than God's own unique name." See Richard Bauckham, "The Worship of Jesus in Philippians 2:9–11," in *Where Christology Began: Essays on Philippians 2*, ed. Ralph P. Martin and Brian J. Dodd (Louisville: Westminster John Knox, 1998), 131. Fee agrees: see *Pauline Christology*,

said of Jesus, directing some to believe that this kind of "judgment" is the same one made in the Nicene use of *homoousios*.[68]

Third, the New Testament speaks of the name of Jesus in the same ways the Old Testament speaks of the divine name. For example, the name of Jesus is said to be magnified (Acts 19:17) and glorified (2 Thess 1:12). His followers are to ask or pray in his name (John 14:13–14; 15:16; 16:23–26), suffer in his name (Acts 5:41; 1 Pet 4:14, 16), and even die for his name (Acts 21:13). In the Gospel of John hearers are called to believe in his name (John 1:12; 2:23; 3:18) so that they may have "life in His name" (John 20:31). This is because "there is no other name under heaven given among mortals by which we must be saved" (Acts 4:12). Those who believe receive forgiveness through his name (Acts 10:43; cf. Luke 24:47) and are sanctified and justified "in the name of the Lord Jesus Christ and in the Spirit of our God" (1 Cor 6:11).

One way of summarizing these three points is to state the divine name is personified in the person and work of Jesus. It is in him that "the whole fullness of deity dwells bodily" (Col 2:9), and he is confessed as "my Lord and my God" (John 20:28). The significance of the name *kyrios* for Jesus is not that it replaces Yahweh. Rather, *kyrios*, as lived out by Jesus, is a further deepening of the being and identity of Yahweh as he was revealed in the Old Testament. This is both a matter of continuity and development first seen in the progressive revelation of the divine name in many names in Exodus, its hypostatic character and doxological element in the Psalms, and now its personification and further revelation in the person and work of Jesus.[69]

396–97, 564. See also Bert-Jan Lietaert Peerbolte, "The Name above All Names (Philippians 2:9)," in *The Revelation of the Name YHWH to Moses: Perspectives from Judaism, the Pagan Graeco-Roman World, and Early Christianity*, ed. Geurt H. van Kooten and Bert-Jan Lietaert Peerbolte (Leiden: Brill, 2006), 187–206. Markus Bockmuehl argues that "it is perhaps not entirely clear whether all shall bow to him because Jesus *has* the name above every name, or because 'Jesus' *is* that name." At the same time, "in assuming the highest name to be 'Jesus' one creates the slight awkwardness that the exalted name here appears quite specifically to be granted upon his exaltation, not at birth (the 'therefore' makes the granting of the name dependent on what goes before, rather than part of it)." Markus Bockmuehl, *The Epistle to the Philippians*, 4th ed., BNTC (London: A&C Black, 1997), 142.

68. Yeago, "The New Testament and Nicene Dogma."

69. One could also add the significance of other titles and metaphors used by and of Jesus. Jesus is called not only Lord but also the Word (John 1:1), Alpha and Omega (Rev 1:8), Son of God (Mark 1:1), Lamb of God (John 1:29, 36), the last Adam (1 Cor 15:45), and many others. The Gospel of John provides another series of insights into the names of Jesus. Two sets of seven "I am" sayings show Jesus naming himself according to Old Testament images and titles that were ascribed to Yahweh, or connecting his self-description to an event that just took place ("I am the bread of life" after the feeding of the five thousand in John 6). In the seven

TRINITARIAN NAMING

The final element of the divine name(s) involves its trinitarian nature throughout the New Testament. First, as I demonstrated in the previous section, Yahweh is not the Father alone but also includes the Son. Accordingly, this identification of Yahweh also extends to the Holy Spirit. For example, Paul writes that "the Lord is the Spirit, and where the Spirit of the Lord is, there is freedom" (2 Cor 3:17).[70] Yahweh is not only revealed to be compassionate, gracious, and slow to anger, but also to be Father, Son, and Holy Spirit. This name (Matt 28:19) further reveals the nature of Yahweh in continuity and development of Old Testament teachings.

Second, while Father, Son, and Holy Spirit are all identified as Yahweh, they are further identified with the same divine character. In the Old Testament, Yahweh is said to be holy (Ezek 34:14) among many other names. In the New Testament, the Father is called holy (John 17:11), the Son is called holy (1 Pet 1:15–16), and the Holy Spirit is clearly holy. Furthermore, "the Father has life in himself" and "has granted the Son also to have life in himself" (John 5:26). Even so, the Holy Spirit is the "Spirit of life" (Rom 8:2), and elsewhere Paul says that "the Spirit gives life" (2 Cor 3:6). To say that the Father is holy, the Son is holy, and the Spirit is holy is not to say there are three

---

"I am" sayings that include predicates, Jesus says "I am" the bread of life (6:35); the light of the world (8:12, 9:5); the door of the sheep (10:7); the good shepherd (10:11); the resurrection and the life (11:25); the way, the truth, and the life (14:6); and the true vine (15:1). The seven absolute "I am" statements can be found in John 4:26; 6:20; 8:24; 8:28; 8:58; 13:19; 18:5, 6, 8. It is debated whether all of these uses can be understood in an ordinary sense ("I am" might mean "It is I") or as a direct or even indirect reference to the "I am" of Exodus. See Richard Bauckham, "Monotheism and Christology in the Gospel of John," in *Contours of Christology in the New Testament*, ed. Richard N. Longenecker (Grand Rapids: Eerdmans, 2005), 154–57. See also Riemer Roukema, "Jesus and the Divine Name in the Gospel of John," in van Kooten and Lietaert Peerbolte, *Revelation of the Name YHWH to Moses*, 207–23. Whether these statements are directly connected to the "I AM" of Exodus 3, or simply mean "it is I," they are Jesus's descriptions of himself that explain something significant about his character.

70. Some take this passage to teach that Jesus is the Spirit. For a response to this position, see Gordon D. Fee, ed., *God's Empowering Presence: The Holy Spirit in the Letters of Paul* (Peabody, MA: Hendrickson, 1994), 296–320. For an in-depth treatment of the divine attributes and the Spirit, see Andrew K. Gabriel, *The Lord Is the Spirit: The Holy Spirit and the Divine Attributes* (Eugene, OR: Pickwick, 2011).

holy ones.[71] This holy name is only said of one God and his simple nature.[72]

CONNECTING THE DIVINE NAME(S) AND DIVINE SIMPLICITY

It might seem that the discussion of the divine name(s) causes a variety of problems for divine simplicity. If the divine name is truly expressible in a multitude of descriptions, then how can someone claim that God is indivisible when the many descriptions seem to imply that there may be parts in God after all? Briefly stated, are not the multiple descriptions a problem for a "partless" God? Herman Bavinck helpfully clarifies this issue, stating that "the simplicity of being does not exclude the many names ascribed to [God], as Eunomius thought, but demands them. God is so abundantly rich that we can gain some idea of his richness only by the availability of many names." In this way, the many descriptions found throughout scripture are necessary on the basis of God's plentiful and rich being. Many descriptions are necessary in order to begin to understand God's greatness. From a creaturely perspective, "every name refers to the same full divine being, but each time from a particular angle, the angle from which it reveals itself to us in his works. . . . [Therefore], every name . . . is an enrichment of our knowledge of his being."[73] Moses knew little about Yahweh when he first learned his name, but as time went on Yahweh revealed what his name means and this required a variety of descriptions.

Both the Old and New Testaments make three main *judgments* about the divine name(s): first, that the divine name is God himself in his self–revelation. What is said of the divine name is also said of Yahweh, and this follows the way that names function throughout the rest of the Old Testament. The two are so closely linked that it is difficult, if not inadvisable, to distinguish between the two. Second,

71. This statement is similar to the patristic statements such as this one found in Augustine: "We do not say three great ones but one great one," and this is "because God is not great by participating in greatness, but he is great with his great self because he is his own greatness" (Augustine, *The Trinity*, ed. John Rotelle, trans. Edmund Hill, WSA [Hyde Park, NY: New City Press, 1991], 5.2 [198]).

72. It is important to remember, as seen in Augustine, that the names Father, Son, and Holy Spirit do not refer to God "substance-wise" but refer to the eternal relations between the three divine persons.

73. Bavinck, *God and Creation*, 177.

there is no conflict in the nature of God. He is called gracious and just, merciful and judge, forgiving and punishing. Far from having a divided nature full of tensions, Yahweh's nature has no conflict but is rich in its diversity. Third, the divine name is revealed through many different descriptions, which appear to be mutual and integrative ways of referring to the being of Yahweh. Love and holiness carry two different meanings, but both refer equally and fully to what Yahweh is.

The display of God's many names, titles, and images is an aid rather than a problem for divine simplicity. They broaden the glimpse we have into God's infinite life without declaring exhaustive knowledge of all that God is. Bavinck draws out this insight with a number of images taken from the theological tradition.

> The diversity of attributes, moreover, does not clash with God's simplicity. For that simplicity does not describe God as an abstract and general kind of being; on the contrary, it speaks of him as the absolute fullness of life. It is for this very reason that God reveals himself to finite creatures by many names. The divine essence is so infinitely and profusely rich that no creature can grasp it all at once. Just as a child cannot picture the worth of a coin of great value but only gains some sense of it when it is counted out in a number of smaller coins, so we too cannot possibly form a picture of the infinite fullness of God's essence unless it is displayed to us now in one relationship, then in another, and now from one angle, then from another [Augustine, *The Trinity* 6.4; *City of God* 12.18]. God remains eternally and immutably the same, but the relation in which he stands to his creatures and they to him varies. The light remains the same even though it breaks up into different colors (Augustine). Fire does not change whether it warms us, illumines us, or consumes us (Moses Maimonides). And grain remains grain even though, depending on the stage in which it comes to us, we call it seed, or food, or fruit (Basil). God is called by different names on account of the varying effects he produces in his creatures by his ever-constant being.[74]

God's revelation discloses his being, *what he is*, as one whose nature is abundant and expressible in many terms and many ways. In short, the many divine names throughout scripture—both proper names and names that function like attributes—do not point to distinct parts of God. Nevertheless, the question still remains: Is this enough to say that God's multifaceted nature is truly indivisible, truly simple? Is

74. Ibid., 127.

all that God is holy, faithful, and wise? One might feel compelled to answer no on the basis that this would imply that God is not completely holy, faithful, or wise. Instead of discussing this issue in the realm of implications and entailments, I believe that the biblical teaching of indivisible operations can provide greater assistance as the second biblical root of divine simplicity.

INDIVISIBLE OPERATIONS

The biblical teaching of indivisible operations (*opera trinitatis ad extra sunt indivisa*) argues that because each of the three persons is not one-third of God (they are indivisible), then each divine person operates indivisibly in all of God's works *ad extra*.[75] As seen throughout the historical chapters, this teaching was common in the tradition in both the East and West and remained an important element of early trinitarian theology. In this section, I will trace some of the key biblical passages that contribute to the second scriptural root of divine simplicity. The goal is to demonstrate that the indivisible work of the divine persons reveals their indivisible nature. This claim supports not only the doctrine of the Trinity but the doctrine of divine simplicity as well.[76]

Having already explored Augustine's example of indivisible

---

75. This teaching also goes by the name of inseparable operation, common operations, and *opera ad extra*.

76. For more background on this issue from within the tradition, see Michel René Barnes, "One Nature, One Power: Consensus Doctrine in Pro-Nicene Polemic," *SP* 29 (1997): 205–23; Barnes, *The Power of God: Δύναμις in Gregory of Nyssa's Trinitarian Theology* (Washington, DC: Catholic University of America Press, 2001); Bruce D. Marshall, "Action and Person: Do Palamas and Aquinas Agree about the Spirit?," *SVTQ* 39 (1995): 379–408; Keith E. Johnson, "Augustine's 'Trinitarian' Reading of John 5: A Model for the Theological Interpretation of Scripture?," *JETS*:52 (2009): 799–810; Kyle Claunch, "What God Hath Done Together: Defending the Historic Doctrine of the Inseparable Operations of the Trinity," *JETS* 56 (2013): 781–800; Stephen R. Holmes, "Trinitarian Action and Inseparable Operations: Some Historical and Dogmatic Reflections," in *Advancing Trinitarian Theology: Explorations in Constructive Dogmatics*, ed. Oliver D. Crisp and Fred Sanders (Grand Rapids: Zondervan, 2014), 60–74; Adonis Vidu, "The Place of the Cross among the Inseparable Operations of the Trinity," in *Locating Atonement: Explorations in Constructive Dogmatics*, ed. Oliver D. Crisp and Fred Sanders (Grand Rapids: Zondervan, 2015), 21–42; Vidu, "Trinitarian Inseparable Operations and the Incarnation," *JAT* 4 (2016): 106–27. Baars's treatment of Calvin is helpful, although his reading of Augustine is highly questionable: Arie Baars, "*Opera Trinitatis ad extra sunt indivisa* in the Theology of John Calvin," in *Calvinus sacrarum literarum interpres: Papers of the International Congress on Calvin Research*, ed. Herman J. Selderhuis (Göttingen: Vandenhoeck & Ruprecht, 2008), 131–41.

operations in the baptism of Jesus,[77] I will offer a different example: the incarnation of the Son of God.[78] Jesus was sent by the Father (John 4:34) and thus obediently "became flesh, and dwelt among us" (John 1:14 NASB). Through the Holy Spirit, he was conceived (Matt 1:20; cf. Luke 1:31, 35) and was anointed (Acts 10:38) when the Spirit came upon him at his baptism (Luke 3:21). It was the Spirit who then led Jesus into the wilderness to be tempted (Matt 4:1) only to return in the power of the Spirit (Luke 4:14). The Spirit empowered Jesus in his ministry, for it was by the Spirit that Jesus cast out demons (Matt 12:28). Jesus obeyed his Father by "finishing the work that you gave me to do" (John 17:4), which is the very work of God since "whatever the Father does, that the Son does likewise" (John 5:19). Jesus's sacrifice was offered "through the eternal Spirit" (Heb 9:14) as he drank the "cup" given to him by the Father (cf. Luke 22:39–46). Although Jesus's resurrection appears to be chiefly attributed to the Father (Acts 2:32; 3:15; 13:30; 1 Cor 15:15; Eph 1:20), it is also said to be an act of the Son (John 2:19–21; 10:17–18) and the Spirit (Rom 1:4; 1 Pet 3:18). At no point in the event of the incarnation—the sending, birth, life, death, resurrection, and ascension of the Son—is there any indication that this is the work of one of the Trinity alone.

To be sure, the incarnation is the becoming human of the Son and not the Father or Spirit. It is the Son who is sent, born, lives, dies, is resurrected, and ascends to the right hand of the Father. But none of this denies that the Father and Spirit are involved in the one action of the incarnation. Even so, the question remains: "Whether there is one single divine operation or three separate divine operations."[79] Is the incarnation the single operation of the Trinity, or is it the separate actions of the three divine persons? Stephen Holmes provides a way forward: "It is surely not just possible, but necessary, to locate the incarnation or passion as part of a wider divine work: God's purpose was not to suffer, but to save. Incarnation, even, is a means to an end,

---

77. See chap. 2.

78. Another example could be the doctrine of creation. "In the beginning God created the heaven and the earth" (Gen 1:1). Yet scripture reveals that it was also the work of the Holy Spirit (Gen 1:2; Job 33:4), the work of the Son (John 1:1–3), and the work of the Father (Mal 2:10). These are not three separate works or operations, but work of the triune God, where the Father creates through the Son and by his Spirit. See Colin E. Gunton, *The Triune Creator: A Historical and Systematic Study* (Grand Rapids: Eerdmans, 1998); Stephen R. Holmes, "Triune Creativity: Trinity, Creation, Art and Science," in *Trinitarian Soundings in Systematic Theology*, ed. Paul L. Metzger (London: T&T Clark, 2006), 73 85; John Webster, "Trinity and Creation," *IJST* 12 (2010): 4–19.

79. Holmes, "Trinitarian Action and Inseparable Operations," 66.

not the end in itself."[80] The incarnation is one element of the much broader series of indivisible actions of the triune God. That is to say, creation is not the work of the Father alone, the incarnation a work of the Son alone, and empowering the work of the Spirit alone. They are one single work of indivisible divine operations carried out by the triune God. The trouble is that "what from our perspective looks like several discrete activities is one single inseparable work in divine intention and execution."[81]

The significance of the indivisible operations is that they point back, or reveal, the indivisible nature of God. This particular issue arose in the early church in response to teachings that the divided or separate acts of the Father, Son, and Holy Spirit clearly revealed separate beings or essences.[82] For example, in seeking to understand the nature of God from his operations, Gregory of Nyssa argued that

> if, then, we see that the operations which are wrought by the Father and the Son and the Holy Spirit differ one from the other, we shall conjecture from the different character of the operations that the natures which operate are also different. For it cannot be that things which differ in their very nature should agree in the form of their operation: fire does not chill, nor ice give warmth, but their operations are distinguished together with the difference between their natures. If, on the other hand, we understand that the operation of the Father, the Son, and the Holy Spirit is one, differing or varying in nothing, the oneness of their nature must needs be inferred from the identity of their operation. The Father, the Son, and the Holy Spirit alike give sanctification, and life, and light, and comfort, and all similar graces. And let no one attribute the power of sanctification in an especial sense to the Spirit, when he hears the Savior in the Gospel saying to the Father concerning His disciples, "Father, sanctify them in Thy name." [cf. John 17:11, 17] So too all the other gifts are wrought in those who are worthy alike by the Father, the Son, and the Holy Spirit: every grace and power, guidance, life, comfort, the change to immortality, the passage to liberty, and every other boon that exists, which descends to us.[83]

---

80. Ibid., 73–74.

81. Ibid., 74. Even though the action is single and indivisible, there is certainly a distinction within the one divine operation. The early church eventually presented this logic in terms of the proper ordering of the triune action: the Father inaugurates, the Son carries it out, and the Spirit perfects or completes. In short, there is genuine distinction without division.

82. See chap. 2.

83. Gregory of Nyssa, *On the Holy Trinity*, in *NPNF2* 5:328.

Just as the divine name(s) reveal Yahweh's divine nature, the indivisible operations of the three divine persons reveal their indivisible nature.[84] They are not separable from one another, nor are they separable from the divine essence, which they all equally and eternally share. Nevertheless, they are genuinely distinct, but not divided.

It should also be noted that the indivisible operations of the triune God aim to avoid two extremes: (1) Any implication that the action of the divine persons is merely an act of cooperation. If this is so, it is difficult to avoid a form of tritheistic divine action in which, at best, each person is a divine agent and, at worst, a separate divine being. (2) The indivisible operations must not be taken to mean that the distinct works of the three divine persons are identical in a way that flattens out all distinction among the persons and their actions. This would be akin to saying that the entire Trinity became incarnate and would represent a modalistic form of divine action. A more balanced and biblical account of the indivisible operations affirms that the work of God is single, indivisible, and yet distinct (that is, only the Son is incarnate) because the very nature of God is indivisible, distinct, and yet there is one will, one power, and so forth.

The indivisible nature of Father, Son, and Holy Spirit is crucial for recognizing the indivisible attributes of God. Yet one might object that the indivisible operations only teach that the three divine persons are indivisible and not the indivisibility of the divine attributes. It may appear this way, but it is vital to see that the indivisible operations refer to the indivisibility of *who* and *what* God is. If this were not so, could the divine persons truly be indivisible if their shared divine nature or attributes were divisible or separable? Is God one power, or three powers? The goal is to recognize, from scripture, that the actions of the three divine persons are not the actions of three separate beings. Salvation is not the act of the Son alone, nor is creation the act of the Father alone. The triune God is creator and savior. But, if there is only one savior or one creator, then the indivisible operations also teach that there is only one power, one light, or one life. Father, Son, and Holy Spirit are all-powerful and have light and life, but their power, light, and life are all as one God. This power, light, and life is indivisible—it is simple—and when God's power is on display

84. John Webster makes a similar connection when he writes of "the simplicity of the triune God as one essence in a threefold modal or personal differentiation. This *is* God's life, and so this is the basis on which we may go on to speak of the indivisibility of the outer works of God" (John Webster, "Trinity and Creation," *IJST* 12 [2010]: 8).

before his creation, it is not just the power of the Father, the Son, or the Holy Spirit alone. God's holiness, kingship (Lordship), or rocklike character describes God as he reveals himself, but does not represent separate parts of his being. What is said of God is completely true of who and what he is.

CONCLUSION

Scripture abounds with descriptions of God in its use of names, images, metaphors, and titles. These descriptions point to something true about God's nature and works, but scripture never explicitly defines the relationship between the descriptions and his character. Nevertheless, questions arise: What *is* God's holiness, righteousness, or life? If he is "the faithful God" (Deut 7:9) or "a jealous God" (Exod 20:5), to what is "faithful" and "jealous" referring? When scripture says that "the Lord is righteous in all his ways and kind in all his works" (Ps 145:17), what does it mean for God to *be* righteous?

This chapter has argued that the Bible's descriptions of God as holy, faithful, or righteous refer to his indivisible nature and operations. God is the Righteous One because he *is* righteous. God is King because he is the Lord who is sovereign over all things. These names refer to what God is because scripture demonstrates that God's name is God himself in his self-revelation. This name is "hypostaticized" as many attributes and works are attributed to it and, in actuality, are therefore attributed to God himself. The question of the identity of the divine name(s) becomes even more serious when we recognize the doxological element that places the doctrine of divine simplicity within the context of worship. God can only be praised for being faithful, good, and glorious if these are actually statements about *who* and *what* he is. If they are not, then what is being praised? Failure to answer this question places one in serious risk of idolatrous worship.

The divine name is further revealed through its personification in the life of Jesus Christ. His life and works represent the rich diversity of the character of Yahweh revealed to Moses (grace and justice). There is no conflict within the nature of God or the life of Jesus. To admit of conflict or contradiction, as Brueggemann does, is to speak of two opposing forces in God—justice versus mercy—as though parts of God's character jockey for primacy. God's name—who and what he is—is inherently rich and is therefore revealed in many ways throughout scripture, all of which are adequate predicates of his nature that further deepen the understanding of his abundant and simple being.

Finally, the indivisible operations of the triune God reveal that the threeness, or multiplicity of the attributes and names of God, do not represent parts, divisions, or separations among either the three divine persons or the divine attributes. The work of creation, salvation, or sanctification is not the work of one divine person alone. As one God, the three divine persons work not as a harmony but as one God and one power.[85] These three are one, and these three are distinct; God's attributes and names are one, and yet they are distinct as well. Nothing that God is or that is "in" God is divided. Holiness, justice, and mercy are not parts of God that can be in conflict, greater or lesser than one another, or govern one another. God is not governed by his anger, nor is he so greatly governed by his love that he fails to be righteous (Rom 3:25–26). Similar to Barth's statement, God is all that he is in all that he does, never failing to be loving or just since these are not parts of his nature that can be lost, limited, or overruled.[86]

This chapter is also the most crucial chapter for furthering the overall argument that divine simplicity's primary origin is in scripture. If I am correct about the two biblical roots and the judgments equated with them, then the concept of divine simplicity is an extension and elaboration of the divine name(s) and indivisible operations. God is revealed through many names and many operations that truly reflect what he is. Nevertheless, this multiplicity of names and operations do not reveal God to be partially holy, partially good, or partially loving. Nor does scripture reveal that the incarnation is the work of the Son alone. Instead, all that God is *is* holy, good, and loving, and the work of the incarnation is the indivisible operation of the three divine persons. Rather than natural theology, perfect being theism, or some other source, this chapter has argued that the origin of divine simplicity is found in these two biblical roots, which shaped its development and content. Finally, this chapter has also begun to relate divine simplicity to the doctrine of the Trinity through its connection to the biblical teaching of indivisible operations. Scripture is the starting point and the origin of the doctrine of divine simplicity, but I will show in the next chapter that the doctrine of the Trinity

85. See Barnes, "One Nature, One Power," 205–23.

86. For example, "in all that He is and does, He is wholly and undividedly Himself" (*CD* II/1, 445).

provides divine simplicity with the crucial framework and theological judgments necessary to understand it as a particularly Christian teaching.

6.

A Trinitarian Account of Divine Simplicity

The fact that a later age may find it harder to understand traditional ideas is not a sufficient reason for replacing them. It simply shows how necessary it is to open up these ideas to later generations by interpretation and thus to keep their meaning alive.

—Wolfhart Pannenberg, *Systematic Theology*

The previous chapters demonstrated that divine simplicity developed in opposition to false teaching (e.g., gnostics, Eunomius), subsequently received further development and clarification (by, for example, Basil, Gregory of Nyssa, and others), and remained a standard Christian doctrine until later in the nineteenth century. Its biblical roots, implicit throughout the tradition, were identified in the last chapter as deriving from scripture's habits of (1) using the many names or descriptions of God's nature and (2) ascribing God's various works to the indivisible operations of the Trinity *ad extra*. If this is correct, then the critics of divine simplicity have misunderstood the teaching's biblical origins and should reevaluate their claims. This chapter will argue that when drawn from its biblical roots, divine simplicity is a theological concept which teaches that the divine essence is identical with the divine attributes, whereas the divine attributes remain distinct, though not independent or separable from one another. The simple nature of God admits of no composition or parts. The task of the doctrine of divine simplicity, therefore, is to properly confess the nature of God set forth in scripture in ways that avoid either dividing God into parts or removing all distinctions.

In order to fully articulate an account of divine simplicity, it is important to clear away common distortions and potential errors. Therefore, I will begin by presenting one major distortion of divine simplicity—its origin—and will then outline four potential errors. Next, I will clarify the relation of divine simplicity to the doctrine of the Trinity by demonstrating how the Trinity provides a formal analogy for simplicity that helps it draw a careful distinction among the divine attributes.[1] Based on this claim, I will begin to articulate a doctrine of divine simplicity that recognizes the rich multiplicity of God's attributes without compromising the claim of simplicity or challenging the nature of the triune God.

DISTORTIONS OF DIVINE SIMPLICITY

One of the keys to understanding divine simplicity as a part of Christian theological and biblical reflection is to understand how it has been distorted. While it is possible to list many examples, I will argue that the most common distortions fall under the broader distortion of the doctrine's origin. What is the main cause, source, or reason for a doctrine of divine simplicity? If we recall chapter 1, contemporary answers vary: natural theology, apophatic theology, perfect being theology, metaphysics, speculation (or abstraction), or hellenization. Whichever one chooses, the problems attributed to divine simplicity are often connected to a serious questioning of its origins. If it is a product of "classical theism," and one is prone to reject "classical theism," then divine simplicity becomes an immediate problem.[2] If divine simplicity is the result of apophatic theology, then it may be viewed as a primarily negative teaching with nothing positive to say

---

1. This statement does not ignore the importance of the OT or ignore its role in formulating a doctrine of divine simplicity. As the previous chapter argued, the OT's revelation of the divine name(s) forms one biblical root. Furthermore, although the Trinity is primarily a NT teaching, the OT is necessary for any doctrine of the Trinity and is therefore assumed in this chapter to critically inform the statements being made.

2. For example, see Bruce L. McCormack, "The Actuality of God: Karl Barth in Conversation with Open Theism." In *Engaging the Doctrine of God: Contemporary Protestant Perspectives*, ed. Bruce L. McCormack(Grand Rapids: Baker Academic, 2008), 187–88, 201. Brian Davies does not reject divine simplicity, but for an example of how it might be positively related to classical theism, see Davies, "Classical Theism and the Doctrine of Divine Simplicity," in *Language, Meaning, and God: Essays in Honour of Herbert McCabe*, ed. Brian Davies [London: Cassell, 1987], 51–74). For an argument that the God of classical theism is "the engaged, personally present, responsive God of the Bible," see Eleonore Stump, *The God of the Bible and the God of the Philosophers*, AL (Marquette: Marquette University Press, 2016).

about God.[3] If it is merely the inevitable result of some form of metaphysics (for example, Platonic), speculation, or abstraction, then one who is wary of metaphysics (or is postmetaphysical) will also be cautious or even hostile to divine simplicity.[4] Finally, if divine simplicity can be shown to originate in Greek philosophy and have no relation to scripture, then it raises serious questions to its function in Christian theology.[5] Noticeably, this distortion is expressed in many forms, but the root cause of the distortion is trying to locate divine simplicity on the basis of some form of natural rather than revealed theology.[6]

The goal is not to respond to each point one by one, but to acknowledge that the distortion in its various forms has already been exposed. By identifying the two roots of divine simplicity in scripture, simplicity should no longer be questioned according to its supposedly doubtful origins. If so many throughout the tradition have called the Trinity "revealed" even though the concept is not directly or explicitly found in scripture, then why is divine simplicity not afforded the same conclusion? It, too, has roots in scripture. It, too, is the result of borrowed concepts that aim to faithfully translate and expand on biblical claims. Divine simplicity never grew into a full doctrine by cutting off or ignoring its biblical roots, but flourished

3. For example, Paul Hinlicky understands traditional doctrines of divine simplicity to be entirely apophatic. See Paul Hinlicky, *Divine Complexity: The Rise of Creedal Christianity* (Minneapolis: Fortress Press, 2010), xi, 176, 191. See also Barry D. Smith, *The Oneness and Simplicity of God* (Eugene, OR: Pickwick, 2013), 126.

4. For examples, see Emil Brunner, *The Christian Doctrine of God*, trans. Olive Wyon (London: Lutterworth, 1949), 1:293; Robert Jenson, *Systematic Theology*, vol. 1, *The Triune God* (New York: Oxford University Press, 1997), 111.

5. For example, see R. T. Mullins, "Simply Impossible: A Case against Divine Simplicity," *JRT* 7 (2013): 190, and Clark H. Pinnock, *Most Moved Mover: A Theology of the Divine Openness* (Grand Rapids: Baker Academic, 2001), 68–79.

6. One might also add the distortion of divine simplicity in perfect being theism. For one example, see Katherin A. Rogers, *Perfect Being Theology*, RR (Edinburgh: Edinburgh University Press, 2000). Generally, this approach attempts to establish God's nature and attributes via a concept of perfection or "that than which a greater cannot be conceived." Although few might deny that God is perfect or great in some sense, the danger rests on how one defines perfect or great. Perfect being theology often defines these terms apart from scripture or other crucial doctrines, focusing more on the logic of perfections or other forms of argument. This makes the approach more general, and in Rogers's project, for example, it allows her to work "within the Christian tradition, though as much of the discussion of the divine nature will be sufficiently general it could apply to Judaism and Islam" (ibid., 1). The context of perfect being theism, at least in Rogers's form, is so broad that divine simplicity cannot be claimed to be a Christian doctrine. However, the most significant weakness and reason for caution is that a concept of perfection is too easily defined a priori and a doctrine of God is molded to fit such a concept. This weakness also occurs when "simple" or "complex" is defined and analyzed prior to any relation to scripture or other distinctly Christian teachings.

because of its relationship to and dependence on them. As a revealed doctrine, divine simplicity is not the outcome of classical theism, apophatic theology, metaphysics, speculation, abstraction, or Greek philosophy. It may contain some of these elements just as many Christian doctrines do, but none of these aspects form the true source or motivation for divine simplicity.[7]

FOUR ERRORS TO AVOID

Divine simplicity may be capable of distortion, but it is also in danger of falling into a variety of errors. The first error to be avoided is a general conception of deity defined prior to God's works. This occurs when divine simplicity is first defined in contrast to predefined understandings of complexity, division, or compositeness. For example, if *composite* is defined as "having distinct parts" then one may be tempted to define simplicity as "having no distinctions." Although there is some truth to such a definition, it ignores how God reveals himself in scripture—one name and many names, titles, images, and his indivisible operations—and particularly through the incarnation and work of the Holy Spirit. Defining God's nature a priori too easily predetermines how his works should be interpreted and fails to listen well to scripture or other theological pushback.

If God's simple nature should not be defined *prior* to his works, a second error must equally be avoided: God's simple nature should not be defined *only* in relation to God's works. This approach tends to focus on God's economic activity to the exclusion of his immanent life. For example, knowledge of divine love is not only limited to God's revelation of his love in creation. The triune love of God preexists in the eternal life of Father, Son, and Holy Spirit, and knowledge of this love is not limited to earthly historical events. Some have expressed serious concern over such claims (for example, Bruce McCormack), worried that knowledge of God apart from Jesus is speculative or abstract.[8] This view and others similar to it may appear to pay more attention to scripture by emphasizing God's revelation

7. To clarify, I am not defending every account of divine simplicity from these labels. As Eunomius and others have shown, it is certainly possible for divine simplicity to be misused or constructed from these other sources. A form of divine simplicity *may* come from one or more of these sources, but as I have argued, it would be a distortion of the biblically rooted doctrine of divine simplicity.

8. See McCormack, "Actuality of God." For a critique of a christological doctrine of God, see

in Jesus, but it can ignore the significance, for example, of God's self-revelation before Jesus (for example, the Old Testament).[9] It also suffers from the necessity of defining God's nature according to history or the limits of human knowledge.

Moving forward from the relation of God's nature and his works, the third error represents an extreme version of divine simplicity: radical unity. This form of simplicity is most clearly found in Eunomius, who argued that God has only one real attribute: unbegottenness. This attribute defines God's essence, and all other attributes are identical to this attribute. More accurately stated, all other attributes exist by name only since they are actually nothing other than God's unbegotten essence. This view also stipulates that there are no distinctions in God whatsoever. Such a conception of simplicity inevitably results in a monad and also risks defining God's nature prior to his works.[10]

The fourth error represents the opposite extreme: radical diversity. If we recall, not only did the Socinians reject the doctrine of the Trinity, but they also posited a real distinction between God's essence and his power (that is, they are two separate essences or things). Not all of God's perfections were necessary to God *ad intra*; therefore, some were seen as separable from the divine essence, which admitted composition in the being of God.[11] Recent analytic philosophical accounts of divine simplicity come perilously close to this extreme when they refer to God's attributes as properties possessed by a divine essence in a univocal sense.[12] A position like this will have great difficulty avoiding division in God's essence, explaining the problems of

Katherine Sonderegger, *Systematic Theology*, vol. 1, *The Doctrine of God* (Minneapolis: Fortress Press, 2015).

9. For example, see Kevin J. Vanhoozer, *Remythologizing Theology: Divine Action, Passion, and Authorship*, CSCD (Cambridge: Cambridge University Press, 2010), 202–5.

10. This error is analogous to the trinitarian heresy of modalism.

11. See Richard A. Muller, *Post-Reformation Reformed Dogmatics*, vol. 3, *The Divine Essence and Attributes*, 2nd ed. (Grand Rapids: Baker Academic, 2003), 288. Hereafter *PRRD* with volume number and page number. For more on Socinianism, see Martin Mulsow and Jan Rohls, eds., *Socinianism and Arminianism: Antitrinitarians, Calvinists, and Cultural Exchange in Seventeenth-Century Europe*, BSIH (Leiden: Brill, 2005); Sarah Mortimer, *Reason and Religion in the English Revolution: The Challenge of Socinianism*, CSEMBH (Cambridge: Cambridge University Press, 2010); Paul C. H. Lim, *Mystery Unveiled: The Crisis of the Trinity in Early Modern England*, OSHT (Oxford: Oxford University Press, 2012).

12. To be clear, I am not saying that analytic accounts are guilty of Socinianism. I mean that some err on the side of radical diversity due to particular views concerning God and his "properties."

independent properties, or accepting a doctrine of divine simplicity if it is understood from this perspective.[13]

To summarize, the doctrine of divine simplicity is capable of distortion when one fails to recognize its basis in scripture and therefore its revealed nature. Alternative accounts of its origins take on many forms: Greek philosophy, classical theism, perfect being theism, substance metaphysics, and so forth. It is surely possible to understand and present divine simplicity in these ways, but it stems from a failed realization that divine simplicity grows out of its biblical roots in the divine name(s) and indivisible operations. Attending this multifaceted distortion are four possible errors: defining God's nature *prior* to his works; defining God's nature *only* in his works; radical unity; and radical diversity. A biblical and theological account of divine simplicity must avoid these errors, and in the following sections I will develop a doctrine of divine simplicity that does these very things.

LEARNING FROM THE TRINITY

As the last chapter argued, scripture presents a window into the unity-in-diversity present in the nature of God. God reveals his name Yahweh, which is further revealed by other names, attributes, titles, and metaphors. From the Psalms, it became clearer that each name or attribute describes what God is since he can only be praised by these names and attributes if they are truly God himself. Scripture also teaches that the works of the three divine persons are indivisible. There are not three different works as though creation, salvation, or sanctification could be said to be the work of the Father, but not the Holy Spirit. The three persons are one God and therefore operate with one power, love, and righteousness. God is not defined as indivisible prior to his works, but is recognized to be indivisible and simple through his revealed works. It begins to appear that the Trinity might provide an analogy for how to properly distinguish among God's attributes.

If we recall, Barth was critical of the "older Protestant orthodoxy" that "usually adopted much the same arguments and explanations

---

13. Plantinga does not argue that God is divisible, but his Platonic realist view of properties as universals leads him to find serious problems with Thomas's view of divine simplicity. See chap. 1 and Alvin Plantinga, *Does God Have a Nature?* (Milwaukee: Marquette University Press, 1980). See Jeffrey E. Brower, "Making Sense of Divine Simplicity," *FPh* 25 (2008): 7–8, for more on Plantinga's view of Platonic realism.

[i.e., logical and metaphysical arguments found in Augustine and Anselm] when it placed and expounded the simplicity of God first among the divine attributes."[14] The further "trouble is that [the arguments] are put at the head, and not, as we are trying to do here, in their proper turn," which is after the doctrine of the Trinity.[15] While I do not fully agree with Barth's critical reading of the tradition, he is correct to point out that simplicity should not have doctrinal authority over the Trinity. The logic must be reversed, and in this sense, the doctrine of the Trinity reveals how to parse the unity-in-diversity question of the divine attributes.

RECENT WORK ON THE TRINITY AND SIMPLICITY

What has been said about the relationship of the Trinity and divine simplicity? Much recent scholarship has asserted the importance of the two doctrines, both historically and theologically. On the one hand, Stephen Holmes writes that "to believe in divine simplicity was to be an orthodox trinitarian, and to deny simplicity was to attack the doctrine of the Trinity."[16] But how does this work? How do they relate? Why were they so interrelated? On the other hand, those who do attempt to describe the relationship between the two often see the issue as a problem of compatibility or coherency.[17] For example, James E. Dolezal's argument attempts to "show the harmony between

14. Barth, *CD* II/1, 447.

15. Ibid. Barth argues that this inevitably leads to a general understanding of "being as truly one" (God defined *prior* to his works) and to some form of nominalism (radical unity). Others, such as Robert Jenson, worry that divine simplicity had so much authority for someone like Augustine that there was an "unquestioning commitment to the axiom" (Jenson, *Triune God*, 111).

16. Stephen R. Holmes, "The Attributes of God," in *The Oxford Handbook of Systematic Theology*, edited by John Webster, Kathryn Tanner, and Iain Torrance (Oxford: Oxford University Press, 2007), 65. Muller adds that the Reformed orthodox believed that "divine simplicity was understood as a support of the doctrine of the Trinity" and that these "doctrines are interdependent." See Muller, *PRRD*, 3:276, 282, cf. 298. Like Holmes, this point is merely asserted, and it remains difficult to sufficiently understand how these two doctrines were interdependent.

17. See Keith Goad, "Simplicity and Trinity in Harmony," *Eusebeia* 8 (2007): 97–118; James E. Dolezal, "Trinity, Simplicity and the Status of God's Personal Relations," *IJST* 16 (2014): 79–98; Thomas H. McCall, "Trinity Doctrine, Plain and Simple," in *Advancing Trinitarian Theology: Explorations in Constructive Dogmatics*, ed. Oliver D. Crisp and Fred Sanders (Grand Rapids: Zondervan, 2014), 21–41; K. Scott Oliphint, "Simplicity, Triunity, and the Incomprehensibility of God," in *One God in Three Persons: Unity of Essence, Distinction of Persons, Implications for Life*, ed. Bruce A. Ware and John Starke (Wheaton, IL: Crossway, 2015), 215–35; Steven J. Duby, *Divine Simplicity: A Dogmatic Account*. SST (London: Bloomsbury T&T Clark, 2015), 207–33.

God's subsistence in three persons and his simplicity."[18] This claim requires clarity on the "real yet non-accidental character of the divine relations," which leads to the conclusion that the divine persons "are simply the divine essence subsisting in a threefold manner."[19] This helps Dolezal express the harmony and agreeability between the Trinity and simplicity; yet it is unclear what such harmony is meant to offer either doctrine or if this was merely a problem to be solved.

Thomas McCall argues that there is not one version of divine simplicity; rather, it is possible to distinguish three different forms. He labels the first version Strict Simplicity, which he summarizes in four points:

> (i) There is no composition whereby God is made up of parts or pieces that are ontologically prior to or more basic than God; (ii) there is no metaphysical or moral complexity of any kind; (iii) there are no genuine distinctions within God, and (iv) everything in God is identical (divine properties are identical with one another, and the divine persons are all identical with the divine essence).[20]

This view "reflects most tradition-based (Latin) versions of the doctrine," and McCall admits that his version "is an open question."[21] Second, Formal Simplicity affirms the first two points but argues that "there are no genuine distinctions within God other than formal distinctions (recall: inseparability)."[22] Finally, Generic Simplicity also affirms the first two points but differs on points three and four: "(iii) There are genuine distinctions within the divine nature; and (iv) all essential divine attributes are mutually entailing and coextensive."[23] McCall locates this final version of divine simplicity in Gregory of Nyssa; however, it is debatable that these four points accurately describe Gregory's view based on my earlier reading of him in chapter 2.

McCall finds the Formal and Generic versions of simplicity to be consistent with a doctrine of the Trinity. Strict Simplicity, on the other hand, faces problems because of its claims that the divine persons are identical to the divine essence but not identical to one

---

18. Dolezal, "Trinity, Simplicity," 81.
19. Ibid., 83, 94.
20. McCall, "Trinity Doctrine, Plain and Simple," 54–55.
21. Ibid., 58n66.
22. Ibid., 55.
23. Ibid.

another. In more logical form, McCall finds the following claims contradictory: (1) "The Father is not identical to the Son," (2) "the Father is identical to the divine essence," (3) "the Son is identical to the divine essence." The problem is that these three points entail that "the Father is identical to the Son."[24]

Steven Duby provides a convincing response to critiques of the relation between the Trinity and simplicity similar to McCall's. He argues two main points: (1) that scripture teaches the unity and singularity of God but does not teach three distinct wills; (2) that the modal or real relative distinctions among the three divine persons is "compatible" with a doctrine of the Trinity.[25] Duby's first point expresses the difficulty of finding compatibility between divine simplicity and "social" accounts of the Trinity.[26] In turn, social trinitarians may struggle to see a way forward for "Latin" versions of the Trinity. These are important steps that begin to clarify the relationship between these two crucial teachings, but they do not go far enough in describing how these two doctrines relate and what, if anything, they do for one another.[27]

The tension felt by many between the Trinity and simplicity is understandable. At first glance, the Trinity appears to allow for distinctions within the Godhead that admit some form of genuine difference without causing or admitting of three divine essences.

24. Ibid., 57. He remarks that "relative identity" may be the best way forward with the hopes of avoiding or solving these problems (ibid., 55n67). If McCall's critique is correct, then a large majority of traditional accounts of the Trinity would be in jeopardy. For a historical argument in which these trinitarian claims are seen as broadly traditional, see Stephen R. Holmes, *The Quest for the Trinity: The Doctrine of God in Scripture, History and Modernity* (Downers Grove, IL: IVP Academic, 2012).

25. See Duby, *Divine Simplicity*, 207–33.

26. The issue of social trinitarianism may be part of the problem for McCall. For his views on the Trinity, see Thomas McCall, *Which Trinity? Whose Monotheism? Philosophical and Systematic Theologians on the Metaphysics of Trinitarian Theology* (Grand Rapids: Eerdmans, 2010); McCall, *Forsaken: The Trinity and the Cross, and Why It Matters* (Downers Grove, IL: IVP Academic, 2012).

27. See also Thomas Joseph White, "Divine Simplicity and the Holy Trinity," *IJST* 18 (2016): 66–93. In relation to Aquinas's formulation of divine simplicity, White argues that "affirmation of the simplicity of God co-exists . . . with the possibility of belief in the revelation of the Holy Trinity" (ibid., 85). This coexistence is accomplished once one understands Aquinas's expression of the subsistent mode of being and the personal mode of subsistence (see esp. ibid., 85–89). He makes a similar argument in "Nicene Orthodoxy and Trinitarian Simplicity," *ACPQ* 90 (2016): 727–50. I agree with White that "even a cursory consideration of the historical origins of [divine simplicity] can help us realize that some version of it is required even for the most basic enunciation of Trinitarian doctrine" (ibid., 728). However, I would qualify that the doctrine of the Trinity *first* informs divine simplicity and only then does divine simplicity mutually inform the Trinity.

However, divine simplicity is often understood to present a view of God's essence in which all that he is is identical to his essence. How can a doctrine of divine simplicity ever claim to accommodate the divine persons who are not identical to one another (for example, the Father is not the Son)? The root of the problem is this: *the Trinity seems to require greater distinctions than divine simplicity will allow.* Most of the time this is where the problem emerges, creating a puzzle that must be solved with the primary goal of harmony, compatibility, and coherency.

TRADITIONAL DISTINCTIONS AMONG THE DIVINE ATTRIBUTES

Claiming that the Trinity is incompatible with divine simplicity due to a clash of distinctions raises the following question: What kind of distinctions, if any, does the doctrine of divine simplicity permit? The historical chapters showed that the tradition found a number of ways to distinguish among the divine attributes, but it is important here to summarize the various distinctions that were drawn throughout the tradition. Richard Muller helpfully describes four kinds of distinctions commonly found in the medieval scholastics that were influential for later accounts:

(1) *Distinctio realis*, a real distinction, such as exists between two independent things; (2) *Distinctio formalis*, a formal distinction, such as exists between two (or more) formal aspects of the essence of a thing; as, e.g., between intellect and will, which are not separate things but which are also distinguishable within the thing, in this case, the soul or spirit of which they are predicated. The formal distinction is also called the *distinctio formalis a parte rei*, the formal distinction on the part of the thing. (3) *Distinctio rationis ratiocinatae*, a distinction by reason of analysis, sometimes qualified or explicated as *distinctio rationis ratiocinatae quae habet fundamentum in re* ("a distinction by reason of analysis that has its basis or foundation in the thing"). Since this distinction is neither between things nor in a thing, it is purely rational; yet it is argued as a distinction expressive of extramental reality since it is grounded in the thing and therefore preserved from being merely a product of the mind. In other words, the *distinctio rationis ratiocinatae* represents no distinction in the thing but a truth of reason concerning the thing. (4) *Distinctio rationis rationans*, a distinction by reason reasoning; i.e., a merely rational

distinction resting only on the operation of the reason and not on the thing.[28]

As Muller points out elsewhere, a real distinction can be understood in three ways: "between different things of different essences (e.g., between a flower and a table), or between two things of the same essence (e.g., between two tables)," and finally, "between the separable parts of a composite thing (e.g., between the tabletop and the legs of the table)."[29] A real distinction is one option at the end of the spectrum, and none of these real distinctions have been affirmed of God since this would make him into a composite being.

On the other hand, a rational or conceptual distinction (*distinctio rationis rationans*) forms the other end of the spectrum and has sometimes been called the nominalist position in relation to the well-known teachings of Maimonides and Ockham. The multitude of perfections is only a perceived multitude. God's perfections exist only in the human mind and are true *ad extra* but not true of God *ad intra*. In other words, there is no foundation in God for the multiple perfections because there are no distinctions in God. This distinction was commonly rejected since it rendered all speech and knowledge of God meaningless given that the perfections revealed nothing true about God but only existed in the human mind.[30]

The most common distinction throughout the tradition, and the one often attributed to Aquinas, is a virtual distinction among God's perfections (*rationis ratiocinatae*). Dolezal claims that "as close as this may appear to Ockham's later nominalism, it is a decidedly different position."[31] The vital difference is that nominalism distinguishes the attributes conceptually *without* any foundation in the thing (or in reality). A virtual distinction, on the other hand, distinguishes God's attributes conceptually but argues that there is a foundation in God himself for these distinctions.[32] The human mind "forms conceptions

28. Richard A. Muller, *Dictionary of Latin and Greek Theological Terms: Drawn Principally from Protestant Scholastic Theology* (Grand Rapids: Baker Academic, 1985), 93–94. See also Muller, *PRRD*, 3:41–42, 54–58, 71–73, 278–98.

29. Muller, *PRRD*, 3:286.

30. For more on the issue of nominalism and realism in relation to divine simplicity, see Holmes, "Attributes of God," 63–65.

31. James E. Dolezal, *God without Parts: Divine Simplicity and the Metaphysics of God's Absoluteness* (Eugene, OR: Pickwick, 2011), 133.

32. Edward Feser adds that others also find a difference between a major and minor virtual distinction. See Edward Feser, *Scholastic Metaphysics: A Contemporary Introduction*, ES (Piscataway, NJ: Transaction, 2014), 73–74.

proportional to the perfections flowing from God to creatures, which perfections pre-exist in God unitedly and simply, whereas in creatures they are received, divided and multiplied."[33] Any diversity seen in what flows from God does not correspond to real diversity in his essence, but is a result of our finite inability to understand his simple nature.[34] Nevertheless, the perfections truly reveal God since their "flow" stems from a foundation in him and not only in human thought.

Scotus disagreed with Thomas's virtual distinction and sought to affirm a formal distinction among the divine attributes.[35] This distinction is not as strong as a real distinction, but is stronger than a virtual distinction. According to Richard Cross, Scotus's formal distinction is

> one that obtains between not things but *formalities*—little or diminished things—and the sort of distinction is not real but somehow diminished too. These formalities are inseparable, and thus really identical with each other. Their formal distinction results from the fact that they are different properties: not sharing the same definition, even if in some cases interdefinable.[36]

The trouble for Scotus, as Dolezal and others have pointed out, is that "underlying this formal distinction is Scotus's commitment to univocism in which attributes are said univocally of God and creatures with the difference being located in God's infinite mode of being."[37] According to Dolezal, the ultimate problem is that "this formal distinction weakens the [doctrine of divine simplicity]."[38]

Neither Thomas nor Scotus is guilty of holding the divine attributes to be synonymous, despite what some contemporary critics have tried to argue.[39] The medieval and Reformed scholastics were right

---

33. Thomas Aquinas, *Summa Theologiae*, 1, q. 13, a. 4. Hereafter abbreviated as *ST*.

34. See Aquinas, *Summa Contra Gentiles* 1.31.

35. They also disagreed in that Scotus argued that divine simplicity and divine unity could be demonstrated from divine infinity, whereas Thomas begins with divine simplicity and then seeks to demonstrate divine unity and divine infinity.

36. Richard Cross, *Duns Scotus on God*, ASHPT (Aldershot: Ashgate, 2005), 109. See also Cross, "Scotus's Parisian Teaching on Divine Simplicity," in *Duns Scot à Paris, 1302–2002*, ed. O. Boulnois et al. (Turnhout: Brepols, 2004), 519–62.

37. Dolezal, *God without Parts*, 131. See also Stephen D. Dumont, "Scotus's Doctrine of Univocity and the Medieval Tradition of Metaphysics," in *Was ist Philosophie im Mittelalter*, ed. Jan A. Aertsen and Andreas Speer (Berlin: de Gruyter, 1998), 193–212.

38. Dolezal, *God without Parts*, 131.

39. Thomas repeatedly denies that the attributes are synonymous from the beginning to the end of his writings. For example, see *ST*, 1, q. 13, a. 4. This criticism likely stems from

to argue that the perfections have more than a verbal or rational existence in the human mind. No account of divine simplicity can be
offered that insists on a radical real distinction between the perfections (or the perfections and God's essence) or that makes the opposite
error by locating the distinctions in the human mind alone. However, I am not convinced that the virtual or formal distinctions are the
best options, and it is here that I see the doctrine of the Trinity as a
wise guide for divine simplicity. The virtual distinction may "have a
foundation" in God, but the distinction still only exists in the human
mind since the divine perfections are actually identical to one another
and the divine essence. The distinction remains and always will be
conceptual or rational. When it comes to the Trinity and simplicity, those who adopt this distinction must continue to demonstrate
the compatibility of a virtual distinction among the divine perfections and a real relative distinction among the divine persons. This
compatibility, I believe, cannot be accomplished as long as the virtual
distinction requires a stronger unity or oneness than the real relative
distinction.[40]

The formal distinction attempts to play an intermediate role, but
it also fails in the end. Scotus states that among the divine attributes
there is "a distinction that is in every way prior to the [operation of]
the intellect, and it is this: that wisdom actually exists naturally, and
goodness actually exists naturally, and actual wisdom is formally not
actual goodness."[41] The distinction is neither real nor conceptual, but
as Edward Feser points out, it is "hard to see how [the formal dis-
tinction] can avoid collapsing into either a real distinction or a virtual
(and thus logical) distinction. For either the intellect plays some role
in the distinction or it does not."[42] It may be, as Feser adds, that "there
just doesn't seem to be some third, 'formal' kind of distinction. However, some Scotists would argue that Scotus's formal distinction is in
fact essentially the same as a virtual distinction, the difference with

Plantinga's influential reading and critique of Thomas in *Does God Have a Nature?* Scotus is
especially innocent of this charge since he denied that God's attributes are identical with each
other (Cross, *Duns Scotus*, 29).

40. For example, if the three persons of the Trinity were only distinct "virtually" then one
may fall prey to modalism.

41. *Ordinatio* 1.8.1.4, n. 192 (*Opera Omnia*, ed. C. Balic et al. [Vatican City: Typis Polyglottis
Vaticanis, 1950–]), quoted in Cross, *Duns Scotus*, 43.

42. Feser, *Scholastic Metaphysics*, 75. Feser's "either/or" is not entirely fair since he is assessing
Scotus within the context of Thomistic philosophy and not according to Scotus's own categories. The "either/or" may exist for Thomas, but is not a necessary choice in Scotus's thought.

Aquinas being one of emphasis."[43] Perhaps most difficult, the formal distinction describes the relationship not only among the divine attributes but also between God's essence and his attributes. In other words, God's essence is not identical to his attributes.[44]

To be clear, the virtual and formal distinctions are viable options for constructing a doctrine of divine simplicity. They both ultimately avoid the problems of nominalism and realism, but I am not convinced that the virtual distinction is able to claim sufficient compatibility with a doctrine of the Trinity without making the distinction among the divine attributes primarily epistemological. If this is the case, then as I will point out below, a virtual distinction will have difficulty not clashing with the real relative distinction among the three divine persons.[45] What is still needed is a distinction that can be affirmed of God ontologically—not just the human conception of God epistemologically—without permitting division, and it is here that I believe the doctrine of the Trinity provides a crucial formal analogy.

TRINITARIAN DISTINCTIONS

Trinitarian theology also makes careful distinctions when talking about the divine nature and the divine persons. The question is not *whether* distinctions exist in God, but *which* ones and *where* to recognize them. Two distinctions are especially important for a doctrine of divine simplicity, and their expression will be aided by the clear expressions found in Francis Turretin's work. On the one hand, he notes that "the divine essence is principally distinguished from the persons in having communicability."[46] This is not to say that the divine essence is communicable in that there can be another divine essence. Rather, it means that the divine essence is common, or can be shared, by the three divine persons through generation and spiration. When Turretin says that they are "principally distinguished" he means that "the three persons are not really distinguished from the

43. Ibid., 75–76.
44. See Cross, *Duns Scotus*, 30, 42–45.
45. Once again, defining divine simplicity and its distinctions among the divine attributes prior to engaging the doctrine of the Trinity often results in a stricter form of unity than the doctrine of the Trinity can handle. As stated above, the problem then becomes one of compatibility.
46. Francis Turretin, *Institutes of Elenctic Theology*, ed. James T. Dennison Jr., trans. George Musgrave Giger (Phillipsburg, NJ: P&R, 1992), 3.25.1 (1:265).

essence."[47] If there was a real distinction between the essence and the persons then there would undoubtedly be three essences. If it is not a real distinction, then what kind of distinction should be drawn?

Turretin points out that there has not been agreement on the terms used for this distinction: real, formal, virtual, eminent, personal, and modal.[48] He chooses the modal distinction, "by which the mode is said to be distinguished from some thing" but is clear, again, that "the person may be said to differ from the essence not really (*realiter*), i.e., essentially (*essentialiter*) as thing and thing, but modally (*modaliter*)—as a mode from a thing (*modus a re*)."[49] This modal distinction is basically a form of a conceptual or logical distinction with the goal of affirming the inseparability and indivisibility of the divine essence and the three divine persons. In terms of the divine essence, there is not another even though, as Augustine states, "the essence is nothing else than the Trinity itself."[50]

On the other hand, if the distinction between the divine essence and divine persons is not real but modal (or conceptual), "the distinction of the persons from each other seems to be greater than from the essence."[51] This distinction can be said to be real, but it must be said to be a real *minor* distinction and not a real major distinction.[52] The latter identifies a difference between two things, whereas the former speaks of the distinction between a thing and its modes. This is also commonly referred to as a real relative distinction with reference to the "relative properties" of the divine persons.[53]

Among divine persons there must be "another" in order for there to truly be three persons; otherwise there would only be one real person. Each divine person is nothing but the divine essence in its particular

47. Ibid., 1:270. Gilles Emery agrees that "the three divine persons *are* their identical divine nature. Between the divine persons and the divine nature, there is no real difference, but only a conceptual distinction." See Gilles Emery, *The Trinity: An Introduction to Catholic Doctrine on the Triune God*, trans. Matthew Levering, TRS 1 (Washington, DC: Catholic University of America Press, 2011), 106. Levering agrees, stating that "while there is a real identity of Person and essence, there is a *real distinction*, not only in our mode of speaking but in reality, of the Persons in God" (Matthew Levering, *Scripture and Metaphysics: Aquinas and the Renewal of Trinitarian Theology*, CCT [Oxford: Blackwell, 2004], 221). Vanhoozer puts it this way: "The divine being is the same in each Person" (*Remythologizing Theology*, 146).

48. Turretin, *Institutes*, 1:278.

49. Ibid.

50. Augustine, *Letters Volume 2 (83–130)*, trans. Wilfrid Parsons, FoC (Washington, DC: Catholic University of America Press, 2008), 314.

51. Turretin, *Institutes*, 1:279.

52. Ibid.

53. See ibid., 1:280–81; cf. Emery, *The Trinity*, 106.

mode (or subsisting in a particular manner), and each divine person has the fullness of the divine essence.

These two distinctions are not the result of abstraction, substance metaphysics, or some other form of speculation. These distinctions are an act of theological discernment meant to maintain truths taught in scripture—one God and three distinct yet equal persons—so that worship of God may be true. To affirm a modal or conceptual distinction between the divine essence and the divine persons is to preserve the oneness of God. Another way to state this—if we recall David Yeago's distinction between concepts and biblical judgments—is that divine simplicity preserves the biblical judgment as to the distinction and relation of the three divine persons.[54] There are three divine persons, but there are not three Gods. To insist on a real minor distinction, or real relative distinction, among the divine persons is to declare that the persons are not identical to one another. But notice the crucial theological judgment: the divine persons are genuinely distinct, not identical, and yet not divided.

As Gilles Emery points out in relation to Thomas,

> The real distinction of the relations thus maintains the simplicity and unity of the divine essence, without partitioning it out: it does not divide the single essence of God. The distinction must be seen as the "smallest possible distinction" in so far as the difference it entails is concerned, that is a distinction which is "closest to unity" [citing *ST* I, q. 40, a. 2, ad 3] (the three persons are one single God), even though it has the status of a sovereign distinction, since it is a distinction within God.[55]

Part of the mystery of the Trinity is confessing the oneness, threeness, indivisibility, inseparability, and irreducibility of God through careful theological discernment, especially when it comes to drawing distinctions. It is here, thanks to these fine distinctions, that the Trinity principally contributes to a doctrine of divine simplicity.[56]

54. Yeago, "The New Testament and Nicene Dogma: A Contribution to the Recovery of Theological Exegesis," in *The Theological Interpretation of Scripture: Classic and Contemporary Readings*, ed. Stephen E. Fowl (Oxford: Blackwell, 1997), 87–100.

55. Gilles Emery, *The Trinitarian Theology of Saint Thomas Aquinas*, trans. Francesca Aran Murphy (Oxford: Oxford University Press, 2007), 97.

56. I am not the first to recognize this connection. For example, William G. T. Shedd declared that "the necessary connection between divine unity and divine trinality is like that between divine essence and divine attributes" (William G. T. Shedd, *Dogmatic Theology*, ed. Alan W. Gomes [Phillipsburg, NJ: P&R, 2003], 221), and Barth made a similar connection in *CD* II/1. Yet Shedd did not work out this connection in any detail, and Barth was not always consistent, sometimes calling the divine perfections "identical" to one another and at other

REARTICULATING A DOCTRINE OF DIVINE SIMPLICITY

After describing what divine simplicity is not (that is, the distortions), what it should not be (that is, errors), and what kinds of distinctions were drawn between the divine attributes and divine persons, we must now articulate a doctrine of divine simplicity that clarifies and synthesizes the previously argued material. Having outlined the differences between the distinctions between the divine attributes and divine persons, it is here that the doctrine of the Trinity provides a formal analogy for making two theological claims about distinctions in God.[57] As Robert W. Jenson writes, the doctrine of the Trinity "is not a separate puzzle to be solved but the framework within which all theology's puzzles are to be solved."[58] Although I use the language of "analogy" rather than "framework," the idea is the same: God's revelation of himself as the triune God, three in one, directs what can be

---

times claiming that they were genuinely "multiple." Thomas Aquinas seems to deny the connection. He writes that "there must be real distinction in God not, indeed, according to that which is absolute—namely, essence, wherein there is supreme unity and simplicity—but according to that which is relative" (*ST* I, q. 28, a. 3). This relative distinction carries with it a form of opposition that admits of distinction without division. In one of the objections, an argument is raised that just as paternity and filiation are *by name* distinguished from the divine essence, so are goodness and power. In his reply, Thomas notes that "power and goodness do not import any opposition in their respective natures; and hence there is no parallel argument" (*ST* I, q. 28, a. 3, ad 2). There is a real relative opposition between paternity and filiation, whereas this does not exist between power and goodness. To be sure, what Thomas may be saying is that "power and goodness" are not relational terms like Father and Son and therefore possess no form of opposition as well as no real distinction of any kind. Either way, he is clear that the distinction between the many names is not real but is only conceptual though with a foundation in God and not just in the mind (see *ST* I, q. 13, a. 4).

57. In some ways this analogy is an extension of Barth's insight. He writes that "we have an exact parallel to the concern of the doctrine of the Holy Trinity. In this doctrine the one God in His three modes of being corresponds to the Lord of glory. As it is of decisive importance to recognise the three modes of being, not only economically as modalism does, but, according to the seriousness of the divine presence and power in the economy of His works, as modes of being of the one eternal God Himself, so it is equally important to understand that God in Himself is not divested of His glory and perfections, that He does not assume them merely in connexion with His self-revelation to the world, but that they constitute His own eternal glory. Again, as it is of decisive importance not to dissolve the unity of the Godhead tritheistically into three gods, but to understand the three modes of being strictly as the modes of being of the one God with whom we have to do in all His works, so it is of equal importance to interpret God's glory and perfections, not in and for themselves, but as the glory of the Lord who alone is able to establish, disclose and confirm them as real glory" (*CD* II/1, 326–27).

58. Robert W. Jenson, "Karl Barth," in *The Modern Theologians: An Introduction to Christian Theology in the Twentieth Century*, ed. David Ford, 2nd ed. (Oxford: Blackwell, 1997), 31.

said of God's simple nature and how we must articulate the distinctions among the divine attributes.

The particular analogy I have in mind is what I call the *analogia diversitatis* (an "analogy of diversity").[59] This analogy states that as the triune God is one nature in three distinct persons, so the simplicity of God affirms one nature in multiple perfections. For those concerned about the doctrine of the Trinity being an arbitrary choice for this analogy, I would argue that the doctrine of appropriations might serve as the basis for this choice. The doctrine of appropriations is a hermeneutical tool which states that we may "appropriate," assign, or ascribe (1) *names*, such as God, Lord, or Spirit; (2) *attributes*, such as power, wisdom, or love; or (3) *works*, such as creation or salvation, to one particular divine person even though the name, attribute, or work is equally true of all three divine persons. The doctrine of appropriations connects the doctrine of the Trinity to the doctrine of the divine attributes, clarifying that even though one attribute may be most fitting to one divine person (for example, wisdom to the Son), that all of the divine attributes are equally predicated of the three divine persons through the one divine nature. Coupled with the indivisible operations, not only are the three divine persons indivisibly at work, but also their work is by the same power, wisdom, love, and so forth.

As with any analogy, there is resemblance without identity—likeness and unlikeness. Therefore, although the analogy is between the divine persons and the divine attributes and the distinctions drawn between each, the divine persons are not identical to the divine attributes, nor are the distinctions identical. More remains to be said regarding the similarity and dissimilarity, and this will be explained as the analogy is further clarified.

The *analogia diversitatis* can be expressed in two key claims. The first claim is found throughout the tradition and standard to any doctrine of divine simplicity. As the divine persons are only conceptually distinct from the divine essence, so the divine attributes are only conceptually distinct from the divine essence. In other words, the divine essence and the divine attributes are identical since a conceptual distinction exists in the human mind but does not actually exist in God. A conceptual distinction can be drawn between the essence and attributes, but if the distinction between them is real, then either

---

59. Thanks to Kevin Vanhoozer for this suggested term.

(1) there would be multiple essences since each attribute would be really distinct from the others or (2) the attributes would not truly reveal God since they are not actually what God is. But, as the last chapter demonstrated, God is praised for his holiness, faithfulness, and other names. If these are not actually true revelations of who God is and their reality is denied, then our knowledge of God and the biblical statements of divine praise lose their true meaning.

The second claim is unique to my project. The doctrine of the Trinity demonstrates that some form of diversity exists within the nature of God without causing, allowing, or admitting of division, separation, mixture, or conflict. This is seen most clearly in the standard statement that the Father is not the Son, the Son is not the Spirit, and so forth. Therefore, as the divine persons are relatively or modally distinct and not identical to one another, so the divine attributes are *idiomatically* distinct and not identical to one another.[60] This distinction agrees with the majority of the theological tradition that the divine attributes are not synonymous, but it goes one step further by claiming that the divine attributes are not identical to one another.[61] If the attributes are identical to each other, and the distinction among them only exists in the human mind (even if it is "grounded" in the divine essence), then it is difficult to see how this does not lead to a radical unity similar to the account given by Eunomius. If saying "God is righteous" is identical to saying "God is light," then human language falls into meaninglessness.[62]

60. I am not connecting the name of this distinction to the *communicatio idiomatum* or Christology. It does follow the translation of *idiomata* as "proper qualities" or "attributes." In that sense, an idiomatic distinction is a distinction between divine attributes that should be differentiated from the virtual and formal distinctions found in scholastic theology. Therefore, the label for this distinction is meant to be merely descriptive.

61. This claim is not identical to Scotus's formal distinction (or formal nonidentity). First, my account of divine simplicity does not stem from or depend on a prior version of divine infinity. Second, I argue that the divine attributes are identical to the divine essence, and this is a view that Scotus rejects. Third, and most significant, my view does not assume or argue for a univocal view of language. Scotus's doctrine of divine simplicity, with its formal distinction, "is entailed by—though perhaps not explained by—Scotus's univocity theory. . . . Scotus makes the point by arguing that, if these different attributes were not distinct in God, then (given his univocity theory) they would not be distinct in creatures either" (Cross, *Duns Scotus*, 43). Scotus arrives at and makes use of the formal distinction in ways different from my idiomatic distinction.Sonderegger argues a similar point, stating that "Goodness and Power cannot be identical," but that the "Attributes are identical to the Divine Nature. . . . And indeed they just are Deity, the one surpassing and superabundant God. But they are not for all that identical to one another" (*Doctrine of God*, 162–63). Despite these claims, she is not clear as to why or how the attributes are not identical to one another.

62. When I say the attributes are "not identical" to one another, I am referring to absolute

My concern regarding the "identical attributes" claim aligns me with some of the contemporary critics of divine simplicity.[63] However, while I sense the problematic nature of claiming that the divine perfections are identical with one another, my argument for an idiomatic distinction accepts this criticism but still maintains a strong account of divine simplicity.[64] Drawing this kind of distinction recognizes that the mystery of divine simplicity is that God is rich and multiple without being composite or divisible into parts, something that is already mirrored in a different, although analogous way in the doctrine of the Trinity. The nature of God is rich and plentiful—or infinite and transcendent, as others have described—and therefore many different descriptions are necessary to even begin to know and understand who and what God is. As the previous chapter claimed, scripture presents the perfections of God as interwoven or integrated realities.[65] However, the distinctions that are drawn among God's attributes do not exist in the human mind alone (that is, a rational or conceptual distinction), nor do they exist in the human mind with a mere foundation in God himself (that is, a virtual distinction). The virtual distinction admits of the reality of what is being predicated (for example, God is holy and good), but the distinction between "holy" and "good" is only acknowledged because finite and sinful creatures cannot comprehend an infinite God. Of course, this is true,

---

identity in the sense of whether there is absolute sameness. For example, love and justice are not absolutely the same even if each is identical to the divine essence. To be clear, the degree of distinction that I am arguing for is admittedly greater than what is found throughout most of the tradition—perhaps closer to what Scotus tried to say with his formal distinction—but it is still not a real distinction that would admit of independent and really distinct attributes.

63. Barry Smith argues that two unusual implications follow from divine simplicity: the "property-deity identification: there are no true divine attributes or properties because God is identical to his attributes or properties" (*Oneness and Simplicity of God*, 48). Second, the "property-property identity" which states that "each of God's attributes is the same as all the others" (ibid., 50). These worries are similar to Andrew Radde-Gallwitz's concern over the identity thesis in the West (see *Basil of Caesarea, Gregory of Nyssa, and the Transformation of Divine Simplicity*, OECS [Oxford: Oxford University Press, 2009], 5–17). While I do not agree with their descriptions of the West's view as a "property-property identity" or "identity thesis," I remain sympathetic to the conceptual concerns.

64. Recall that nearly all theologians throughout the theological tradition deny that the perfections of God are synonymous. Augustine and others may claim that God's greatness is identical to God's holiness, but the point was that each one is the entirety of the divine essence and not that divine greatness just *is* divine holiness with no difference whatever. Therefore, my theological claim of an idiomatic distinction is not meant to imply that I agree that there are significant problems with traditional renderings of divine simplicity to the extent that it should be rejected. Rather, the function of the idiomatic distinction is to remove the supposed problem of identical attributes and point to a different way forward.

65. Thanks to Daniel Treier for the suggestion of this language.

but the real reason why these distinctions must be acknowledged in God and not just in the human mind is because God has revealed himself to be this way. God's attributes are one and yet not synonymous; they are also diverse and yet not divisible into parts.[66]

As with all analogies, there is an imperfect likeness between the two things being compared, and the likeness has already been described above. The unlikeness of the *analogia diversitatis* can be expressed in two main ways. First, the divine persons are distinct due to their personal properties (paternity, filiation, and procession) that express their distinct relations and origins (the Father generates, the Son is begotten, the Spirit proceeds). The divine attributes are not personal and are not distinguished via relations or origins. No divine attribute was ever begotten or proceeds from one of the divine persons or the divine essence. The attributes have always been identical to the divine essence, and their multiplicity is an expression of the rich, abundant, and simple life of God, meaning that divine persons and divine attributes are not identical.

The second way that the analogy breaks down can be located in the difference in the unity of divine persons and the unity of divine attributes. What is common is that the divine persons and the divine attributes are identical to the divine essence. However, the divine persons are united to one another not only through their relations and origin but also through their perichoretic unity.[67] The divine attributes, however, are *not* united to one another through perichoresis. However, while the idiomatic distinction claims that the divine attributes are not identical to one another, this distinction does not posit or allow a division or separation of God's essence into parts.

66. Is not this claim merely an account of divine unity or divine oneness? Critics may argue this point, and it must be admitted that divine simplicity is a form of divine unity. Theologians have drawn a distinction between God's singularity (*unitas singularitatis*) and God's simplicity (*unitas simplicitatis*). Others, like Barth, located divine simplicity and God's uniqueness under the larger heading of God's unity (*CD* II/1, 440–61). Scholastic philosophy provides one way to draw distinctions between different forms of unity. As Bernard Wuellner points out, it distinguished between two kinds of unity. Real unity consists of metaphysical, physical, artificial, and moral unity, which are all distinct from logical unity. Metaphysical unity includes simplicity, which can be unique—consisting of simplicity of being or essence—or common. Divine unity is also regularly understood in the context of a doctrine of the Trinity, referring to the unity of three divine persons and one divine essence. Divine simplicity, a form of real and metaphysical unity, refers to the unity of the divine perfections and the one divine essence, but this is not to say that divine simplicity is identical to an account of divine unity in general (Bernard Wuellner, *Dictionary of Scholastic Philosophy* [Fitzwilliam, NH: Loreto, 2013], 129).

67. On perichoresis, see Charles C. Twombly, *Perichoresis and Personhood: God, Christ, and Salvation in John of Damascus*, PTM (Eugene, OR: Pickwick, 2015).

These statements, based on the *analogia diversitatis* drawn above, lead to seven implications regarding divine simplicity. First, any perfection predicated of God refers to the entire divine essence. Denys articulates this well when he writes of God's many names such as life, light, truth, good, wise, power, King of kings, and so forth. He says that

> in scripture all the names appropriate to God are praised regarding the whole, entire, full, and complete divinity rather than any part of it, and that they all refer indivisibly, absolutely, unreservedly, and totally to God in his entirety.[68]

Many throughout the tradition agree with this statement, but my rearticulation of divine simplicity argues that the recognition of the multiple divine attributes is not merely a finite, human conception (that is, nominalism), nor does it represent a real multiplicity where each divine attribute is "really" distinct, or independent of the others (that is, realism). Rather, it follows the *analogia divinitatis*, learning from the Trinity and realizing, as Barth claims, that Trinity and simplicity go together: "He is One even in the distinctions of the divine persons of the Father, the Son and the Holy Spirit. He is One even in the real wealth of His distinguishable perfections."[69] This kind of predication is not of a general essence, but to the triune God, for "every kindly name of God, even when applied to any one of the divine persons, must be taken as belonging, without distinction, to the entire Godhead."[70] The divine perfections are perfections of the triune God and not a divine essence in general.[71]

Second, while each attribute is predicated of the entire nature of God, this does not mean that God's nature can be reduced to one particular attribute. Divine simplicity is not a reductive doctrine; rather, it recognizes and confesses the depth of God's character such that many descriptions are necessary. Another way to state this is that divine simplicity teaches that God is *irreducible*. This also means that

---

68. Dionysius, "The Divine Names," in *Pseudo-Dionysius: The Complete Works*, trans. Colm Luibheid and Paul Rorem (Mawhaw, NJ: Paulist, 1987), 58.

69. *CD* II/1, 445.

70. Ibid., 67.

71. My goal is not to develop a trinitarian articulation of the divine perfections, even though I believe the two are closely connected. For an example of this move, see Colin E. Gunton, *The Christian Faith: An Introduction to Christian Doctrine* (Oxford: Blackwell, 2002), 188–91, and Christopher R. J. Holmes, "Eberhard Jüngel and Wolf Krötke: Recent Contributions toward a Trinitarian Doctrine of God's Attributes," *TJT* 22 (2006): 159–80.

God does not have a primary attribute because, first, he does not "have" attributes, and second, because every divine perfection predicated of him is the divine essence in its entirety and is also distinct from the other divine perfections.

Third, the divine perfections are nothing but the divine essence, but the perfections are not identical or synonymous with the other divine perfections. They are idiomatically distinct from one another, but not so distinct that they are separable. In this sense, divine simplicity teaches not only God's irreducibility but also his *inseparability*. This claim flows from theological judgments found within the doctrine of the Trinity. For example, Gregory of Nazianzus wrote that "no sooner do I conceive of the One than I am illumined by the Splendour of the Three; no sooner do I distinguish Them than I am carried back to the One."[72] Placing this claim in the context of the divine attributes, it may be possible to imagine God's holiness without thinking of his Lordship, faithfulness, or oneness. But there is no full and true understanding of God's holiness without considering the other revealed divine perfections that are equally and entirely the divine essence as well. Stated briefly, no divine attribute is an island.[73]

Fourth, as Peter Sanlon states, "When [God] loves us, he gives himself to us."[74] To speak truly of God's love is not to speak of a feeling God has, a part of who God is, or an experience a person has of God. God's love is God himself in his entirety. There is nothing missing when God reveals or demonstrates his love toward his creation. In this sense, divine love is not an abstract property that can be analyzed apart from the rest of God's attributes or God himself. Neither is divine love a general concept or an idea *about* God. Rather, God's love is the entirety of God himself revealed to his finite and sinful creation. Yet God's love is just one example. All of the other revealed divine perfections should be understood and contemplated in the same way: as God himself in his entirety.

Fifth, my articulation of divine simplicity also implies that God's nature is not a mixture of his attributes. Even though I claim that

---

72. Gregory Nazianzus, *Oration 40: On Holy Baptism*, in *NPNF2* 7:375.

73. This claim is in contrast to theologians who attempt to make a single divine perfection primary or all encompassing. For examples, see Stanley J. Grenz, *Theology for the Community of God* (Grand Rapids: Eerdmans, 2000), 72–75; Gerald L. Bray, *The Doctrine of God*, Contours of Christian Theology (Downers Grove, IL: InterVarsity Press, 1993), 103. Even Bavinck seems to prefer aseity; however, this is not entirely clear. See Bavinck, *PRRD*, 2:124, 152.

74. Peter Sanlon, *Simply God: Recovering the Classical Trinity* (Nottingham, UK: Inter-Varsity Press, 2014), 125.

the divine attributes are not identical to one another, my account still strongly rejects any composition in God. God is without parts, and therefore there are no parts in God that can be mixed. God's love is rich in that it is a love that is good, wise, righteous, and faithful, but this is not because of a mixture of these attributes but is due to his rich, simple, and incomprehensible nature.

Sixth, divine simplicity implies that God's attributes cannot be in conflict. On the one hand, there are no parts in God that can come in conflict with one another. God's love is his essence and God's justice is his essence. These are not parts that form tensions or can push against one another, but reveal that God's love is just and his justice is loving. God's love and justice, for example, are richly displayed on the cross. As Herman Bavinck states, "There is no fact that so powerfully brings those perfections of God to the fore as Christ's incarnation and satisfaction. Not just one attribute is brilliantly illumined by these events but all of them together."[75]

Finally, divine simplicity implies that there is no difference of degrees among his attributes. God's love is not greater than his justice, nor is God's dynamic life stronger than his immutability. This implication was best expressed by Gregory of Nyssa when he wrote that God is "unlimited in goodness, and unlimited is the same as infinite. But to apply the concepts of greater and less to the infinite and unlimited is utterly absurd."[76] In God there is "no addition, no subtraction, no variation of quantity or quality generating change."[77] God's love does not become more holy; his knowledge does not become wiser; nor does his justice ever triumph his patience. God is all of these things, equally, fully, indivisibly, and simply.

75. Bavinck, *PRRD*, 3:371. Henri Blocher also states that "in the central event of the cross, biblically considered, all of God's attributes—which are one—shine forth in one way or another" (Henri Blocher, "God and the Cross," in McCormack, *Engaging the Doctrine of God*, 138).

76. Gregory of Nyssa, *A Refutation of the First Book of the Two Published by Eunomius after the Decease of Holy Basil*, in *El "Contra Eunomium I" en la Producción Literaria de Gregorio de Nisa*, ed. Lucas F Mateo-Seco and Juan L. Bastero, trans. Stuart G. Hall (Pamplona: Ediciones Universidad de Navarra, SA, 1988), 169. For more on divine infinity in Gregory, see Mark Weedman, "The Polemical Context of Gregory of Nyssa's Doctrine of Divine Infinity," *JECS* 18 (2010): 81–104; Albert-Kees Geljon, "Divine Infinity in Gregory of Nyssa and Philo of Alexandria," *VC* 59 (2005): 152–77.

77. Gregory of Nyssa, *The Second Book against Eunomius*, in *Gregory of Nyssa: Contra Eunomium II*, ed. Lenka Karfíková, Scot Douglass, and Johannes Zachhuber, trans. Stuart George Hall, SVC 82 (Leiden: Brill, 2007), 489.

CONCLUSION

This account of divine simplicity avoids the four errors I pointed out above. It does not begin with a general account of the divine being, but begins with an account of the nature of the triune God. It recognizes that God's revealed perfections are true and distinct not just according to human intellect, but according to God's very nature as well. Furthermore, it avoids the final two errors by finding a middle ground between a radical unity and a radical plurality. God's attributes are neither really nor conceptually distinct, but, analogous to the real relative distinction among the divine persons, they are idiomatically distinct.

I have been able to make these claims because they are first rooted in the teachings of scripture seen in the previous chapter. In particular, scripture's testimony to the multiple divine names of the one God and the indivisible operations of the triune God form the principal exegetical basis of the doctrine of divine simplicity. God is worthy of being called Yahweh, the Holy One, jealous, love, light, and so forth, and none of these descriptions describe only part of who God is, but all that he is. God is not partially faithful or partially holy, but fully faithful and completely holy. However, the divine name(s) alone do not secure the fact that he is indivisible. It is only when the teaching of indivisible operations of the Trinity *ad extra* is viewed in relation to the divine name(s) that the picture begins to become clearer.

This also leads to the doctrine of the Trinity as the theological source and analogy for the doctrine of divine simplicity. To begin describing God as simple requires that one first recognize that God is triune. The doctrine of the Trinity helps orient divine simplicity to properly define and explain the unity, plurality, and distinctions in God's nature. Finally, once divine simplicity is reconceived in light of the doctrine of the Trinity, it can be seen as a consequential doctrine (that is, it follows from the Trinity) rather than a teaching that defines itself prior to engaging with other doctrines. Divine simplicity supports the doctrine of the Trinity, but it does not govern it. Rather, it is internally informed and directed by the *analogia divinitatis* and therefore finds its true home in Christian theology.

We can now sufficiently state that divine simplicity is a theological concept which teaches that the divine attributes and the divine essence are identical, whereas the divine attributes are idiomatically distinct from one another. Defining it this way resolves two significant problems in contemporary accounts of divine simplicity. First, this understanding of divine simplicity does not require a stricter form of unity than what is found in the Trinity. My argument does not need to demonstrate the compatibility between divine simplicity and the Trinity, but instead has shown that the supposed incompatibility is actually not the problem if divine simplicity draws a proper distinction among the divine attributes that are analogous to the distinction between the divine persons. The Trinity and simplicity are revealed doctrines that find their roots in scripture, and both aim to make sense of the unity, diversity, and distinctions in God—one according to divine persons, the other according to divine attributes—in order to oppose false teachings and worship God in truth.

Second, this perspective offers a new answer to the problem of identical attributes. This issue has caused great confusion and, for many, is one of the major reasons to reject divine simplicity. My account demonstrates that the divine perfections are not identical to each other nor are they synonymous, but this does not threaten or weaken the claim of divine simplicity. The divine perfections are the divine essence in its entirety, but it should not be said that one attribute is identical to another (for example, justice is identical to love). They are distinct attributes; however, they eternally remain inseparable from one another in that God's justice is always loving and his love is always just. Such a claim does not require that they be identical—analogous to how the divine persons are not identical—even though both attributes equally describe the divine essence in its entirety.

To be clear, the argument I am making is not a departure from the tradition, but is a development from within the tradition. Stated differently, this project is a renewal of divine simplicity. Simplicity was never a monolithic teaching; rather, it advanced and matured in response to false teaching, scripture, and the needs of each new time and location. This project, similar to previous advances, aims to extend the ongoing dialogue surrounding divine simplicity in light of contemporary criticisms and concerns. On the other hand, because this argument is intended as a development from within the tradition, it claims to have a degree of continuity with the tradition in claiming divine simplicity as an inherently Christian teaching rooted in scripture and informed by the Trinity. In short, the doctrine of divine simplicity I have attempted to outline is a theological restatement, not a repetition.

Further research will do well to focus on four particular areas: (1) Divine simplicity and Christology. How do the life, death, and resurrection of Jesus reveal divine simplicity? Or do these doctrines conflict? Do only some versions of Christology conflict with divine simplicity? (2) Divine simplicity and the atonement. Adam Johnson has moved the conversation forward in significant ways, but as he admits in his work, divine simplicity is not a central focus of the book.[78] Is the atonement primarily about God's love or primarily about his holiness? Can justice and mercy truly be on display in Jesus's life and on the cross? Are divine justice and mercy different "things"? (3) Divine simplicity and the knowledge of God. Attention has been given to God's revelation in creation, in Jesus, and through the Holy Spirit, but little focus has been given to the way that God's works are expressions of his divine perfections—his very essence—and how they reveal God to his creation. To know God's love is not to know love in general, but to know God himself. (4) Further studies of the divine perfections will be wise to avoid isolated accounts of God's perfections. For example, the study of God's love cannot merely be a study of scripture's use of love, his particular displays of love, or a general understanding of love itself. If divine simplicity is true, then God's love is holy love, wise love, sovereign love, and so forth. When God judges, he does so in love. When God remains silent, he does so in love.[79] In short, God never fails to be loving, holy, sovereign, and so forth because God is these very things in the entirety of his being as Father, Son, and Holy Spirit.

---

78. Adam J. Johnson, *God's Being in Reconciliation: The Theological Basis of the Unity and Diversity of the Atonement in the Theology of Karl Barth*, SST (London: T&T Clark, 2012). See also Ken Oakes, "The Divine Perfections and the Economy: The Atonement," in *Theological Theology: Essays in Honour of John Webster*, ed. R. David Nelson, Darren Sarisky, and Justin Stratis (London: Bloomsbury T&T Clark, 2015), 237–46.

79. As stated early, no perfection is an island, and they should not be treated in isolation.

Bibliography

Ables, Travis. *Incarnational Realism: Trinity and the Spirit in Augustine and Barth*. SST. London: Bloomsbury T&T Clark, 2013.

Adams, Marilyn McCord. *William Ockham*. 2 vols. Notre Dame: University of Notre Dame Press, 1987.

Allen, Michael. "Divine Attributes." In *Christian Dogmatics: Reformed Theology for the Church Catholic*, edited by Michael Allen and Scott R. Swain, 57–77. Grand Rapids: Baker Academic, 2016.

_____. "Exodus 3 after the Hellenization Thesis." *JTI* 3 (2009): 179–96.

_____. *Justification and the Gospel: Understanding the Contexts and Controversies*. Grand Rapids: Baker Academic, 2013.

Anastos, Milton V. "Basil's Κατά Ευνομίου: A Critical Analysis." In *Basil of Caesarea, Christian, Humanist, Ascetic: A Sixteen-Hundredth Anniversary Symposium*, edited by Paul Fedwick, 1:67–136. Toronto: PIMS, 1981.

Anatolios, Khaled. *Retrieving Nicaea: The Development and Meaning of Trinitarian Doctrine*. Grand Rapids: Baker Academic, 2011.

Anselm of Canterbury. *Anselm of Canterbury: The Major Works*. Edited by Brian Davies and Gareth Evans. Translated by Simon Harrison. Oxford: Oxford University Press, 1998.

Athanasopoulos, C., and C. Schneider, eds. *Divine Essence and Divine Energies: Ecumenical Reflections on the Presence of God in Eastern Orthodoxy*. Cambridge: James Clarke, 2013.

Athenagoras. *Plea for the Christians*. In *Ante-Nicene Fathers*, vol. 2. Edited by Alexander Roberts, James Donaldson, and A. Cleveland Coxe. Translated by B. P. Pratten. Peabody, MA: Hendrickson, 1994.

Augustine. *The City of God against the Pagans*. Translated by R. W. Dyson. CTHPT. Cambridge: Cambridge University Press, 1998.

_____. *Letters Volume 2 (83–130)*. Translated by Wilfrid Parsons. FoC. Washington, DC: Catholic University of America Press, 2008.

_____. "Sermon 52." In *Sermons 51–94 (III/3)*, translated by Edmund Hill, 50–65. WSA. Hyde Park, NY: New City Press, 1991.

_____. *The Trinity*. Edited by John Rotelle. Translated by Edmund Hill. WSA. Hyde Park, NY: New City Press, 1991.

Ayres, Lewis. *Augustine and the Trinity*. Cambridge: Cambridge University Press, 2010.

_____. "The Fundamental Grammar of Augustine's Trinitarian Theology." In *Augustine and His Critics: Essays in Honour of Gerald Bonner*, edited by Robert Dodaro and George Lawless, 51–76. New York: Routledge, 2000.

_____. "'Giving Wings to Nicaea': Reconceiving Augustine's Earliest Trinitarian Theology." *AugStud* 38 (2007): 21–40.

_____. *Nicaea and Its Legacy: An Approach to Fourth-Century Trinitarian Theology*. Oxford: Oxford University Press, 2006.

_____. "Not Three People: The Fundamental Themes of Gregory of Nyssa's Trinitarian Theology as Seen in *To Ablabius: On Not Three Gods*." *ModTheo* 18 (2002): 445–74.

_____. "'Remember That You Are Catholic' (serm. 52.2): Augustine on the Unity of the Triune God." *JECS* 8 (2000): 39–82.

Ayres, Lewis, and Andrew Radde-Gallwitz. "Doctrine of God." In *The Oxford Handbook of Early Christian Studies*, edited by Susan Ashbrook Harvey and David Hunter, 864–85. Oxford: Oxford University Press, 2008.

Baars, Arie. "*Opera Trinitatis ad extra sunt indivisa* in the Theology of John Calvin." In *Calvinus sacrarum literarum interpres: Papers of the International Congress on Calvin Research*, edited by Herman J. Selderhuis, 131–41. Göttingen: Vandenhoeck & Ruprecht, 2008.

Baddorf, Matthew. "An Argument from Divine Beauty against Divine Simplicity." *Topoi*. Forthcoming.

_____. "Divine Simplicity, Aseity, and Sovereignty." *Sophia*. Forthcoming.

Baglow, Christopher. *"Modus Et Forma": A New Approach to the Exegesis of Saint Thomas Aquinas with an Application to the "Lectura Super Epistulam Ad Ephesios."* Analecta Biblica Dissertationes. Rome: Gregorian & Biblical Press, 2002.

Barnes, Michel R. "The Arians of Book V, and the Genre of *De Trinitate*." *JTS* 44 (1993): 185–95.

_____. "Augustine in Contemporary Trinitarian Theology." *TS* 56 (1995): 237–50.

_____. "The Background and Use of Eunomius' Causal Language." In *Arianism after Arius: Essays on the Development of the Fourth Century Trinitarian Conflicts*, edited by Michel R. Barnes and Daniel H. Williams, 217–36. Edinburgh: T&T Clark, 1993.

_____. "De Régnon Reconsidered." *AugStud* 26 (1995): 51–79.

_____. "*De Trinitate* VI and VII: Augustine and the Limits of Nicene Orthodoxy." *AugStud* 38 (2007): 189–202.

_____. "Divine Unity and the Divided Self: Gregory of Nyssa's Trinitarian Theology in Its Psychological Context." *ModTheo* 18 (2002): 475–96.

_____. "Exegesis and Polemic in Augustine's *De Trinitate* I." *AugStud* 30 (1999): 43–59.

_____. "Eunomius of Cyzicus and Gregory of Nyssa: Two Traditions of Transcendent Causality." *VC* 52 (1998): 59–87.

_____. "One Nature, One Power: Consensus Doctrine in Pro-Nicene Polemic." *SP* 29 (1997): 205–23.

_____. *The Power of God: Δύναμις in Gregory of Nyssa's Trinitarian Theology.* Washington, DC: Catholic University of America Press, 2001.

_____. "Rereading Augustine's Theology of the Trinity." In *The Trinity: An Interdisciplinary Symposium on the Trinity*, edited by Stephen T. Davis, Daniel Kendall, and Gerald O'Collins, 145–76. Oxford: Oxford University Press, 1999.

Barth, Karl. *Church Dogmatics.* Edited by Geoffrey Bromiley and Thomas F. Torrance. Translated by G. W. Bromiley, J. C. Campbell, Ian Wilson, and J. Strathearn McNab. 4 vols in 14 parts. Edinburgh: T&T Clark, 1956–1975.

_____. *The Göttingen Dogmatics: Instruction in the Christian Religion.* Edited by Hannelotte Reiffen. Translated by Geoffrey W. Bromiley. Vol. 1. Grand Rapids: Eerdmans, 1991.

Basil of Caesarea. *Against Eunomius.* Translated by Mark DelCogliano and Andrew Radde-Gallwitz. FoC. Washington, DC: Catholic University of America Press, 2011.

Bauckham, Richard. *God Crucified: Monotheism and Christology in the New Testament.* Grand Rapids: Eerdmans, 1999.

_____. *Jesus and the God of Israel: God Crucified and Other Studies on the New Testament's Christology of Divine Identity.* 2nd ed. Grand Rapids: Eerdmans, 2008.

_____. "Monotheism and Christology in the Gospel of John." In *Contours of Christology in the New Testament*, edited by R. N. Longenecker, 148–66. Grand Rapids: Eerdmans, 2005.

_____. "The Worship of Jesus in Philippians 2:9–11." In *Where Christology Began: Essays on Philippians 2*, edited by Ralph P. Martin and Brian J. Dodd, 128–39. Louisville: Westminster John Knox, 1998.

Bauerschmidt, Frederick Christian. *Thomas Aquinas: Faith, Reason, and Following Christ.* CTC. Oxford: Oxford University Press, 2013.

Bavinck, Herman. *Reformed Dogmatics: God and Creation.* Edited by John Bolt. Translated by John Vriend. Vol. 2. Grand Rapids: Baker Academic, 2006.

Behr, John. *Irenaeus of Lyons: Identifying Christianity.* Oxford: Oxford University Press, 2013.

_____. *The Nicene Faith: Part Two: One of the Holy Trinity.* Vol. 2. FCT. Crestwood, NY: St. Vladimir's Seminary Press, 2004.

Bennett, Daniel C. "The Divine Simplicity." In *Logical Analysis and Contemporary Theism*, edited by John Donnelly, 94–105. New York: Fordham University Press, 1972.

Bergmann, Michael, and Jeffrey Brower. "A Theistic Argument against Platonism (and in Support of Truthmakers and Divine Simplicity)." In *Oxford Studies in Metaphysics*, edited by Dean Zimmerman, 2:357–86. Oxford: Clarendon, 2006.

Blackburn, W. Ross. *The God Who Makes Himself Known: The Missionary Heart of the Book of Exodus.* NSBT. Downers Grove, IL: IVP Academic, 2012.

Blocher, Henri. "God and the Cross." In *Engaging the Doctrine of God: Contemporary Protestant Perspectives*, edited by Bruce L. McCormack, 125–41. Grand Rapids: Baker Academic, 2008.

Bockmuehl, Markus. *The Epistle to the Philippians.* 4th ed. BNTC. London: A&C Black, 1997.

Bohmbach, Karl G. "Names and Naming in the Biblical World." In *Women in Scripture: A Dictionary of Named and Unnamed Women in the Hebrew Bible, The Apocryphal/Deuteroconomical Books, and the New Testament*, edited by Carol Meyers, 33–39. Boston: Houghton Mifflin, 2000.

Bonino, Serge-Thomas. "La simplicité de Dieu." In *Istituto San Tommaso, Studi 1996*, edited by Dietrich Lorenz, 117–51. Rome: Pontifical University of St. Thomas Aquinas, 1996.

Bradshaw, David. *Aristotle East and West: Metaphysics and the Division of Christendom*. Cambridge: Cambridge University Press, 2007.

_____. "Augustine the Metaphysician." In *Orthodox Readings of Augustine*, edited by Aristotle Papanikolaou and George E. Demacopoulos, 227–51. Crestwood, NY: St. Vladimir's Seminary Press, 2008.

_____. "The Concept of Divine Energies." *P&T* 18 (2006): 93–120.

_____. "The Divine Energies in the New Testament." *SVTQ* 50 (2006): 189–223.

_____. "The Divine Glory and the Divine Energies." *FPh* 23 (2006): 279–98.

_____. "Divine Simplicity and Divine Freedom in Maimonides and Gersonides." *PACPA* 86 (2012): 75–87.

Bray, Gerald L. *The Doctrine of God*. ConCT. Downers Grove, IL: InterVarsity Press, 1993.

Brouwer, Rinse H. Reeling. "The Conversation between Karl Barth and Amandus Polanus on the Question of the Reality of Human Speaking of the Simplicity and the Multiplicity in God." In *The Reality of Faith in Theology: Studies on Karl Barth (Princeton-Kampen Consultation, 2005)*, edited by Bruce L. McCormack and Gerrit Neven, 51–110. New York: Peter Lang, 2007.

_____. *Karl Barth and Post-Reformation Orthodoxy*. BS. Burlington, VT: Ashgate, 2015.

Brower, Jeffrey E. "Making Sense of Divine Simplicity." *FPh* 25 (2008): 3–30.

_____. "Simplicity and Aseity." In *The Oxford Handbook of Philosophical Theology*, edited by Thomas P. Flint and Michael C. Rea, 105–28. Oxford: Oxford University Press, 2009.

Brueggemann, Walter. "Exodus." In *The New Interpreter's Bible*. Vol. 1, *Genesis to Leviticus*, edited by Leander Keck, 675–982. Nashville: Abingdon, 1994.

_____. *Theology of the Old Testament: Testimony, Dispute, Advocacy*. Minneapolis: Fortress Press, 2005.

Brunner, Emil. *The Christian Doctrine of God*. Translated by Olive Wyon. Vol. 1. London: Lutterworth, 1949.

Burns, Peter. "The Status and Function of Divine Simpleness in *Summa theologiae* Ia, qq.2–13." *Thomist* 57 (1993): 1–26.

Burns, Robert. "The Divine Simplicity in St. Thomas." *RelS* 25 (1989): 271–93.

Burrell, David B. *Aquinas: God and Action*. Notre Dame: University of Notre Dame Press, 1979.

_____. "Aquinas on Naming God." *TS* 24 (1963): 183–212.

_____. "The Attributes of God: Simpleness." In *Philosophy of Religion*, edited by Brian Davies, 71–75. Washington, DC: Georgetown University Press, 1998.

_____. "Creator/Creatures Relation: 'The Distinction' vs. 'Onto-theology.'" *FPh* 25 (2008): 177–89.

_____. "Distinguishing God from the World." In *Language, Meaning, and God: Essays in Honour of Herbert McCabe*, edited by Brian Davies, 75–91. London: Chapman, 1987.

_____. *Knowing the Unknowable God: Ibn-Sina, Maimonides, Aquinas*. Notre Dame: University of Notre Dame Press, 1992.

_____. "Maimonides, Aquinas, and Ghazali on Naming God." In *The Return to Scripture in Judaism and Christianity: Essays in Postcritical Scriptural Interpretation*, edited by Peter Ochs, 233–55. Theological Inquiries. Mahwah, NJ: Paulist, 1993.

Butner, D. Glenn, Jr. "For and against de Régnon: Trinitarianism East and West." *IJST* 17 (2015): 399–412.

Calvin, John. *Calvin's Calvinism: Treatises on "The Eternal Predestination of God" and "The Secret Providence of God."* Translated by Henry Cole. Grand Rapids: Reformed Free, 1987.

_____. *Institutes of the Christian Religion*. Edited by John T. McNeill. Translated by Ford Lewis Battles. 2 vols. LCC 20–21. Philadelphia: Westminster, 1960.

Childs, Brevard S. *The Book of Exodus: A Critical, Theological Commentary*. OTL. Philadelphia: Westminster, 1974.

Clarke, Samuel. *A Demonstration of the Being and Attributes of God and Other Writings*. Edited by Ezio Vailati. CTHP. Cambridge: Cambridge University Press, 1998.

Claunch, Kyle. "What God Hath Done Together: Defending the Historic Doctrine of the Inseparable Operations of the Trinity." *JETS* 56 (2013): 781–800.

Coakley, Sarah, and Charles M. Stang, eds. *Re-thinking Dionysius the Areopagite*. Oxford: Wiley-Blackwell, 2009.

Cohen, Will. "Augustine and John Zizioulas." In *T&T Clark Companion to Augustine and Modern Theology*, edited by C. C. Pecknold and Tarmo Toom, 223–39. London: Bloomsbury T&T Clark, 2013.

Cole, Graham A. "Exodus 34, the Middoth and the Doctrine of God: The Importance of Biblical Theology to Evangelical Systematic Theology." *SBJT* 12 (2008): 24–36.

Colish, Marcia L. *Peter Lombard*. Vol. 1. Leiden: Brill, 1994.

Coon, George. "A Historical-Theological Analysis of the Doctrine of Divine Simplicity." ThM Thesis, Grand Rapids Baptist Seminary, 2001.

Cotnoir, Aaron J., and Donald L. M. Baxter, eds. *Composition as Identity*. Oxford: Oxford University Press, 2014.

Cowan, Steven B. "Purely and Simply God: A Defense of the Classical View of Divine Simplicity." MA Thesis, University of Arkansas, 1993.

Craig, William Lane. "Toward a Tenable Social Trinitarianism." In *Philosophical and Theological Essays on the Trinity*, edited by Thomas McCall and Michael C. Rea, 89–99. Oxford: Oxford University Press, 2009.

Cremer, Hermann. *The Christian Doctrine of the Divine Attributes*. Edited by Helmut Burkhardt. Translated by Robert B. Price. Eugene, OR: Pickwick, 2016.

Crisp, Oliver D. *Jonathan Edwards among the Theologians*. Grand Rapids: Eerdmans, 2015.

_____. "Jonathan Edwards's God: Trinity, Individuation, and Divine Simplicity." In *Engaging the Doctrine of God: Contemporary Protestant Perspectives*, edited by Bruce L. McCormack, 83–106. Grand Rapids: Baker Academic, 2008.

_____. "Jonathan Edwards on Divine Simplicity." *RelS* 39 (2003): 23–41.

_____. *Jonathan Edwards on God and Creation*. Oxford: Oxford University Press, 2012.

_____. "On the Orthodoxy of Jonathan Edwards." *SJT* 67 (2014): 304–22.

Cross, Richard. "Divine Simplicity and the Doctrine of the Trinity: Gregory of Nyssa and Augustine." In *Philosophical Theology and the Christian Tradition: Russian and Western Perspectives*, edited by David Bradshaw, 53–66. Washington, DC: The Council for Research in Values and Philosophy, 2012.

_____. *Duns Scotus*. GMT. Oxford: Oxford University Press, 1999.

_____. *Duns Scotus on God*. ASHPT. Aldershot: Ashgate, 2005.

_____. "Scotus's Parisian Teaching on Divine Simplicity." In *Duns Scot à Paris, 1302–2002*, edited by O. Boulnois, E. Karger, J. L. Solère, and G. Sondag, 519–62. Textes et Études du Moyen Âge 26. Turnhout: Brepols, 2004.

Dauphinais, Michael, Barry David, and Matthew Levering, eds. *Aquinas the Augustinian.* Washington, DC: Catholic University of America Press, 2007.

Dauphinais, Michael, and Matthew Levering, eds. *Reading John with St. Thomas Aquinas: Theological Exegesis and Speculative Theology.* Washington, DC: Catholic University of America Press, 2005.

Davies, Brian. "Classical Theism and the Doctrine of Divine Simplicity." In *Language, Meaning, and God: Essays in Honour of Herbert McCabe*, edited by Brian Davies, 51–74. London: Cassell, 1987.

———. *An Introduction to the Philosophy of Religion.* 3rd ed. Oxford: Oxford University Press, 2004.

———. "A Modern Defence of Divine Simplicity." In *Philosophy of Religion: A Guide and Anthology*, edited by Brian Davies, 549–64. Oxford: Oxford University Press, 2000.

———. "Simplicity." In *The Cambridge Companion to Christian Philosophical Theology*, edited by Charles Taliaferro and Chad Meister, 31–45. Cambridge: Cambridge University Press, 2010.

DeHart, Paul J. *Beyond the Necessary God: Trinitarian Faith and Philosophy in the Thought of Eberhard Jüngel.* Oxford: Oxford University Press, 1999.

DelCogliano, Mark. *Basil of Caesarea's Anti-Eunomian Theory of Names: Christian Theology and Late-Antique Philosophy in the Fourth Century Trinitarian Controversy.* SVC 103. Leiden: Brill, 2010.

Dempster, Stephen G. "LORD." In *The Routledge Encyclopedia of the Historical Jesus*, edited by Craig A. Evans, 375–80. New York: Routledge, 2008.

Dever, Vincent M. "Divine Simplicity: Aquinas and the Current Debate." PhD diss., Marquette University, 1994.

Dewan, Lawrence. "Saint Thomas, Alvin Plantinga, and the Divine Simplicity." *MSch* 66 (1989): 141–51.

Dionysius the Areopagite. "The Divine Names." In *The Mystical Theology and The Divine Names*, translated by C. E. Rolt, 50–190. Mineola, NY: Dover, 2004.

———. *The Divine Names.* In *Pseudo-Dionysius: The Complete Works*, translated by Colm Luibheid and Paul Rorem, 47–131. Mahwah, NJ: Paulist, 1987.

Dolezal, James E. *All That Is in God: Evangelical Theology and the Challenge of Classical Theism.* Grand Rapids, MI: Reformation Heritage Books, 2017.

_____. *God without Parts: Divine Simplicity and the Metaphysics of God's Absoluteness*. Eugene, OR: Pickwick, 2011.

_____. "Trinity, Simplicity and the Status of God's Personal Relations." *IJST* 16 (2014): 79–98.

Dorner, Isaak A. *Divine Immutability: A Critical Reconsideration*. TMT. Minneapolis: Fortress Press, 2000.

Duby, Steven J. "Divine Simplicity, Divine Freedom, and the Contingency of Creation: Dogmatic Responses to Some Analytic Questions." *JRT* 6 (2012): 115–42.

_____. *Divine Simplicity: A Dogmatic Account*. SST. London: Bloomsbury T&T Clark, 2015.

Dumont, Stephen D. "Scotus's Doctrine of Univocity and the Medieval Tradition of Metaphysics." In *Was ist Philosophie im Mittelalter*, edited by Jan A. Aertsen and Andreas Speer, 193–212. Berlin: de Gruyter, 1998.

Ebeling, Gerhard. "Schleiermacher's Doctrine of the Divine Attributes." In *Schleiermacher as Contemporary*, 125–75. New York: Herder & Herder, 1970.

Eglinton, James. *Trinity and Organism: Towards a New Reading of Herman Bavinck's Organic Motif*. SST. London: T&T Clark, 2012.

Eichrodt, Walther. *Theology of the Old Testament*. Translated by J. A. Baker. 2 vols. Philadelphia: Westminster, 1961.

Emery, Gilles. "Biblical Exegesis and the Speculative Doctrine of the Trinity in St. Thomas Aquinas' Commentary on St. John." In *Reading John with St. Thomas Aquinas: Theological Exegesis and Speculative Theology*, edited by Michael Dauphinais and Matthew Levering, 23–61. Washington, DC: Catholic University of America Press, 2005.

_____. "Essentialism or Personalism in the Treatise on God in Saint Thomas Aquinas?" *Thomist* 64 (2000): 521–63.

_____. *The Trinitarian Theology of Saint Thomas Aquinas*. Translated by Francesca Aran Murphy. Oxford: Oxford University Press, 2007.

_____. *The Trinity: An Introduction to Catholic Doctrine on the Triune God*. Translated by Matthew Levering. TRS 1. Washington, DC: Catholic University of America Press, 2011.

Erickson, Millard J. *God the Father Almighty: A Contemporary Exploration of the Divine Attributes*. Grand Rapids: Baker, 1998.

Farley, Edward. *Divine Empathy: A Theology of God*. Minneapolis: Fortress Press, 1996.

Farlow, Gregory. "Simplicity or Priority?" In *Oxford Studies in Philosophy of Religion*, edited by Jonathan Kvanvig, 114–38. Oxford: Oxford University Press, 2015.

Farrow, Douglas. *Ascension and Ecclesia: On the Significance of the Doctrine of the Ascension for Ecclesiology and Christian Cosmology*. Edinburgh: T&T Clark, 1999.

Fee, Gordon D. *God's Empowering Presence: The Holy Spirit in the Letters of Paul*. Peabody, MA: Hendrickson, 1994.

_____. "Paul and the Trinity: The Experience of Christ and the Spirit for Paul's Understanding of God." In *The Trinity: An Interdisciplinary Symposium on the Trinity*, edited by Stephen T. Davis, Daniel Kendall, and Gerald O'Collins, 49–72. Oxford: Oxford University Press, 2002.

_____. *Pauline Christology: An Exegetical-Theological Study*. Peabody, MA: Hendrickson, 2007.

Feinberg, John S. *No One Like Him: The Doctrine of God*. FET. Wheaton, IL: Crossway, 2001.

Feldmeier, Reinhard, and Hermann Spieckermann. *God of the Living: A Biblical Theology*. Translated by Mark E. Biddle. Waco, TX: Baylor University Press, 2011.

Feser, Edward. *Scholastic Metaphysics: A Contemporary Introduction*. Editiones Scholasticae. Piscataway, NJ: Transaction, 2014.

Frame, John. *The Doctrine of God*. A Theology of Lordship. Phillipsburg, NJ: P&R, 2002.

_____. *Systematic Theology*. Phillipsburg, NJ: P&R, 2013.

Franks, Christopher A. "The Simplicity of the Living God: Aquinas, Barth, and Some Philosophers." *ModTheo* 21 (2005): 275–300.

Fretheim, Terence E. *Exodus*. IBC. Louisville: Westminster John Knox, 2010.

Friedman, Russell L. *Medieval Trinitarian Thought from Aquinas to Ockham*. Cambridge: Cambridge University Press, 2010.

Gabriel, Andrew K. *The Lord Is the Spirit: The Holy Spirit and the Divine Attributes*. Eugene, OR: Pickwick, 2011.

Gehring, Allen Stanley, Jr. "Divine Simplicity as Actus Purus." MA thesis, Texas A&M University, 2005.

Geljon, Albert-Kees. "Divine Infinity in Gregory of Nyssa and Philo of Alexandria." *VC* 59 (2005): 152–77.

Gerber, Chad Tyler. *The Spirit of Augustine's Early Theology: Contextualizing Augustine's Pneumatology*. ASPTLA. Burlington, VT: Ashgate, 2012.

Gericke, J. W. "Philosophical Interpretations of Exodus 3:14—A Brief Historical Overview." *Journal for Semitics* 21 (2012): 125–36.

Gerrish, B. A. "Theology within the Limits of Piety Alone: Schleiermacher and Calvin's Notion of God." In *The Old Protestantism and the New: Essays on the Reformation Heritage*, 196–207. Chicago: University of Chicago Press, 1982.

Gilson, Étienne. *The Spirit of Mediaeval Philosophy.* Translated by A. H. C. Downes. New York: Charles Scribner's Sons, 1940.

Gioia, Luigi. *The Theological Epistemology of Augustine's "De Trinitate."* OTM. Oxford: Oxford University Press, 2008.

Goad, Keith. "Simplicity and Trinity in Harmony." *Eusebeia* 8 (2007): 97–118.

Goudriaan, Aza. *Reformed Orthodoxy and Philosophy, 1625–1750: Gisbertus Voetius, Petrus Van Mastricht, and Anthonius Driessen.* BSCH. Leiden: Brill, 2006.

Grant, W. Matthews. "Aquinas, Divine Simplicity, and Divine Freedom." *PACPA* 77 (2003): 129–44.

_____. "Divine Simplicity, Contingent Truths, and Extrinsic Models of Divine Knowing." *FPh* 29 (2012): 254–74.

Green, Bradley G. *Colin Gunton and the Failure of Augustine: The Theology of Colin Gunton in Light of Augustine.* DDCT. Eugene, OR: Pickwick, 2011.

Gregory of Nazianzus. *Oration 40: On Holy Baptism.* In *Nicene and Post-Nicene Fathers*, Series 2, vol. 7. Edited by Philip Schaff and Henry Wace. Translated by Charles Gordon Browne and James Edward Swallow. 1886–1889. Reprint, Peabody, MA: Hendrickson, 1994.

Gregory of Nyssa. *Concerning We Should Not Think of Saying That There Are Not Three Gods to Ablabius.* In *The Trinitarian Controversy.* Edited and translated by William G. Rusch. SECT. Philadelphia: Fortress Press, 1980.

_____. *On the Holy Trinity.* In *Nicene and Post-Nicene Fathers*, Series 2, vol. 5. Edited by Philip Schaff and Henry Wace. Translated by H. A. Wilson. 1886–1889. Reprint, Peabody, MA: Hendrickson, 1994.

_____. *A Refutation of the First Book of the Two Published by Eunomius after the Decease of Holy Basil.* In *El "Contra Eunomium I" en la Producción Literaria de Gregorio de Nisa.* Edited by Lucas F Mateo-Seco and Juan L. Bastero. Translated by Stuart G. Hall. Pamplona: Ediciones Universidad de Navarra, SA, 1988.

_____. *The Second Book against Eunomius.* In *Gregory of Nyssa: Contra Eunomium II.* Edited by Lenka Karfíková, Scot Douglass, and Johannes Zachhuber. Translated by Stuart George Hall. SVC 82. Leiden: Brill, 2007.

Greig, Jonathan. "Plotinus and Aristotle on the Simplicity of the Divine Intellect." MSc thesis, University of Edinburgh, 2013.

Grenz, Stanley J. *Theology for the Community of God.* Grand Rapids: Eerdmans, 2000.

Guichardan, P. Sébastien. *Le Problème de la simplicité divine en Orient et en Occident aux XIVe et XVe siècles: Grégoire Palamas, Duns Scot, Georges Scholarios: étude de théologie comparée.* Lyon: Legendre, 1933.

Gunton, Colin E. *Act and Being: Towards a Theology of the Divine Attributes.* Grand Rapids: Eerdmans, 2003.

_____. "Augustine, the Trinity and the Theological Crisis of the West." *SJT* 43 (1990): 33–58.

_____. *Becoming and Being: The Doctrine of God in Charles Hartshorne and Karl Barth.* Oxford: Oxford University Press, 1978.

_____. "The Being and Attributes of God: Eberhard Jüngel's Dispute with the Classical Philosophical Tradition." In *The Possibilities of Theology: Studies in the Theology of Eberhard Jüngel,* edited by John Webster, 7–22. London: T&T Clark, 1994.

_____. *The Christian Faith: An Introduction to Christian Doctrine.* Oxford: Blackwell, 2002.

_____. *The One, the Three and the Many: God, Creation and the Culture of Modernity.* Cambridge: Cambridge University Press, 1993.

Hanson, Richard P. C. *The Search for the Christian Doctrine of God: The Arian Controversy, 318–381.* 1988. Reprint, Grand Rapids: Baker Academic, 2006.

Haring, Nicholas M. "Notes on the Council and the Consistory of Rheims (1148)." *MS* 28 (1966): 39–59.

Hart, David Bentley. *The Beauty of the Infinite: The Aesthetics of Christian Truth.* Grand Rapids: Eerdmans, 2004.

_____. *The Experience of God: Being, Consciousness, Bliss.* New Haven: Yale University Press, 2013.

_____. "The Hidden and the Manifest: Metaphysics after Nicaea." In *Orthodox Readings of Augustine,* edited by Aristotle Papanikolaou and George E. Demacopoulos, 191–26. Crestwood, NY: St. Vladimir's Seminary Press, 2008.

Hasker, William. "Is Divine Simplicity a Mistake?" *ACPQ* 90 (2016): 699–725.

_____. *Metaphysics and the Tri-personal God*. OSAT. Oxford: Oxford University Press, 2013.

_____. "Simplicity and Freedom: A Response to Stump and Kretzmann." *FPh* 3 (1986): 192–201.

Hays, Richard B. "The God of Mercy Who Rescues Us from the Present Evil Age: Romans and Galatians." In *The Forgotten God: Perspectives in Biblical Theology*, edited by A. Andrew Das and Frank J Matera, 123–43. Louisville: Westminster John Knox, 2002.

Hector, Kevin W. "Apophaticism in Thomas Aquinas: A Re-formulation and Recommendation." *SJT* 60 (2007): 377–93.

_____. *Theology without Metaphysics: God, Language, and the Spirit of Recognition*. CIT. Cambridge: Cambridge University Press, 2011.

Hennessy, Kristin. "An Answer to de Régnon's Accusers: Why We Should Not Speak of 'His' Paradigm." *HTR* 100 (2007): 179–97.

Henry, Carl F. H. *God, Revelation and Authority*. Vol. 5, *God Who Stands and Stays*. 2nd ed. Wheaton, IL: Crossway, 1999.

Herrera, Juan José. *La simplicidad divina según santo Tomás de Aquino*. Salta, Argentina: Ediciones de la Universidad del Norte Santo Tomás de Aquino, 2011.

Hertog, Cornelis Den. *The Other Face of God: "I Am That I Am" Reconsidered*. HBM. Sheffield: Sheffield Phoenix, 2012.

Highfield, Ron. *Great Is the Lord: Theology for the Praise of God*. Grand Rapids: Eerdmans, 2008.

Hildebrand, Stephen M. *The Trinitarian Theology of Basil of Caesarea: A Synthesis of Greek Thought and Biblical Truth*. Washington, DC: Catholic University of America Press, 2007.

Hillman, T. Allan. "Substantial Simplicity in Leibniz: Form, Predication, and Truthmakers." *Review of Metaphysics* 63 (2009): 91–138.

Hinlicky, Paul R. *Beloved Community: Critical Dogmatics after Christendom*. Grand Rapids: Eerdmans, 2015.

_____. *Divine Complexity: The Rise of Creedal Christianity*. Minneapolis: Fortress Press, 2010.

_____. *Divine Simplicity: Christ the Crisis of Metaphysics*. Grand Rapids: Baker Academic, 2016.

Hodge, Charles. *Systematic Theology*. Vol. 1. 1871. Reprint, Peabody, MA: Hendrickson, 2003.

Holmes, Christopher R. J. "Eberhard Jüngel and Wolf Krötke: Recent Contributions toward a Trinitarian Doctrine of God's Attributes." *TJT* 22 (2006): 159–80.

_____. "The Glory of God in the Theology of Eberhard Jüngel." *IJST* 8 (2006): 343–55.

_____. *Revisiting the Doctrine of the Divine Attributes: In Dialogue with Karl Barth, Eberhard Jüngel, and Wolf Krötke.* IST. New York: Peter Lang, 2006.

Holmes, Stephen R. "The Attributes of God." In *The Oxford Handbook of Systematic Theology*, edited by John Webster, Kathryn Tanner, and Iain Torrance, 54–71. Oxford: Oxford University Press, 2007.

_____. "Divine Attributes." In *Mapping Modern Theology: A Thematic and Historical Introduction*, edited by Bruce L. McCormack and Kelly M. Kapic, 47–65. Grand Rapids: Baker Academic, 2012.

_____. "Does Jonathan Edwards Use a Dispositional Ontology? A Response to Sang Hyun Lee." In *Jonathan Edwards: Philosophical Theologian*, edited by Paul Helm and Oliver Crisp, 99–114. Aldershot: Ashgate, 2003.

_____. *The Quest for the Trinity: The Doctrine of God in Scripture, History and Modernity.* Downers Grove, IL: IVP Academic, 2012.

_____. "A Simple Salvation? Soteriology and the Perfections of God." In *God of Salvation: Soteriology in Theological Perspective*, edited by Ivor Davidson and Murray Rae, 35–46. Aldershot: Ashgate, 2011.

_____. "'Something Much Too Plain to Say': Towards a Defence of the Doctrine of Divine Simplicity." *NZSTR* 43 (2001): 137–54.

_____. "'Something Much Too Plain to Say': Towards a Defence of the Doctrine of Divine Simplicity." In *Listening to the Past: The Place of Tradition in Theology*, 50–67. Grand Rapids: Baker Academic, 2002.

_____. "Trinitarian Action and Inseparable Operations: Some Historical and Dogmatic Reflections." In *Advancing Trinitarian Theology: Explorations in Constructive Dogmatics*, edited by Oliver D. Crisp and Fred Sanders, 60–74. Grand Rapids: Zondervan, 2014.

Houtman, C. *Exodus.* Vol. 3. HCOT. Kampen: Peeters, 1999.

Hughes, Christopher. *On a Complex Theory of a Simple God: An Investigation in Aquinas' Philosophical Theology.* CSPR. Ithaca, NY: Cornell University Press, 1989.

Hughes, Gerard J. *The Nature of God.* PP. London: Routledge, 1995.

Hunsinger, George. "Robert Jenson's Systematic Theology: A Review Essay." *SJT* 55 (2002): 161–200.

Hurtado, Larry W. *Lord Jesus Christ: Devotion to Jesus in Earliest Christianity.* Grand Rapids: Eerdmans, 2003.

Immink, F. G. *Divine Simplicity.* Utrecht: J. H. Kok, 1987.

_____. "The One and Only: The Simplicity of God." In *Understanding the Attributes of God,* edited by Gijsbert van den Brink and Marcel Sarot, 99–118. Contributions to Philosophical Theology 1. Frankfurt: Peter Lang, 1999.

Ip, Pui Him. "Re-imagining Divine Simplicity in Trinitarian Theology." *IJST* 18 (2016): 274–89.

Irenaeus of Lyons. *Five Books against Heresies.* Vol. 2. Edited by W. Wigan Harvey. Cambridge: Cambridge University Press, 1857.

Jenson, Robert W. "The Attributes of God." In *Christian Dogmatics,* edited by Carl E. Braaten and Robert W. Jenson, 1:181–92. Philadelphia: Fortress Press, 1984.

_____. "A Decision Tree of Colin Gunton's Thinking." In *The Theology of Colin Gunton,* edited by Lincoln Harvey, 8–16. London: T&T Clark, 2010.

_____. "*Deus est ipsa pulchritudo* (God Is Beauty Itself)." In *Theology as Revisionary Metaphysics: Essays on God and Creation,* edited by Stephen John Wright, 207–15. Eugene, OR: Cascade, 2014.

_____. "Karl Barth on the Being of God." In *Thomas Aquinas and Karl Barth: An Unofficial Catholic-Protestant Diaologue,* edited by Bruce L. McCormack and Thomas Joseph White, 43–51. Grand Rapids: Eerdmans, 2013.

_____. *Systematic Theology.* Vol. 1, *The Triune God.* New York: Oxford University Press, 1997.

_____. *Systematic Theology.* Vol. 2, *The Works of God.* New York: Oxford University Press, 1999.

_____. *The Triune Identity: God according to the Gospel.* 1982. Reprint, Eugene, OR: Wipf & Stock, 2002.

John of Damascus. *Exposition of the Orthodox Faith.* In *Nicene and Post-Nicene Fathers,* Series 2, vol. 9. Edited by Philip Schaff and Henry Wace. Translated by S. D. F. Salmond. 1886–1889. Reprint, Peabody, MA: Hendrickson, 1994.

Johnson, Adam J. *God's Being in Reconciliation: The Theological Basis of the Unity and Diversity of the Atonement in the Theology of Karl Barth.* SST. London: T&T Clark, 2012.

Johnson, Keith E. "Augustine's 'Trinitarian' Reading of John 5: A Model for the Theological Interpretation of Scripture?" *JETS* 52 (2009): 799–810.

Jones, John D. "(Mis?)-Reading the Divine Names as a Science: Aquinas' Interpretation of the Divine Names of (Pseudo) Dionysius Areopagite." *SVTQ* 52 (2008): 143–72.

Jones, Mark. *God Is: A Devotional Guide to the Attributes of God.* Wheaton, IL: Crossway, 2017.

Jordan, Mark D. "The Names of God and the Being of Names." In *The Existence and Nature of God,* edited by Alfred J. Freddoso, 161–90. Notre Dame: University of Notre Dame Press, 1983.

Jowers, Dennis W. "The Inconceivability of Subordination within a Simple God." In *The New Evangelical Subordinationism? Perspectives on the Equality of God the Father and God the Son,* edited by Dennis W. Jowers and H. Wayne House, 375–410. Eugene, OR: Pickwick, 2012.

Jüngel, Eberhard. *God as the Mystery of the World: On the Foundation of the Theology of the Crucified One in the Dispute between Theism and Atheism.* Translated by Darrell L. Guder. Grand Rapids: Eerdmans, 1983.

_____. "Theses on the Relation of the Existence, Essence and Attributes of God." Translated by Philip G. Ziegler. *TJT* 17 (2001): 107–24.

Kaufman, Dan. "Divine Simplicity and the Eternal Truths in Descartes." *BJHP* 11 (2003): 553–79.

Kelly, Douglas. "A Rehabilitation of Scholasticism? A Review Article on Richard A. Muller's *Post-Reformation Reformed Dogmatics,* vol. 1, *Prolegomena To Theology.*" *SBET* 6 (1988): 112–22.

Kerr, Fergus. *After Aquinas: Versions of Thomism.* Oxford: Blackwell, 2002.

_____. "God in the *Summa Theologiae*: Entity or Event." In *Philosophy of Religion for a New Century: Essays in Honor of Eugene Thomas Long,* edited by Jeremiah Hackett and Jerald Wallulis, 63–80. Boston: Springer, 2004.

_____. "Recent Theology: Divine Simplicity." *NBf* 79 (2007): 154–57.

Kilby, Karen. "Aquinas, the Trinity and the Limits of Understanding." *IJST* 7 (2005): 414–27.

Klauber, Martin I. "Continuity and Discontinuity in Post-Reformation Reformed Theology: An Evaluation of the Muller Thesis." *JETS* 33 (1990): 467–75.

Klubertanz, George P. *St. Thomas Aquinas on Analogy: A Textual Analysis and Systematic Synthesis.* 1960. Reprint, Eugene, OR: Wipf & Stock, 2009.

Knowles, Michael P. *The Unfolding Mystery of the Divine Name: The God of Sinai in Our Midst.* Downers Grove, IL: IVP Academic, 2012.

Kooi, Cornelis van der. *As in a Mirror: John Calvin and Karl Barth on Knowing God.* Translated by Donald Mader. SHCT. Leiden: Brill, 2005.

Kooten, Geurt H. van, ed. *The Revelation of the Name YHWH to Moses: Perspectives from Judaism, the Pagan Graeco-Roman World, and Early Christianity.* Themes in Biblical Narrative 9. Leiden: Brill, 2006.

Kraal, Anders. "Logic and Divine Simplicity." *Philosophy Compass* 6 (2011): 282–94.

Kretzmann, Norman. "Abraham, Isaac and Euthyphro: God and the Basis of Morality." In *Hamartia: The Concept of Error in the Western Tradition; Essays in Honor of John M. Crossett*, edited by Donald V. Stump, James A. Arieti, Lloyd Gerson, and Eleonore Stump, 27–50. Lewston, NY: Edwin Mellen, 1983.

Krivochéine, Basile. "Simplicity of the Divine Nature and the Distinctions in God, according to St. Gregory of Nyssa." *SVTQ* 21 (1977): 76–104.

Krötke, Wolf. *Gottes Klarheiten: Eine Neuinterpretation der Lehre von Gottes "Eigenschaften."* Tübingen: Mohr Siebeck, 2001.

La Croix, Richard R. "Augustine on the Simplicity of God." In *What Is God? The Selected Essays of Richard R. La Croix*, 96–108. Buffalo, NY: Prometheus, 1993.

———. "Wainwright, Augustine, and God's Simplicity: A Final Word." In *What Is God? The Selected Essays of Richard R. La Croix*, 130–33. Buffalo, NY: Prometheus, 1993.

Lamont, J. "Aquinas on Divine Simplicity." *Monist* 80 (1997): 521–39.

Lane, Nathan C. *The Compassionate, but Punishing God: A Canonical Analysis of Exodus 34:6–7.* Eugene, OR: Pickwick, 2010.

Langston, Scott M. *Exodus: Through the Centuries.* BBC. Oxford: Wiley-Blackwell, 2005.

Leftow, Brian. "Aquinas, Divine Simplicity and Divine Freedom." In *Metaphysics and God: Essays in Honor of Eleonore Stump*, edited by Kevin Timpe, 21–38. New York: Routledge, 2009.

———. "Divine Simplicity." *FPh* 23 (2006): 365–80.

———. "Is God an Abstract Object?" *Noûs* 24 (1990): 581–98.

———. "Simplicity and Eternity." PhD diss., Yale University, 1984.

———. *Time and Eternity.* Ithaca, NY: Cornell University Press, 1991.

Lekkas, Georgios. "Simplicité et caractère inengendré de Dieu selon Plotin, Eunome et Grégoire de Nysse." In *Gregory of Nyssa: Contra Eunomium II*, edited by Lenka Karfíková, Scot Douglass, and Johannes Zachhuber, 423–32. SVC 82. Leiden: Brill, 2007.

Levering, Matthew. "God and Greek Philosophy in Contemporary Biblical Scholarship." *JTI* 4 (2010): 169–86.

_____. *Paul in the "Summa Theologiae."* Washington, DC: Catholic University of America Press, 2014.

_____. *Scripture and Metaphysics: Aquinas and the Renewal of Trinitarian Theology*. CCT. Oxford: Blackwell, 2004.

Levering, Matthew, and Michael Dauphinais, eds. *Reading Romans with St. Thomas Aquinas*. Washington, DC: Catholic University of America Press, 2012.

Lim, Paul C. H. *Mystery Unveiled: The Crisis of the Trinity in Early Modern England*. OSHT. Oxford: Oxford University Press, 2012.

Lombard, Peter. *The Sentences*. Book 1, *The Mystery of the Trinity*. Translated by Giulio Silano. MST 42. Toronto: PIMS, 2007.

Long, D. Stephen. *The Perfectly Simple Triune God: Aquinas and His Legacy*. Minneapolis: Fortress Press, 2016.

_____. *Speaking of God: Theology, Language, and Truth*. EES. Grand Rapids: Eerdmans, 2009.

Louth, Andrew. *Denys the Areopagite*. OCT. London: Continuum, 2002.

Macierowski, Edward Michael. "The Thomistic Critique of Avicennian Emanationism from the Viewpoint of Divine Simplicity: With Special Reference to the 'Summa Contra Gentiles.'" DPhil Diss., University of Toronto, 1979.

Maimonides, Moses. *The Guide of the Perplexed*. Translated by Shlomo Pines. Chicago: University Of Chicago Press, 1963.

Mann, William E. "The Divine Attributes." *APQ* 12 (1975): 151–59.

_____. "Divine Simplicity." *RelS* 18 (1982): 451–71.

_____. "Simplicity and Immutability in God." In *The Concept of God*, edited by Thomas V. Morris, 253–67. ORP. Oxford: Oxford University Press, 1987.

_____. "Simplicity and Properties: A Reply to Morris." *RelS* 22 (1986): 343–53.

Marion, Jean-Luc. "*Idipsum*: The Name of God according to Augustine." In *Orthodox Readings of Augustine*, edited by Aristotle Papanikolaou and George E. Demacopoulos, 167–89. Crestwood, NY: St. Vladimir's Seminary Press, 2008.

Marshall, Bruce D. "Action and Person: Do Palamas and Aquinas Agree about the Spirit?" *SVTQ* 39 (1995): 379–408.

Martin, C. B. "God, the Null Set, and Divine Simplicity." In *The Challenge of Religion Today*, edited by John King-Farlow, 138–43. New York: Neale Watson, 1976.

Maspero, Giulio. "Energy." In *The Brill Dictionary of Gregory of Nyssa*, edited by Lucas F. Mateo-Seco and Giulio Maspero, 258–62. Translated by Seth Cherney. SVC 99. Leiden: Brill, 2010.

_____. *Trinity and Man: Gregory of Nyssa's "Ad Ablabium."* SVC 86. Leiden: Brill, 2007.

Maurer, Armand. "St. Thomas on the Sacred Name 'Tetragrammaton.'" *MS* 34 (1972): 275–86.

Maxwell, Paul. "The Formulation of Thomistic Simplicity: Mapping Aquinas's Method for Configuring God's Essence." *JETS* 57 (2014): 371–403.

McCall, Thomas H. *Forsaken: The Trinity and the Cross, and Why It Matters.* Downers Grove, IL: IVP Academic, 2012.

_____. "Trinity Doctrine, Plain and Simple." In *Advancing Trinitarian Theology: Explorations in Constructive Dogmatics*, edited by Oliver D. Crisp and Fred Sanders, 21–41. Grand Rapids: Zondervan, 2014.

_____. *Which Trinity? Whose Monotheism? Philosophical and Systematic Theologians on the Metaphysics of Trinitarian Theology.* Grand Rapids: Eerdmans, 2010.

McCann, Hugh J. "Divine Will and Divine Simplicity." In *Creation and the Sovereignty of God*, 213–35. Indiana Series in the Philosophy of Religion. Indianapolis: Indiana University Press, 2012.

McCarthy, Dennis J. "Exodus 3:14: History, Philosophy, and Theology." *CBQ* 40 (1978): 311–22.

McClymond, Michael J. "Hearing the Symphony: A Critique of Some Critics of Sang Lee's and Amy Pauw's Accounts of Jonathan Edwards' View of God." In *Jonathan Edwards as Contemporary: Essays in Honor of Sang Hyun Lee*, edited by Don Schweitzer, 67–92. New York: Peter Lang, 2010.

McClymond, Michael J., and Gerald R. McDermott. *The Theology of Jonathan Edwards*. Oxford: Oxford University Press, 2012.

McCormack, Bruce L. "The Actuality of God: Karl Barth in Conversation with Open Theism." In *Engaging the Doctrine of God: Contemporary Protestant Perspectives*, edited by Bruce L. McCormack, 185–242. Grand Rapids: Baker Academic, 2008.

_____. "Not a Possible God but the God Who Is: Observations on Friedrich Schleiermacher's Doctrine of God." In *The Reality of Faith in Theology: Studies on Karl Barth (Princeton-Kampen Consultation 2005)*, edited by Bruce L. McCormack and Gerrit Neven, 111–39. Bern: Peter Lang, 2007.

_____. "The Only Mediator: The Person and Work of Christ in Evangelical Perspective." In *Renewing the Evangelical Mission*, edited by Richard Lints, 250–69. Grand Rapids: Eerdmans, 2013.

_____. Preface to *Engaging the Doctrine of God: Contemporary Protestant Perspectives*, edited by Bruce L. McCormack, 7–10. Grand Rapids: Baker Academic, 2008.

McCormack, Bruce L., and Thomas Joseph White, eds. *Thomas Aquinas and Karl Barth: An Unofficial Catholic-Protestant Dialogue*. Grand Rapids: Eerdmans, 2013.

McDermott, Gerald. "Jonathan Edwards and God's Inner Life: A Response to Kyle Strobel." *Themelios* 39 (2014): 241–50.

McFadden, William. "The Exegesis of I Cor. 1:24, 'Christ the Power of God and the Wisdom of God' until the Arian Controversy." PhD diss., Pontifical Gregorian University, 1963.

McInerny, Ralph M. *Aquinas and Analogy*. Washington, DC: Catholic University of America Press, 1998.

McIntosh, Adam. "The Doctrine of Appropriation as an Interpretative Framework for Karl Barth's Ecclesiology of the *Church Dogmatics*." DTheol diss, Melbourne College of Divinity, 2006.

Miller, Barry. *A Most Unlikely God: A Philosophical Enquiry into the Nature of God*. Notre Dame: University of Notre Dame Press, 1996.

_____. "On 'Divine Simplicity: A New Defense.'" *FPh* 11 (1994): 474–77.

_____. "Theism and the Principle of Simplicity." *Sophia* 13 (1974): 17–21.

Moad, Edward R. "Between Divine Simplicity and the Eternity of the World: Ghazali on the Necessity of the Necessary Existent in the Incoherence of the Philosophers." *P&T* 27 (2015): 55–73.

Moberly, R. W. L. *At the Mountain of God: Story and Theology in Exodus 32–34.* JSOTSup. Sheffield: Sheffield Academic, 1983.

_____. *Old Testament Theology: Reading the Hebrew Bible as Christian Scripture.* Grand Rapids: Baker Academic, 2013.

Moreland, J. P., and William Lane Craig. *Philosophical Foundations for a Christian Worldview.* Downers Grove, IL: InterVarsity Press, 2003.

Morreal, John. "Divine Simplicity and Divine Properties." *Journal of Critical Analysis* 7 (1978): 67–70.

Morris, Thomas V. "Dependence and Divine Simplicity." *IJPR* 23 (1988): 161–74.

_____. "On God and Mann: A View of Divine Simplicity." In *Anselmian Explorations: Essays in Philosophical Theology,* 98–123. Notre Dame: University of Notre Dame Press, 1987.

_____. *Our Idea of God: An Introduction to Philosophical Theology.* Downers Grove, IL: InterVarsity Press, 1991.

_____. "Problems with Divine Simplicity." In *Philosophy of Religion: A Guide and Anthology,* edited by Brian Davies, 545–48. Oxford: Oxford University Press, 2000.

_____. "Review: Divine Simplicity, by F. G. Immink." *JAAR* 56 (1988): 579–81.

Morrison, Chris. "Reconsidering Divine Simplicity." MA thesis, Luther Rice Seminary, 2011.

Mortimer, Sarah. *Reason and Religion in the English Revolution: The Challenge of Socinianism.* CSEMBH. Cambridge: Cambridge University Press, 2010.

Muller, Richard A. *Dictionary of Latin and Greek Theological Terms: Drawn Principally from Protestant Scholastic Theology.* Grand Rapids: Baker, 1985.

_____. "Incarnation, Immutability, and the Case for Classical Theism." *WTJ* 45 (1983): 22–40.

_____. *Post-Reformation Reformed Dogmatics.* Vol. 3, *The Divine Essence and Attributes.* 2nd ed. Grand Rapids: Baker Academic, 2003.

_____. *Post-Reformation Reformed Dogmatics.* Vol. 1, *Prolegomena to Theology.* 2nd ed. Grand Rapids: Baker Academic, 2003.

_____. *The Unaccommodated Calvin: Studies in the Foundation of a Theological Tradition.* New York: Oxford University Press, 2001.

Mullins, R. T. "An Analytic Response to Stephen R. Holmes, with a Special Treatment of His Doctrine of Divine Simplicity." In *The Holy Trinity Revisited: Essays in Response to Stephen Holmes*, edited by Thomas Noble and Jason Sexton, 82–96. Milton Keynes, UK: Paternoster, 2015.

_____. *The End of the Timeless God*. OSAT. Oxford: Oxford University Press, 2016.

_____. "Simply Impossible: A Case against Divine Simplicity." *JRT* 7 (2013): 181–203.

Mulsow, Martin, and Jan Rohls, eds. *Socinianism and Arminianism: Antitrinitarians, Calvinists, and Cultural Exchange in Seventeenth-Century Europe*. BSIH. Leiden: Brill, 2005.

Nash-Marshall, Siobhan. "God, Simplicity, and the *Consolatio Philosophiae*." *CPQ* 78 (2005): 225–46.

_____. "Properties, Conflation, and Attribution: The Monologion and Divine Simplicity." *SAJ* 4 (2007): 19–36.

Nash, Ronald H. *The Concept of God: An Exploration of Contemporary Difficulties with the Attributes of God*. Grand Rapids: Zondervan, 1983.

Neele, Adriaan C. *Petrus van Mastricht (1630–1706), Reformed Orthodoxy: Method and Piety*. BSCH. Leiden: Brill, 2009.

_____. "A Study of Divine Spirituality, Simplicity, and Immutability in Petrus Van Mastricht's Doctrine of God." ThM thesis, Calvin Theology Seminary, 2002.

Niebuhr, Richard R., and Robert W. Funk. "Schleiermacher and the Names of God." In *Schleiermacher as Contemporary*, 176–215. New York: Herder & Herder, 1970.

Norris, Richard A. "The Transcendence and Freedom of God: Irenaeus, the Greek Tradition and Gnosticism." In *Early Christian Literature and the Classical Intellectual Tradition: In Honorem Robert M. Grant*, edited by William R. Schoedel and Robert L. Wilken, 87–100. Théologie Historique. Paris: Beauchesne, 1979.

_____. "Who Is the Demiurge? Irenaeus' Picture of God in *Adversus haereses* 2." In *God in Early Christian Thought: Essays in Memory of Lloyd G. Patterson*, edited by Andrew B. T. McGowan, Brian E. Daley, and Timothy J. Gaden, 9–38. Leiden: Brill, 2009.

Oakes, Kenneth. "The Divine Perfections and the Economy: The Atonement." In *Theological Theology: Essays in Honour of John Webster*, edited by R. David Nelson, Darren Sarisky, and Justin Stratis, 237–46. London: Bloomsbury T&T Clark, 2015.

_____. *Karl Barth on Theology and Philosophy*. Oxford: Oxford University Press, 2012.

O'Connor, Timothy. "Simplicity and Creation." *FPh* 16 (1999): 405–12.

O'Leary, Joseph S. "Divine Simplicity and the Plurality of Attributes (*CE* II 359–386; 445–560)." In *Gregory of Nyssa: Contra Eunomium II*, edited by Lenka Karfíková, Scot Douglass, and Johannes Zachhuber, 307–37. SVC 82. Leiden: Brill, 2007.

_____. "The Simplicity of the Ultimate: East and West." In *Aquinas, Education and the East*, edited by Thomas Brian Mooney and Mark Nowacki, 133–45. New York: Springer, 2013.

Oliphint, K. Scott. "Simplicity, Triunity, and the Incomprehensibility of God." In *One God in Three Persons: Unity of Essence, Distinction of Persons, Implications for Life*, edited by Bruce A. Ware and John Starke, 215–35. Wheaton, IL: Crossway, 2015.

O'Meara, Thomas F. *Thomas Aquinas Theologian*. Notre Dame: University of Notre Dame Press, 1997.

Oppy, Graham. "The Devilish Complexities of Divine Simplicity." *Philo* 6 (2003): 10–22.

O'Rourke, Fran. *Pseudo-Dionysius and the Metaphysics of Aquinas*. Notre Dame: University of Notre Dame Press, 2005.

Ortlund, Gavin. "Divine Simplicity in Historical Perspective: Resourcing a Contemporary Discussion." *IJST* 16 (2014): 436–53.

Osthövener, Claus-Dieter. *Die Lehre von Gottes Eigneschaften bei Friedrich Schleiermacher und Karl Barth*. Theologische Bibliotek Töpelmann 76. Berlin: de Gruyter, 1996.

Owen, H. P. *Concepts of Deity*. New York: Herder & Herder, 1971.

Owen, John. *Vindiciae Evangelicae: The Mystery of the Gospel Vindicated and Socinianism Examined*. WJO 12. Edinburgh: Banner of Truth, 1966.

Palakeel, Joseph. *The Use of Analogy in Theological Discourse: An Investigation in Ecumenical Perspective*. Rome: Gregorian University Press, 1995.

Pannenberg, Wolfhart. "The Appropriation of the Philosophical Concept of God as a Dogmatic Problem of Early Christian Theology." In *Basic Questions in Theology: Collected Essays*, translated by George H. Kehm, 2:119–83. Philadelphia: Fortress Press, 1971.

_____. *Systematic Theology*. Translated by Geoffrey W. Bromiley. 2 vols. Grand Rapids: Eerdmans, 1991–1994.

Pauw, Amy Plantinga. "'One Alone Cannot Be Excellent': Edwards on Divine Simplicity." In *Jonathan Edwards: Philosophical Theologian*, edited by Paul Helm and Oliver Crisp, 115–25. Aldershot: Ashgate, 2003.

———. *"The Supreme Harmony of All": The Trinitarian Theology of Jonathan Edwards*. Grand Rapids: Eerdmans, 2002.

Pedersen, Daniel J. "Schleiermacher and Reformed Scholastics on the Divine Attributes." *IJST* 17 (2015): 413–31.

Peerbolte, Bert-Jan Lietaert. "The Name above All Names (Philippians 2:9)." In *The Revelation of the Name YHWH to Moses: Perspectives from Judaism, the Pagan Graeco-Roman World, and Early Christianity*, edited by Geurt H. van Kooten, 187–206. Leiden: Brill, 2006.

Pelikan, Jaroslav. *The Christian Tradition*. Vol. 3, *The Growth of Medieval Theology*. Chicago: University of Chicago Press, 1980.

Pessin, Andrew. "Divine Simplicity and the Eternal Truths: Descartes and the Scholastics." *Philosophia* 38 (2010): 69–105.

Pettit, Gordon. "Moral Objectivity, Simplicity, and the Identity." *PC* 11 (2009): 126–44.

Philippe, Marie-Dominique. "La simplicité de Dieu." In *Hommage aux catholiques suisses*, 304–15. Fribourg: Éditions universitaires, 1954.

Pickard, Stephen. "Barth on Divine Simplicity: Some Implications for Life in a Complex World." In *Karl Barth: A Future for Postmodern Theology?*, edited by Geoff Thompson and Christiaan Mostert, 210–23. Hindmarsh: Australian Theological Forum, 2000.

Pinnock, Clark H. *Most Moved Mover: A Theology of the Divine Openness*. Grand Rapids: Baker Academic, 2001.

Plantinga, Alvin. *Does God Have a Nature?* Milwaukee: Marquette University Press, 1980.

Plastaras, James. *The God of Exodus: The Theology of the Exodus Narratives*. Milwaukee: Bruce, 1966.

Pokrifka, Todd. *Redescribing God: The Roles of Scripture, Tradition, and Reason in Karl Barth's Doctrines of Divine Unity, Constancy, and Eternity*. PTM. Eugene, OR: Pickwick, 2010.

Prestige, G. L. *God in Patristic Thought*. London: SPCK, 1952.

Price, Robert B. *Letters of the Divine Word: The Perfections of God in Karl Barth's Church Dogmatics*. SST. London: T&T Clark, 2011.

Prügl, T. "Thomas Aquinas as Interpreter of Scripture." In *The Theology of Thomas Aquinas*, edited by R. Van Nieuwenhove and J. Wawrykow, 386–415. Notre Dame: University of Notre Dame Press, 2005.

Pruss, A. "On Two Problems of Divine Simplicity." In *Oxford Studies in Philosophy of Religion*, edited by J. Kvanvig, 150–67. Oxford: Oxford University Press, 2008.

Radde-Gallwitz, Andrew. *Basil of Caesarea, Gregory of Nyssa, and the Transformation of Divine Simplicity*. OECS. Oxford: Oxford University Press, 2009.

Rahner, Karl. *The Trinity*. Translated by Joseph Donceel. MCT. New York: Crossroad, 1997.

Raynall, Charles Edward, III. "Karl Barth's Conception of the Perfections of God." PhD diss., Yale University, 1973.

Régnon, Théodore de. *Études de théologie positive sur la sainté Trinité*. 4 vols. Paris: Victor Retaux, 1892–1898.

Rehnman, Sebastian. "The Doctrine of God in Reformed Orthodoxy." In *A Companion to Reformed Orthodoxy*, edited by Herman Selderhuis, 353–401. BCCT. Leiden: Brill, 2013.

_____. "Theistic Metaphysics and Biblical Exegesis: Francis Turretin on the Concept of God." *RelS* 38 (2001): 167–86.

Richards, Jay Wesley. "Divine Simplicity: The Good, the Bad, and the Ugly." In *For Faith and Clarity: Philosophical Contributions to Christian Theology*, edited by James K. Beilby, 157–77. Grand Rapids: Baker Academic, 2006.

_____. *The Untamed God: A Philosophical Exploration of Divine Perfection, Immutability, and Simplicity*. Downers Grove, IL: InterVarsity Press, 2003.

Ricoeur, Paul. "From Interpretation to Translation." In *Thinking Biblically: Exegetical and Hermeneutical Studies*, 331–61. Translated by David Pellauer. Chicago: University of Chicago Press, 1998.

Robinson, Howard. "Can We Make Sense of the Idea That God's Existence Is Identical to His Essence?" In *Reason, Faith and History: Philosophical Essays for Paul Helm*, 127–43. Aldershot: Ashgate, 2008.

Rocca, Gregory P. *Speaking the Incomprehensible God: Thomas Aquinas on the Interplay of Positive and Negative Theology*. Washington, DC: Catholic University of America Press, 2008.

Rogers, Eugene F. *Thomas Aquinas and Karl Barth: Sacred Doctrine and the Natural Knowledge of God*. Notre Dame: University of Notre Dame Press, 1995.

Rogers, Katherin A. *Perfect Being Theology*. RR. Edinburgh: Edinburgh University Press, 2000.

_____. "The Traditional Doctrine of Divine Simplicity." *RelS* 32 (1996): 165–86.

Rooney, James Dominic. "Being as Iconic: Aquinas on 'He Who Is' as the Name for God." *IJST* 19 (2017): 163–74.

Rorem, Paul. *Pseudo-Dionysius: A Commentary on the Texts and an Introduction to Their Influence.* New York: Oxford University Press, 1993.

Ross, James F. "Comments on 'Absolute Simplicity.'" *FPh* 2 (1985): 383–91.

Roukema, Riemer. "Jesus and the Divine Name in the Gospel of John." In *The Revelation of the Name YHWH to Moses: Perspectives from Judaism, the Pagan Graeco-Roman World, and Early Christianity*, edited by Geurt H. van Kooten, 207–23. Leiden: Brill, 2006.

Rowe, C. Kavin. "Biblical Pressure and Trinitarian Hermeneutics." *ProEccl* 11 (2002): 295–312.

_____. *Early Narrative Christology: The LORD in the Gospel of Luke.* Grand Rapids: Baker Academic, 2009.

_____. "God, Greek Philosophy, and the Bible: A Response to Matthew Levering." *JTI* 4 (2010): 69–80.

_____. "Romans 10:13: What Is the Name of the Lord?" *HBT* 22 (2000): 135–73.

Rowe, W. V. "Adolf von Harnack and the Concept of Hellenization." In *Hellenization Revisited: Shaping a Christian Response within the Greco-Roman World*, edited by Wendy E. Helleman, 69–99. Lanham, MD: University Press of America, 1994.

Rubio, Mercedes. *Aquinas and Maimonides on the Possibility of the Knowledge of God: An Examination of the* Quaestio de attributis. ASJP. Dordrecht, Netherlands: Springer, 2010.

Ryan, Thomas. *Thomas Aquinas as Reader of Psalms.* Notre Dame: University of Notre Dame Press, 2000.

Sadler, Gregory B. "A Perfectly Simple God and Our Complicated Lives." *SAJ* 6 (2008): 39–61.

Sadler, Mark Davidson. "Simply Divine: Simplicity as Fundamental to the Nature of God." PhD diss., Southwestern Baptist Theological Seminary, 2004.

Saenz, Noël B. "Against Divine Truthmaker Simplicity." *FPh* (2014): 460–74.

Sammon, Brendan Thomas. *The God Who Is Beauty: Beauty as a Divine Name in Thomas Aquinas and Dionysius the Areopagite.* PTM. Eugene, OR: Pickwick, 2013.

Sanders, Fred. *The Triune God*. NSD. Grand Rapids: Zondervan, 2016.

Saner, Andrea. *"Too Much to Grasp": Exodus 3:13–15 and the Reality of God*. JTISup. Winona Lake, IN: Eisenbrauns, 2015.

Sanlon, Peter. *Simply God: Recovering the Classical Trinity*. Nottingham, UK: Inter-Varsity Press, 2014.

Schleiermacher, Friedrich. *Christian Faith*. Edited by Catherine L. Kelsey and Terrence N. Tice. Translated by Terrence N. Tice, Catherine L. Kelsey, and Edwina Lawler. 2 vols. Louisville: Westminster John Knox, 2016.

Schmitt, Yann. "The Deadlock of Absolute Divine Simplicity." *IJPR* 71 (2012): 117–30.

Schubert, Aaron Matthew. "The Importance of Divine Simplicity." MA thesis, Dallas Theological Seminary, 2014.

Schweitzer, Don. "Karl Barth's Critique of Classical Theism." *TJT* 18 (2002): 231–44.

Schwöbel, Christoph. *God: Action and Revelation*. SPT. Kampen: Kok Pharos, 1992.

_____. "God as Conversation: Reflections on a Theological Ontology of Communicative Relations." In *Theology and Conversation: Towards a Relational Theology*, edited by J. Haers and P. De Mey, 43–67. Leuven: Leuven University Press, 2003.

_____, ed. *Gott in Beziehung: Studien Zur Dogmatik*. Tübingen: Mohr Siebeck, 2002.

Scobie, Charles H. H. *The Ways of Our God: An Approach to Biblical Theology*. Grand Rapids: Eerdmans, 2003.

Seitz, Christopher. "The Divine Name in Christian Scripture." In *Word without End: The Old Testament as Abiding Theological Witness*, 251–62. Grand Rapids: Eerdmans, 1998.

_____. "Handing Over the Name: Christian Reflection on the Divine Name YHWH." In *Figured Out: Typology and Providence in Christian Scripture*, 131–44. Minneapolis: Fortress Press, 2001.

Shedd, William G. T. *Dogmatic Theology*. Edited by Alan W. Gomes. Phillipsburg, NJ: P&R, 2003.

Sherman, Robert. "Isaak August Dorner on Divine Immutability: A Missing Link between Schleiermacher and Barth." *JR* 77 (1997): 380–401.

Smith, Barry D. *The Indescribable God: Divine Otherness in Christian Theology*. Eugene, OR: Pickwick, 2012.

_____. *The Oneness and Simplicity of God*. Eugene, OR: Pickwick, 2013.

Smith, J. Warren. "Divine Ecstasy and Divine Simplicity: The Eros Motif in Pseudo-Dionysius's Soteriology." *ProEccl* 21 (2012): 211–27.

Sonderegger, Katherine. "Barth and the Divine Perfections." *SJT* 67 (2014): 450–63.

_____. *Systematic Theology*. Vol. 1, *The Doctrine of God*. Minneapolis: Fortress Press, 2015.

Soskice, Janet Martin. "The Gift of the Name: Moses and the Burning Bush." In *Silence and the Word: Negative Theology and Incarnation*, edited by Oliver Davies and Denys Turner, 61–75. Cambridge: Cambridge University Press, 2002.

_____. "Naming God: A Study in Faith and Reason." In *Reason and the Reasons of Faith*, edited by Paul J. Griffiths and Reinhard Hütter, 241–54. Theology for the Twenty-First Century. New York: T&T Clark, 2005.

Soulen, R. Kendall. *The Divine Name(s) and the Holy Trinity*. Vol. 1, *Distinguishing the Voices*. Louisville: Westminster John Knox, 2011.

_____. "'The Name above Every Name': The Eternal Identity of the Second Person of the Trinity and the Covenant of Grace." In *Advancing Trinitarian Theology: Explorations in Constructive Dogmatics*, edited by Oliver D. Crisp and Fred Sanders, 114–29. Grand Rapids: Zondervan, 2014.

Spear, John Peter. "Aquinas and Bonaventure: Two Medieval Theories of Divine Simplicity." MA thesis, Fordham University, 2006.

Spencer, Archie J. *The Analogy of Faith: The Quest for God's Speakability*. SIET. Downers Grove, IL: IVP Academic, 2015.

Spencer, Jeffrey. "Mystical Theology and the Transcendence of God: The Problem of Deification and Divine Simplicity in Palamism and Thomism." MA thesis, Georgia State University, 1998.

Spencer, Mark K. "The Flexibility of Divine Simplicity: Aquinas, Scotus, Palamas." *IPQ* 57 (2017): 123–39.

Stead, Christopher. "Divine Simplicity as a Problem for Orthodoxy." In *The Making of Orthodoxy: Essays in Honour of Henry Chadwick*, edited by Rowan Williams, 255–69. Cambridge: Cambridge University Press, 1989.

_____. *Divine Substance*. Oxford: Clarendon, 1977.

Stefan, Jan. "Gottes Vollkommenheiten nach KD II/1." In *Karl Barth im europäischen Zeitgeschehen (1935–1950): Widerstand—Bewährung—Orientierung*, edited by Michael Beintker, Christian Link, and Michael Trowitzsch, 83–108. Zürich: Theologischer Verlag, 2010.

Steineger, Joseph. "John of Damascus on the Simplicity of God." *SP* 68 (2013): 337–54.

Strobel, Kyle C. *Jonathan Edwards's Theology: A Reinterpretation.* SST. Bloomsbury T&T Clark, 2013.

Stump, Eleonore, and Norman Kretzmann. "Absolute Simplicity." *FPh* 2 (1985): 353–82.

_____. "Simplicity Made Plainer: A Reply to Ross." *FPh* 4 (1987): 198–201.

Stump, Eleonore. *Aquinas.* London: Routledge, 2003.

_____. "Aquinas on Being, Goodness, and Divine Simplicity." In *Die Logik des Transzendentalen: Festschrift für Jan A. Aertsen zum 65. Geburtstag,* edited by Martin Pickave, 212–25. Miscellanea Mediaevalia 30. Berlin: de Gruyter, 2003.

_____. "Aquinas's Account of Divine Simplicity." In *Theologie Negative,* edited by Marco M. Olivetti, 575–84. Casa Editrice Dott: Antonio Milani, 2002.

_____. "Eternity, Simplicity, and Presence." In *God, Time, and Eternity,* edited by Christian Tapp and Edmund Runggaldier, 29–45. Aldershot: Ashgate, 2011.

_____. *The God of the Bible and the God of the Philosophers.* AL. Milwaukee: Marquette University Press, 2016.

_____. "God's Simplicity." In *The Oxford Handbook of Aquinas,* edited by Brian Davies and Eleonore Stump, 135–46. Oxford: Oxford University Press, 2011.

_____. "The Nature of a Simple God." *PACPA* 87 (2013): 33–42.

_____. "Review of Does God Have a Nature? (The Aquinas Lecture: 1980) by Alvin Plantinga." *Thomist* 47 (1983): 616–22.

_____. "Simplicity." In *A Companion to Philosophy of Religion,* edited by Philip L. Quinn and Charles Taliaferro, 250–56. Blackwell Companions to Philosophy. Oxford: Blackwell, 1997.

Surls, Austin. "Finding the Meaning of the Divine Name in the Book of Exodus: From Etymology to Literary Onomastics." PhD diss., Wheaton College, 2014.

_____. *Finding the Meaning of the Divine Name in the Book of Exodus: From Etymology to Literary Onomastics.* BBRSup. Winona Lake, IN: Eisenbrauns, 2017.

Swain, Scott R. "The Being and Attributes of God." In *Reformation Theology: A Systematic Summary,* edited by Matthew Barrett, 217–39. Wheaton, IL: Crossway, 2017.

_____. *The God of the Gospel: Robert Jenson's Trinitarian Theology*. SIET. Downers Grove, IL: IVP Academic, 2013.

_____. "On Divine Naming." In *Aquinas Among the Protestants*, edited by Manfred Svensson and David VanDrunen, 207–27. Oxford: Wiley-Blackwell, 2018.

Sweeney, Douglas A. *Edwards the Exegete: Biblical Interpretation and Anglo-Protestant Culture on the Edge of the Enlightenment*. Oxford: Oxford University Press, 2015.

Swinburne, Richard. *The Christian God*. Oxford: Clarendon, 1994.

Teske, Roland J. "Properties of God and the Predicaments in *De Trinitate* V." In *To Know God and the Soul: Essays on the Thought of Saint Augustine*, 93–111. Washington, DC: Catholic University of America Press, 2008.

Thomas Aquinas. *The Academic Sermons*. Translated by Mark-Robin Hoogland. Washington, DC: Catholic University of America Press, 2010.

_____. *Compendium of Theology*. Translated by Richard J. Regan. Oxford: Oxford University Press, 2009.

_____. *On the Power of God*. Translated by Lawrence Shapcote. Westminster, MD: Newman Press, 1952.

_____. *Summa contra gentiles*. 4 vols. Translated by Anton C. Pegis. Notre Dame: University of Notre Dame Press, 1955–1975.

_____. *Summa theologiae*. 61 vols. London: Eyre & Spottiswoode, 1964–1981.

Titus, Eric J. "The Perfections of God in the Theology of Karl Barth: A Consideration of the Formal Structure." *Kairos* 4 (2010): 203–22.

Tollefson, Torstein. "Essence and Activity (Energeia) in St. Gregory's Anti-Eunomian Polemic." In *Gregory of Nyssa: Contra Eunomium II*, edited by Lenka Karfíková, Scot Douglass, and Johannes Zachhuber, 433–44. SVC 82. Leiden: Brill, 2007.

Torrance, Alexis. "Precedents for Palamas' Essence-Energies Theology in the Cappadocian Fathers." *VC* 63 (2009): 47–70.

Torrell, Jean-Pierre. *Saint Thomas Aquinas: Spiritual Master*. Translated by Robert Royal. Vol. 2. Washington, DC: Catholic University of America Press, 2003.

Trueman, Carl R. *John Owen: Reformed Catholic, Renaissance Man*. Aldershot: Ashgate, 2007.

Turner, Denys. *Thomas Aquinas: A Portrait*. New Haven: Yale University Press, 2013.

Turretin, Francis. *Institutes of Elenctic Theology*. Edited by James T. Dennison Jr. Translated by George Musgrave Giger. Vol. 1. Phillipsburg, NJ: P&R, 1992.

Twetten, Walter S. "The Doctrine of Divine Simplicity in Thomas Aquinas and a Contemporary Defense." MA thesis, Trinity Evangelical Divinity School, 1987.

Vaggione, Richard P. *Eunomius: The Extant Works*. OECT. Oxford: Oxford University Press, 1987.

———. *Eunomius of Cyzicus and the Nicene Revolution*. OECS. Oxford: Oxford University Press, 2001.

Valkenberg, Wilhelmus. *Words of the Living God: Place and Function of Holy Scripture in the Theology of St. Thomas Aquinas*. PTUNS 6. Louvain: Peeters, 2000.

Vallicella, William F. "Divine Simplicity: A New Defense." *FPh* 9 (1992): 508–25.

———. "On Property Self-Exemplification: Rejoinder to Miller." *FPh* 11 (1994): 478–81.

Vanhoozer, Kevin J. *Remythologizing Theology: Divine Action, Passion, and Authorship*. CSCD. Cambridge: Cambridge University Press, 2010.

Velde, Dolf te. *The Doctrine of God in Reformed Orthodoxy, Karl Barth, and the Utrecht School: A Study in Method and Content*. SRT. Leiden: Brill, 2013.

———. "Eloquent Silence: The Doctrine of God in the *Synopsis of Purer Theology*." *CHRC* 92 (2012): 581–608.

———, ed. *Synopsis Purioris Theologiae/Synopsis of a Purer Theology: Latin Text and English Translation: Disputations 1–23*. Translated by Riemer Faber. SMRT. Leiden: Brill, 2014.

Velde, Rudi A. te. *Aquinas on God: The "Divine Science" of the Summa Theologiae*. ASHPT. Aldershot: Ashgate, 2006.

———. *Participation and Substantiality in Thomas Aquinas*. STGM 46. Leiden: Brill, 1995.

Vidu, Adonis. "The Place of the Cross among the Inseparable Operations of the Trinity." In *Locating Atonement: Explorations in Constructive Dogmatics*, edited by Oliver D. Crisp and Fred Sanders, 21–42. Grand Rapids: Zondervan, 2015.

———. "Trinitarian Inseparable Operations and the Incarnation." *JAT* 4 (2016): 106–27.

Wainwright, William J. "Augustine on God's Simplicity: A Reply to Richard La Croix." *NS* 53 (1979): 118–23.

Waltke, Bruce K., and Charles Yu. *An Old Testament Theology: An Exegetical, Canonical, and Thematic Approach.* Grand Rapids: Zondervan, 2007.

Ware, Kallistos. "God Hidden and Revealed: The Apophatic Way and the Essence-Energies Distinction." *Eastern Churches Review* 7 (1975): 125–36.

Warfield, B. B. "Calvin's Doctrine of God." In *Calvin and Calvinism*, edited by Samuel G. Craig, 133–85. New York: Oxford University Press, 1931.

Webster, John. "Attributes, Divine." In *The Cambridge Dictionary of Christian Theology*, edited by Ian A. McFarland, David A. S. Fergusson, Karen Kilby, and Iain R. Torrance, 45–48. Cambridge: Cambridge University Press, 2011.

_____. *Essays in Christian Dogmatics.* Vol. 2, *Confessing God.* Edinburgh: T&T Clark, 2005.

_____. *The Domain of the Word: Scripture and Theological Reason.* London: Bloomsbury T&T Clark, 2012.

_____. "God's Perfect Life." In *God's Life in Trinity*, edited by Miroslav Volf and Michael Welker, 143–52. Minneapolis: Fortress Press, 2006.

_____. *God without Measure: Working Papers in Christian Theology.* Vol. 1, *God and the Works of God.* London: Bloomsbury T&T Clark, 2016.

_____. *Holiness.* Grand Rapids: Eerdmans, 2003.

_____. "Life in and of Himself: Reflections on God's Aseity." In *Engaging the Doctrine of God: Contemporary Protestant Perspectives*, edited by Bruce L. McCormack, 107–24. Grand Rapids: Baker Academic, 2008.

_____. "Principles of Systematic Theology." *IJST* 11 (2009): 56–71.

_____. "Trinity and Creation." *IJST* 12 (2010): 4–19.

Weedman, Mark. "The Polemical Context of Gregory of Nyssa's Doctrine of Divine Infinity." *JECS* 18 (2010): 81–104.

Weigel, Peter. *Aquinas on Simplicity: An Investigation into the Foundations of His Philosophical Theology.* New York: Peter Lang, 2008.

Weinandy, Thomas G. *Does God Change? The Word's Becoming in the Incarnation.* Still River, MA: St. Bede's, 1985.

_____. *Does God Suffer?* Notre Dame: University of Notre Dame Press, 2000.

Weinandy, Thomas, Daniel Keating, and John Yocum, eds. *Aquinas on Scripture: An Introduction to His Biblical Commentaries.* London: T&T Clark, 2005.

White, Thomas Joseph. "Divine Simplicity and the Holy Trinity." *IJST* 18 (2016): 66–93.

_____. *Exodus.* BTCB. Grand Rapids: Brazos, 2016.

_____. "Nicene Orthodoxy and Trinitarian Simplicity." *ACPQ* 90 (2016): 727–50.

Wielenberg, Erik. "Dawkins's Gambit, Hume's Aroma, and God's Simplicity." *PC* 11 (2009): 111–25.

Wilkinson, Robert J. *Tetragrammaton: Western Christians and the Hebrew Name of God: From the Beginnings to the Seventeenth Century.* SHCT. Leiden: Brill, 2015.

Williams, Anna. "Mystical Theology Redux: The Pattern of Aquinas' *Summa Theologiae.*" *ModTheo* 13 (1997): 53–74.

Williams, Robert R. *Schleiermacher the Theologian: The Construction of the Doctrine of God.* Philadelphia: Fortress Press, 1978.

Williams, Rowan. "*Sapientia* and the Trinity: Reflections on *De Trinitate.*" In *Collectanea Augustiniana: mélanges T. J. van Bavel,* edited by B. Bruning, M. Lamberigts, and J. van Houtem, 1:317–32. BETL 92-A. Leuven: Leuven University Press, 1990.

Wisse, Maarten. *Trinitarian Theology beyond Participation: Augustine's "De Trinitate" and Contemporary Theology.* SST. London: T&T Clark, 2011.

Wittman, Tyler R. "The End of the Incarnation: John Owen, Trinitarian Agency and Christology." *IJST* 15 (2013): 284–300.

_____. "'Not a God of Confusion but of Peace': Aquinas and the Meaning of Divine Simplicity." *ModTheo* 32 (2016): 151–69.

Wolterstorff, Nicholas. "Divine Simplicity." In *Inquiring about God: Selected Essays,* edited by Terence Cuneo, 91–111. Cambridge: Cambridge University Press, 2010.

Wright, Stephen John. *Dogmatic Aesthetics: A Theology of Beauty in Dialogue with Robert W. Jenson.* ES. Minneapolis: Fortress Press, 2014.

Wynn, Mark. "Simplicity, Personhood, and Divinity." *IJPR* 41 (1997): 91–103.

Yazawa, Reita. "John Howe (1630–1705) on Divine Simplicity: A Debate over Spinozism." In *Church and School in Early Modern Protestantism,* edited by Jordan J. Ballor, David Sytsma, and Jason Zuidema, 629–40. Leiden: Brill, 2013.

Yeago, David S. "The New Testament and Nicene Dogma: A Contribution to the Recovery of Theological Exegesis." In *The Theological Interpretation of Scripture: Classic and Contemporary Readings,* edited by Stephen E. Fowl, 87–100. Oxford: Blackwell, 1997.

Young, Frances, and David F. Ford. *Meaning and Truth in 2 Corinthians.* Grand Rapids: Eerdmans, 1987.

Zimmerli, Walther. *Old Testament Theology in Outline.* Translated by David E. Green. Louisville: John Knox, 1978.

Zizioulas, John D. *Being as Communion: Studies in Personhood and the Church.* Crestwood, NY: St. Vladimir's Seminary Press, 1985.

_____. *Communion and Otherness: Further Studies in Personhood and the Church.* Edited by Paul McPartlan. London: T&T Clark, 2006.

Index